Celebrities'
Most Wanted™

D1529121

Other "Most Wanted™" Titles from Potomac Books

Hollywood's Most Wanted™: The Top 10 Book of Lucky Breaks, Prima Donnas, Box Office Bombs, and Other Oddities
by Floyd Conner

TV's Most Wanted™: The Top 10 Book of Crazy Casting, Off-Camera Clashes, and Other Oddities
by Douglas Tonks

Broadway's Most Wanted™: The Top 10 Book of Dynamic Divas, Surefire Showstoppers, and Box Office Busts
by Tom Shea

Celebrities' Most Wanted™

The Top 10 Book of Lavish Lifestyles, Tabloid Tidbits, and Superstar Oddities

Marjorie Hallenbeck-Huber

POTOMAC BOOKS, INC.
WASHINGTON, D.C.

Library of Congress Cataloging-in-Publication Data

Hallenbeck-Huber, Marjorie.
Celebrities' most wanted : the top 10 book of lavish lifestyles,
tabloid tidbits, and other superstar oddities / Marjorie
Hallenbeck-Huber. — 1st ed.
p. cm.
Includes bibliographical references and index.
ISBN 978-1-59797-510-0 (pbk. : acid-free paper)
1. Celebrities—Humor. 2. Celebrities—Miscellanea. I. Title.
PN6231.C25H35 2010
818'.607—dc22
2010013559

Printed in the United States of America on acid-free paper that meets
the American National Standards Institute Z39-48 Standard.

Potomac Books, Inc.
22841 Quicksilver Drive
Dulles, Virginia 20166

First Edition

10 9 8 7 6 5 4 3 2 1

To my husband, Jeremy, who learned more about
celebrity culture than he ever wanted.

To my daughter, Charlotte, whose impending birth kept the
writing process eventful and on track.

And to Anastasia and Oliver, my faithful writing
companions and sounding boards.

"The whole celebrity culture thing—
I'm fascinated by it, and repelled by it,
and yet I end up knowing about it"

-Anderson Cooper

Contents

Part Two: Celebrity Spotlight

Part Three: Celebrity Looks

Part Four: Celebrity Life

Photographs

Introduction

The Merriam-Webster dictionary defines *celebrity* as "the state of being celebrated;" and throughout the history of man, society has designated its celebrities. However, who is celebrated has changed considerably over time. The gods of Greece and Rome could be considered celebrities. The masses were fascinated by stories of the lives of their gods and even created tabloid-worthy scandals among them. No one living commanded such broad appeal or notoriety. The first non-celestial celebrities were products of the first Olympic games in 776 B.C.E. Winning Olympic athletes were set apart from the populous because they achieved feats most people could not. Winners returned to their home cities and were worshiped as heroes. While many professional athletes achieve some level of celebrity status today, this status does not have the permanence the Greeks and Romans gave theirs, for I have yet to see Michael Jordan's face on a coin, or a statue erected to Tiger Woods. Endorsement deals may be lucrative, but they are fleeting.

Rulers have been viewed as celebrities to their people throughout history. Julius Caesar, Napoleon, Alexander the Great, and Louis XIV were all exceptionally admired by their people and received "rock star" treatment. They inspired clothing and diet trends, and their personal traits were admired and emulated. With the rare exception of the Kennedys, Princess Diana, Michelle Obama, and a few international personalities, few modern day politicians or their families would really be considered celebrities. They are the exception, not the rule. Being a respected, rather than celebrated, politician is all one can hope for nowadays.

Religious leaders, in addition to rulers, rose in fame during the Dark Ages because frankly there weren't any other people who stood out from the crowd. Saints and martyrs received special notice, the most famous of whom was Thomas Becket. The site of his death was the "in" destination for pilgrimages. The literary classic *The Canterbury Tales* by Geoffrey Chaucer centered on such a journey. Somewhat similarly today, people visit Graceland and pay tribute to Elvis. . . though Becket died for his beliefs and Elvis died of a drug overdose. How times change!

During the Renaissance, artists achieved widespread fame and admiration. These "average Joes" became famous without the help of social status. Instead, they were noticed because of their talent. Though not all the noted artists from this period were famous during their lifetime, many were, and their talents catapulted them into upper class circles, along with fame and fortune.

The nineteenth century welcomed the industrial revolution, which led to more widespread printing, lower cost of paper, and a rise in literacy that helped the novel and writers come to fame. This seems to be the period in which the entertainment industry began to dominate the field of celebrity, for since then the most celebrated figures in our society come from within various fields of the entertainment industry. After the novel came radio, film, TV—first scripted and then Reality TV—and the Internet, all of which produce celebrities.

These modern entertainment celebrities display special talents in their industry, but what does it say about our society that more and more people become famous just because they have a talent for attracting attention? Reality TV shows abound, and it seems viewers never tire of watching people fight it out for "true love" (or at least a one night stand with Brett Michaels or Flavor Flav), struggle to survive in the wilderness, or to achieve their dreams.

Enjoy the juicy factoids and salacious gossip that follows, but also consider how today's celebrities differ from the celebrities of the past. These are the people we currently deem worthy of celebration. As you read through this lighthearted primer about celebrities from the past three decades, remember that celebrities are always making headlines.

Celebrity
Relationships

They Met, They Wed, They Split

Short marriages among celebrities are the norm, but the marriages on this list make even other celebrities scratch their heads and wonder, "What was the point?" If you blinked, you would have missed these marriages that obviously should not have happened.

1. ZSA ZSA GABOR AND FELIPE DE ALBA—24 HOURS

Zsa Zsa Gabor is Paris Hilton's great aunt, as Conrad Hilton was Gabor's second husband. Though not blood relatives, Zsa Zsa was the Paris of her time, becoming famous for being famous. The paparazzi couldn't wait to see what she would do next. She was a regular on talk shows and always knew how to cause a stir with her Hungarian accent, saying such things as, "I'm a marvelous housekeeper. Every time I leave a man I keep his house." Eventually, she decided she was an actress and was cast in a handful of TV and film roles.

In 1982 Felipe de Alba, a Mexican attorney and popular actor, became Gabor's eighth husband (she has had nine total). Technically the marriage was invalid because the ceremony took place on a ship that had not yet reached international waters, and Gabor was not yet legally divorced from her seventh husband (who was the divorce lawyer for her sixth marriage). Gabor had the marriage annulled the following day just to be safe. Apparently she didn't love de Alba enough to marry him again once she was finally divorced.

2. BRITNEY SPEARS AND JASON ALEXANDER—55 HOURS

When someone says, "Let's do something wild, crazy. Let's go get married, just for the hell of it!" as BBC News quotes Jason Alexander, it probably isn't a good idea. One or both of you have probably had too much to drink and it would just be best if you retired to your room(s). You can do plenty of wild and crazy things that you can later regret that will not legally bind you to another person.

Apparently Britney Spears had no one to inform her of this when she and her childhood friend, Jason Alexander, decided to marry at the Little White Wedding Chapel in Las Vegas. Just fifty-five hours later the union was annulled and twenty-two-year-old Spears was a free woman, ready to go out into the world and make better decisions.

According to BBC News, Spears stated that she "lacked understanding of her actions," which would be fair to say if Alexander's 2007 interview with Britain's *Sunday Mirror* is truthful. He stated that Spears was high on ecstasy during much of their Vegas vacation, almost overdosing at one point. According to BBC News, Spears's record company classified the marriage as a "joke that had gone too far." Unfortunately, her idea of a better decision (or maybe this too was a joke that went too far) was marrying Kevin Federline eight months later. We all know how that turned out.

3. CARMEN ELECTRA AND DENNIS RODMAN—9 DAYS

I don't think anyone was surprised that this union didn't last. It is shocking that they married at all. They had been dating for nine months when they decided to wed on November 14, 1998 at the Little Chapel of the Flowers in Las Vegas (is anyone noticing a pattern here?).

Not surprisingly, alcohol played a part in this decision. According to *People* magazine, the couple arrived at the chapel at 7:00 am, two hours before it opened. The chapel owner informed them that they needed a marriage license before they could be married. They returned to the chapel, marriage license in hand, where they were opted for the basic seventy-five dollar, twenty-minute, candlelight service. Nine days later Rodman filed for an annulment stating that he was intoxicated at the wedding. Really?

4. MARIO LOPEZ AND ALI LANDRY—‹ 2 WEEKS

Unlike the previous couples on this list, Mario Lopez and Ali Landry dated for six years before marrying on April 24, 2004, at the Las Alamandas resort in Mexico. However, less than two weeks later, Landry filed for an annulment because of infidelity. *People* magazine made public information from a reputable source that Lopez had been cheating on Landry for several years, and she had just found out the previous week.

Landry's story does have a happy ending, however. Two years after her failed marriage to Lopez, she married film director Alejandro Gomez Monteverde in Mexico, and in July 2007 the couple welcomed a daughter. Lopez is still enjoying the ladies.

5. EDDIE MURPHY AND TRACEY EDMONDS—‹ 2 WEEKS

The couple had been dating since late 2006 and was engaged in July 2007. Their New Year's Day wedding was well-planned. It took place on a beach on Bora Bora with a wedding party and both Murphy's and Edmonds's families in attendance. They even paid for a gazebo to be constructed out of six thousand shells. Less than two weeks later, however, and before the couple made it legal (the ceremony in Bora Bora was a non-binding spiritual union not recognized by the United States) the two decided to go their separate ways. Some claimed that Edmonds refused to sign a prenup, but one source told the *New York Post* that because she had her own money, the prenup was not an issue. A more likely reason was that Murphy had become "physically intimidating." According to Australia's *Herald Sun* on January 25, 2008, "he became very controlling and insisted on bringing his mother" on their honeymoon. A fight led to him grabbing Edmonds, scaring her about what a future with him might hold. Edmonds quickly bounced back showing up to an event in February 2008 with celebrity chef Rocko Dispirito by her side. Eddie got his groove back as well, hooking up with twenty-five-year-old Lara LaRue, (sister of *CSI: Miami* actress Eva LaRue).

6. DARVA CONGER AND RICK ROCKWELL—< 3 WEEKS

You might be asking yourself "Who are Darva Conger and Rick Rockwell?" Think back to the short-lived show *Who Wants to Marry a Multi-Millionaire*. Conger was the lucky woman who won millionaire Rockwell's heart. As this chapter has so far demonstrated, money can't buy you love. Apparently Rockwell was more than Conger was prepared to put up with, even if she did get a 3-carat diamond ring and more than one-hundred thousand dollars worth of prizes.

After the couple returned from their honeymoon Conger immediately filed for an annulment claiming that Rockwell misrepresented himself. The marriage had lasted less than three weeks. Some investigators reported that Rockwell was not a multi-millionaire. Furthermore, he had not disclosed that an ex-fiancée had filed a restraining order against him in 1991. TheSmokingGun.com website explains that the reason for the restraining order was that Rockwell had assaulted and threatened his ex after her repeated attempts at breaking off their engagement. *Brava!* to Conger for ditching the creep, who then went on an "annulment comedy tour." But seriously, what did she expect when she went on the show? I'd be a little wary of a multi-millionaire who couldn't find a wife.

7. DREW BARRYMORE AND JEREMY THOMAS—38 DAYS

After dating for six weeks, then nineteen-year-old actress Drew Barrymore and thirty-two-year-old club owner Jeremy Thomas decided they wanted to be together forever. To prove it, they married on March 20, 1994. Well, it turned out they really only wanted to be together for about a month. Who would have guessed that a marriage that took place at Thomas's club and was performed by a clairvoyant they hired through a psychic hotline an hour before the service wouldn't last? Barrymore filed for divorce on April 28 and went on to have a slightly longer marriage (six months) to comedian Tom Green.

8. NICKY HILTON AND TODD MEISTER—< 3 MONTHS

Nicky Hilton wanted her day in the spotlight, which can be hard to steal from her big sister, Paris. But Nicky found something her sister hadn't yet done: get married. Sure, Paris was engaged, but marriage was a whole new level. And a quickie marriage in Las Vegas? Even more headline grabbing. Following it up with a divorce a mere six weeks later? Even better. The seemingly quiet twenty-year-old Hilton made waves in August 2004 when reports surfaced that she had married her assumed (though not publicly acknowledged) boyfriend and long-time family friend, thirty-three-year-old Todd Meister, in Las Vegas.

While it might seem like a spontaneous decision, they claim it was planned. Apparently Meister proposed to Nicky a few weeks earlier and according to *People* magazine they decided that a 2:30 am Vegas wedding would be more intimate and garner less attention. Um . . . yeah, that *always* happens when celebrities get hitched seemingly out of the blue. Furthermore, Paris, who served as Maid of Honor, was the only family member in the know.

Less than three months later Nicky filed for an annulment. Insiders say the age difference was too great and that at twenty, Nicky wasn't at the right place in her life to settle down. Also, their bicoastal living arrangements made it difficult for the couple to make the relationship work. Next time maybe they will discuss these little details before walking down the aisle—and not in a haze of partying.

9. LISA MARIE PRESLEY AND NICOLAS CAGE—3 MONTHS

Considering Lisa Marie's second marriage was to Michael Jackson, Nicholas Cage was a step in the sane direction. What's creepy is that Cage is a big fan of Elvis Presley, which makes one wonder if the fact that Lisa Marie is Elvis's daughter was part of her appeal. This idea is reinforced by the fact that the couple married in Hawaii in August 2002, the week of the twenty-fifth anniversary of Elvis's death. The wedding was planned, and the couple's respective children from previous relationships participated in the ceremony. Lisa Marie's mother, Priscilla, was present as well.

Just over three months later the bloom was off the rose and Cage filed for divorce, citing irreconcilable differences. According to *People* magazine, Cage refused to comment on the relationship, and Lisa Marie merely claimed that the marriage had been a mistake.

10. R. KELLY AND AALIYAH—< 6 MONTHS

On August 31, 1994, then twenty-seven-year-old R. Kelly married his protégeé, then fifteen-year-old Aaliyah in a secret ceremony. How was this marriage possible? The couple was initially able to marry because Aaliyah lied about her age on the marriage license. However, because she lied, the marriage was invalid. When Aaliyah's parents learned about the marriage, it was annulled. The incident was very hush-hush and the couple denied it ever happened. In 2005 *Vibe* magazine published a copy of the marriage certificate, confirming that the event occurred.

Happily Ever After

While the marriages in the last chapter might turn heads for their brevity, the relationships on this list defy the odds and are admirable by any standard. Though not all of these couples are married, they continue to remain dedicated to each other despite the plethora of temptations that surrounds them daily. Maybe there is such a thing as true love. For now . . .

1. PAUL NEWMAN AND JOANNE WOODWARD—50 YEARS

The second time was the charm for actor Paul Newman. His second marriage to actress Joanne Woodward lasted over fifty years, until his death in 2008. Newman and Woodward met while both were acting on Broadway in William Inge's *Picnic* (1953). At the time Newman was married to actress Jackie Witte with whom he had two children. Nothing happened immediately, but Woodward and Newman reconnected when they worked on the film *The Long Hot Summer* (1958). It was love at first (second) sight, leading Newman to divorce his first wife to marry Woodward in January 1958. The couple wed in a small Los Angeles civil ceremony and bought a farmhouse in Westport, Connecticut, where they lived for the rest of their marriage, raising three daughters and making a lot of salad dressing. Though they owned a house in Hollywood, it was never their primary residence. When asked about the secret to their long relationship, the September 28, 2008 issue of the New York *Daily News* recalled Newman saying there was "the correct amounts of lust and respect" between them and Woodward told the *Daily News* in 2001 "[they] always enjoyed each others company."

2. PATRICK SWAYZE AND LISA NIEMI—34 YEARS

Despite his status as a Hollywood heartthrob in the 1980s, Patrick Swayze was a devoted husband. Swayze and Lisa Niemi were merely teenagers when they met. Niemi was a student at Swayze's mother's dance studio. At the time, she was still a minor, and their age difference raised a few eyebrows, but Swayze insisted they were friends before lovers and slept together for a year before they had sex (until she turned eighteen . . . how convenient). They married on June 2, 1975 when he was twenty-two and she nineteen. As difficult as it is to maintain a marriage in Hollywood, a successful marriage at their young age is rare anywhere. Swayze and Niemi beat the odds and their marriage persisted through numerous hardships, such as two miscarriages and Swayze's battle with pancreatic cancer until his death on September 14, 2009. Swayze admitted, "I like being married. I'm sort of like a loyal sheepdog, sometimes to a fault." More Hollywood couples should read this quote and assess their character before marrying.

3. JAY AND MAVIS LENO—30 YEARS

Jay and Mavis Leno have a unique marriage, and it has worked for them since 1980. There have been numerous rumors that they aren't married or that they have divorced, for they are rarely seen together. However, that could be a result of their views toward marriage. Mavis, a leading feminist in California, said in the February 2003 issue of *O* magazine, "let people go their own way [in a marriage]. . . . He can do any damn thing he wants and it's okay with me." Though I'm sure Jay could do *something* to upset her, Mavis is content to go her own way. She works for numerous non-profits, including the Feminist Majority Foundation and is the founder of the Campaign to Stop Gender Apartheid in Afghanistan. Jay is a major supporter of her causes, and is always there to lend a hand when she asks. He credits their successful relationship to the fact that Mavis doesn't stop him from working . . . or doing anything else he wants.

4. DANNY DEVITO AND RHEA PERLMAN—28 YEARS

Devito has appeared in numerous films including costarring roles in *Twins*, *Junior*, and *Batman Returns*. He owns the production company Jersey Films, which has produced such notable films as *Pulp Fiction*, *Get Shorty*, *Erin Brockovich*, and *Garden State*. He has even directed, including the project in which he costarred with his wife, *Matilda*. They met on the set of the sitcom *Taxi* where Perlman played Zena, Devito's on-screen girlfriend. The real-life couple kept things short and cheap—just like Devito's character on *Taxi*, Lou—by marrying during a lunch break on the set of the show where they met.

After *Taxi*, Perlman became famous for her role on the hit show *Cheers*, for which she received ten Emmy Award nominations. Aside from acting, Perlman is the author of the children's book series *Otto Undercover*.

These Hollywood funny people fit together perfectly, and the fact that they've been married since January 8, 1982, and have three children, is a testament to that.

5. OZZY AND SHARON OSBOURNE—27 YEARS

Ozzy and Sharon's relationship is a model for the mantra "make it work." Their marriage has endured Ozzy's drug and alcohol addictions, rehab, infidelity, as well as Sharon's battle with colon cancer. Though the duo has had many ups and downs over the years, they seem to be in a place now where they are grateful for each other. Metrolyrics.com reported on November 2, 2009 that Ozzy claimed, "Falling in love with Sharon was the best thing that ever happened to me." When they met, Sharon was a mere seventeen and working as a receptionist for her father, who managed Ozzy's band, *Black Sabbath*. At the time, Ozzy was married to Thelma Mayfair and had little interaction with Sharon. Their platonic relationship changed when Sharon literally picked him up off his apartment floor and forced him to clean up his act—no more drugs or alcohol. Soon after Sharon's act of tough love, she and Ozzy married on a beach in Hawaii on July 4, 1982. However, Ozzy continued to battle drug and alcohol addiction throughout the 1980s.

The newlyweds bought Ozzy's contract from Sharon's father and she became his manager, a position she still holds. Unfortunately, this action created bad blood between Sharon and her parents, and when her mother died in 1998 she had never met her three grandchildren: Aimee, Kelly, and Jack. Though the Osbournes look like an odd couple, they are one of the few couples to weather such hardships—even Reality TV—and remain committed.

6. GOLDIE HAWN AND KURT RUSSELL—26 YEARS

Goldie Hawn and Kurt Russell proves that marriage isn't indicative of a lasting relationship. They have been together since March 1983 and their only vow is that they will never marry. Hawn prefers not marrying because she explains, "I wake up everyday knowing I can walk out at any moment. . . . That keeps things fresh." Despite the lack of legal connection, they built a family together; Russell helped Hawn raise her two children from a previous marriage, Kate and Oliver, and share a son, Wyatt. Kate said she considers Russell to be her true "Pa," even granting him the honor of walking her down the aisle at her wedding. Though they have experienced their fair share of ups and downs, upon which the media has been quick to pounce, they remain one of Hollywood's golden couples.

7. DENZEL WASHINGTON AND PAULETTA PEARSON—26 YEARS

Like many Hollywood couples, Denzel Washington and Pauletta Pearson met on a film set. Both actors, they were cast together in the film *Wilma* in 1977; it was Washington's first role. So what's the secret to their marriage that's lasted since 1983? Having faith. Washington's father was a preacher, and family came first. Pearson put her acting career on the back burner to raise the couple's four children. Though Washington works constantly, he remains a devoted family man and still drops everything for his family. Rumors of infidelity and divorce have surfaced at times, but so far they have been unfounded. In 1995 the pair renewed their vows in South Africa in a ceremony officiated by Archbishop Desmond Tutu. Washington divulged in an interview with *Reader's Digest* that the secret to a successful marriage is, "Do whatever your wife tells you." Hey, you can't argue with that.

8. DAN AKROYD AND DONNA DIXON—26 YEARS

One of the original *Blues Brothers* and member of the original cast of *Saturday Night Live*, famous funny man Dan Akroyd is serious when it comes to his marriage. Akroyd met his wife, Donna Dixon, when they costarred in the movie *Doctor Detroit* (1983). While the movie was forgettable, their relationship didn't suffer as many relationships do when partners costar together—think *Gigli*—since their marriage has lasted since April 1983.

Dixon began her career as a model and was Miss Virginia USA 1976 and Miss Washington DC World 1977. As an actress she costarred in the sitcom *Bosom Buddies* alongside

Tom Hanks. Although Akroyd and Dixon have gone on to costar in two more forgettable movies, *Spies Like Us* and *Couch Trip,* they have successfully produced three daughters and maintained one of the longest relationships in Hollywood.

9. SUSAN SARANDON AND TIM ROBBINS—22 YEARS

Susan Sarandon and Tim Robbins have been happily unmarried since 1988. They met on the set of *Bull Durham* and their twelve-year age difference was irrelevant. Sarandon has even commented, "in some ways he's older and more traditional," thus reinforcing the saying that age is just a number. She went on to say that the age gap enlivens their relationship. While I don't want to think about what she meant, this couple seems well matched. They share similar interests, in particular their activism in environmental conservation and politics. And they work well together, Sarandon even winning an Oscar in a movie directed by Robbins.

10. TOM HANKS AND RITA WILSON—21 YEARS

Tom Hanks and Rita Wilson met on the set of his sitcom *Bosom Buddies* in 1981 but did not begin a romantic relationship until their second meeting while filming *Volunteers* in 1985. Hanks admitted to *Esquire* magazine that while he and Wilson were falling in love on the set he had a wife and two children back home. However, he and Wilson both felt it was the real thing and "it just couldn't be denied." Hanks's divorce was finalized in 1987 and he married Wilson on April 20, 1988.

Over twenty years and two children later they continue to be a very close couple and appear to be great friends as well. They also work together when a project presents itself. They have coproduced several films together, including *My Big Fat Greek Wedding* and *Mamma Mia.* They also support various charitable causes through their fundraising efforts.

Cinderella Stories

Remember the posters of teen idols you plastered on your wall as a teenager? You dreamed of them showing up on your doorstep or fantasized about running into them at the mall. Either way, if they met you it would be love at first sight and you'd live happily ever after. Well, it didn't happen for us, but once in a blue moon it does happen, as the men and women on this list prove.

1. VANESSA (LAINE) BRYANT—(KOBE BRYANT)

What high school girl doesn't dream of marrying a rich, famous, hunk to save her from crammed dorm rooms, the freshman fifteen, and Ramen noodle dinners? Well, then-seventeen-year-old Vanessa Laine lived every girl's fantasy when she began dating NBA star Kobe Bryant. Kobe transitioned straight to professional basketball after high school, and was already a star at age twenty-two when he met the high-school senior, Vanessa while she was working as a background dancer on the music video "G'd Up" for the band Tha Eastsidaz. Kobe happened to be in the recording studio at the same time recording an album that was never released. Probably a smart career move. Kobe and Vanessa dated for only six months before they wed on April 18, 2001—*sans* prenup and *sans* Kobe's family or teammates. Kobe's family did not approve of the union.

The couple appeared in the spotlight in 2003 when Kobe was charged with sexual assault. He admitted to committing adultery, but maintained that it was consensual. Throughout the proceedings, Vanessa stood by her husband, though he has done quite a bit of groveling to get back in her good graces. He gave her an eight-carat purple diamond ring worth an estimated four million dollars. He also surprised her with a recommitment ceremony in Laguna Beach, California. Since then, there have been occasional rumblings that their marriage is still on the rocks, but only time will tell.

2. LUCIANA BARROSA—(MATT DAMON)

So this actor walks into a bar . . . and he marries the bartender! Matt Damon made girls swoon—and keep on dreaming that some day their prince would come—when he married Luciana Barrosa whom he met in 2003 while she was bartending at The Crobar, in Miami. Damon was in the area filming *Stuck on You*. Somehow, Barrosa and Damon managed to mingle enough in the nightclub to garner further meetings. He wasn't even scared off by the fact that she had a daughter from a previous marriage! This guy is golden. The Argentine bartender and the A-list actor made it official on December 9, 2005 and have since added two daughters, Isabella and Gia, to their family. While Damon continues acting, Barrosa is now an interior designer, a much more fitting career choice for the wife of *People* magazine's Sexiest Man Alive 2007.

3. JESSICA (SKLAR) SEINFELD—(JERRY SEINFELD)

After Jerry Seinfeld dated seventeen-year-old Shoshanna Lonstein in his late thirties, you'd think anyone he dated thereafter would be less scandalous. Well, the negative press surrounding his wife Jessica Seinfeld has made it a toss-up.

Jessica and Jerry met in 1998 when he approached her at a Manhattan gym. She was twenty-six and worked in fashion PR; he was forty-four and the most famous comedian in the world. She had just returned from her honeymoon after marrying Eric Nederlander, a member of a prominent family in the theater industry. However, according to an interview with the *Telegraph* published on May 4, 2008, Jessica claims there were problems with the relationship before the wedding, and by the time she returned from the honeymoon the marriage was over—at least for her. It had nothing to do with the fact that the most famous and wealthiest comedian in the world was interested in her. Why go ahead with a marriage you knew wasn't right only to abandon it a few weeks later? Probably shouldn't even ask.

Jerry and Jessica married on December 25, 1999 and both the public and industry professionals have been tentative to embrace her. It didn't help that Jessica published a cookbook, *Deceptively Delicious: Simple Secrets to Get Your Kids Eating Good Food* (2007) that was later accused of having been plagiarized. Seinfeld has since been cleared of all charges. Jessica also does her part for charity; in 2001 she founded the Baby Buggy charity, which provides baby clothing and supplies to low-income families in New York. Is she genuine or an opportunist? Only Jerry would know for sure.

4. DANNY MODER—(JULIA ROBERTS)

Danny Moder didn't know it at the time, but landing a job as a cameraman for the movie *The Mexican* would change his life. Or rather meeting Julia Roberts would. When they met in 2000, she was at the top of her game professionally, but in need of a friend to support her through the decline of her relationship with Benjamin Bratt. The couple claims that during shooting they were just friends, as Roberts was still in a relationship with Bratt and Moder was married (to Vera Steimberg Moder). However, rumors of an affair swirled, and when Roberts and Moder tied the knot one month after his divorce from his wife of five years was final, more people began to question how innocent the couple's relationship had been.

While some might wonder what an Academy Award–winning actress and a cameraman have in common, the July 22, 2002 issue of *People* magazine quoted friends as saying that both are solid, nonjudgmental, loving people. Furthermore, Moder accepts Roberts's fame as part of who she is and is very supportive; it is probably a nice change from some of her former performer beaus who couldn't handle the competition for media attention.

5. RYAN SHAWHUGHES—(ETHAN HAWKE)

While Ethan Hawke's relationship with nanny Ryan Shawhughes might not be as well-known as Jude Law's *nannygate*, he actually married his children's former caretaker. Hawke has stood firm, insisting that he and Shawhughes did not become romantically involved until after his divorce from Uma Thurman and Shawhughes was no longer his employee. According to Hawk it was not his relationship with Shawhughes that facilitated his 2004 divorce from his A-list wife of seven years. Still, there are claims that the duo were seeing each other at least during the divorce proceedings, but took extreme precautions not to be seen by the paparazzi because Hawke feared Thurman's wrath. In June 2009, Hawke and Shawhughes made it official a month before they welcomed daughter, Clementine, into the world.

6. CASH WARREN—(JESSICA ALBA)

What does it take to win over one of Hollywood's sexiest leading ladies? Apparently Cash Warren knows the secret, having wooed Jessica Alba down the aisle in May 2008 (though he *may* have been aided by the impending birth of the couple's daughter, Honor Marie). Aside from his dashing good looks, what else comprises Warren's resume? Well, apparently Alba looks for more than an A-list resume; when she and Warren met on the set of *The Fantastic Four* in 2005 he was working as the director's assistant. Having a boyfriend who's used to doing things for others can certainly come in handy.

Us Weekly magazine reported that in July 2007 Alba broke up with Warren, telling him she wasn't in love with him anymore. However, in August the couple was seen together, apparently giving their relationship another try. That try led to their daughter's conception, and a somewhat surprising courthouse wedding in Beverly Hills, California, in May 2008. No one else was in attendance, and apparently not even family members knew about the wedding. Onlookers said Alba looked happy but nervous. On December 19, 2008, the newlyweds and new parents held a commitment celebration with their family and friends.

7. BROOKE MUELLER—(CHARLIE SHEEN)

A history including multiple stints in rehab and a string of failed relationships couldn't keep Brooke Mueller away from Charlie Sheen, who is currently the highest paid comedy star on TV. Mueller, who is twelve years Sheen's junior, was an aspiring actress, but is now a real estate investor. The couple were introduced at a party in May 2006 by Eric Dane and Rebecca Gayhart. *People* magazine reported in its July 20, 2007 issue that Sheen claimed Mueller was, "the coolest gal [he'd] ever met." Hopefully she's cool enough for him to stay on the straight and narrow. Sheen proposed while the couple was vacationing in Costa Rica in June 2007. They married in May 2008, and welcomed twin boys in April 2009. The couple has hit a rough patch after Mueller called 911 on December 25, 2009, saying—according to ABC News on February 8, 2010—"My husband had me with a knife. I was scared for my life and he threatened me." As a result, Sheen was slapped with a restraining order prohibiting him from coming near Mueller, and both Mueller and Sheen have been in and out of rehab since the incident. Hopefully this couple will work out their issues.

8. JILLIAN (FINK) DEMPSEY—(PATRICK DEMPSEY)

Jillian and Patrick Dempsey's meeting could be something out of a chick-lit novel. Former A-list actor walks into salon, falls in love with hair stylist, gets a chance at career redemption, and finally becomes fulfilled both personally and professionally at a level he never enjoyed the first time around in Hollywood. Yes, it's all true. Patrick and Jillian met in 1994 when he walked into Jillian's Delux Beauty salon and she cut his hair. They married in 1999 at Dempsey's family farmhouse in Maine and have been together ever since. The couple welcomed their daughter, Tallulah, in 2002 and twin boys, Sullivan and Darby, in 2007. Since their marriage both Patrick and Jillian have enjoyed career success: Patrick had a big comeback as TV's hottest doctor on *Grey's Anatomy*; and Jillian is the Global Creative Color Director for Avon Products, Inc. and as a makeup artist and hairstylist has worked with some of the biggest stars in the world. This duo seems to be prospering professionally and maintaining their family bond as well. And yes, Jillian still does Patrick's hair.

9. TAMEKA FOSTER RAYMOND—(USHER RAYMOND)

This is a classic case of falling in love with your boss, but this one actually worked out—at least for a while. Tameka Foster was Usher Raymond's stylist. How sweet, right? She watched him date other girls, knowing she was the right one for him, until he came to his senses. Ok, so that's how she tells the story. Others might argue that he's under her gold-digging spell; there certainly wasn't much support for this relationship from either Usher's family (especially his mother) or his fans from the get-go.

Usher, who has won five Grammys and sold over thirty million albums, turned a blind eye to the haters and married a very pregnant Tameka in August 2007. They had planned to marry in a lavish ceremony in the Hamptons on July 28, but called off the event at the last minute. Instead, they tied the knot in an Atlanta law office with a civil ceremony (his mother allegedly chose to spend the day at an Atlanta spa instead of attending the ceremony). A few weeks later, on September 1, they had a big wedding bash for two hundred of their nearest and dearest.

Tameka has three sons from a previous marriage and now shares two sons with Usher. Even while building a family her career flourished: she is the owner of Swanky Image Group, a stylist and image consultant group, and Hides & Dungarees a leather and denim collection based in Atlanta.

In June 2009, Usher filed for divorce from Tameka, and it became final in November 2009.

10. MARSHA GARCES WILLIAMS—(ROBIN WILLIAMS)

This might not be *the* oldest story in the book, but considering it's now shown up twice on this list alone, it's pretty close: the husband and the nanny. While this story didn't end up "happily ever after," it was successful by Hollywood standards. Marsha worked as a nanny for Robin Williams and his first wife, Valerie Velardi. Robin and Valerie's ten-year marriage ended in 1988 and Robin married Marsha the following year. They have two children together and cofounded Blue Wolf Productions, which produced many of Robin's films such as *Mrs. Doubtfire* (1993) and *Patch Adams* (1998), allowing husband and wife to work together—he as an actor and she as a producer.

The marriage lasted nineteen years until Marsha filed for divorce in March 2008 citing irreconcilable differences. *People* magazine reported in April 2008 that friends said the couple's relationship had been rocky since Robin's relapse with alcoholism in 2006. The trust was broken and could not be repaired. Robin and Marsha separated in December 2008, so divorce was not a surprise. Unlike many couples going through divorce, however, Robin and Marsha signed a pact to be honest, cooperative, and civil. Now that is admirable!

Cringeworthy Couples

May—December romances aren't unusual among celebrities. So to make this chapter interesting, couples aren't included on this list for age differences alone, but also for the extra "creep factor" in the relationship.

1. WOODY ALLEN AND SOON-YI PREVIN

One of the most infamous Hollywood relationships, Allen and Priven's relationship received extensive media attention because of their father-daughter relationship. Even in Hollywood a thirty-five year age difference between a couple raises eyebrows, but the fact that Allen played the role of Previn's father for twelve years made the relationship just plain disturbing. Though Allen is not Previn's biological father, he was a father figure to her for almost twelve years during his relationship with her adoptive mother, Mia Farrow (with whom he shares two children). Allen's relationship with Farrow only ended when she found nude pictures of Previn in Allen's apartment, forcing Allen to admit to a sexual relationship with Previn who was then twenty-one. However unlikely, this relationship continues to thrive. Previn and Allen have been married since 1997 and have two adopted children.

2. CELINE DION AND RENE ANGELIL

This relationship is the classic case of a manager falling in love with his talent, (aka his cash cow). Not only is the twenty-six year age difference a little off-putting, but the circumstances surrounding their relationship are creepy as well. Celine Dion's mother and brother started sending out Dion's demo tape when she was only twelve years old. When Angelil heard the tape he immediately offered to manage her, going so far as to mortgage his house to fund Dion's first album. Thus, their professional relationship began when Dion was thirteen and Angelil was thirty-six. They began dating when Dion was twenty, and married six years later at Notre Dame Basilica in Montreal. By that time Dion had become an international superstar, all of which (except for her talent) she owed to Angelil. That kind of power discrepancy makes the relationship a little suspect: What were his motives for marrying Dion? Was he afraid of losing his control over her? Did she really love him, or merely feel obligated to him? Whatever the reason, this May–December marriage has lasted thus far.

3. RANDY JACKSON AND ALEJANDRA OAZIAZA AND JERMAINE JACKSON

Odd relationships seem to run in the Jackson family, with Michael's relationships and marriages being the most infamous. His less well-known brothers, Jermaine and Randy, however, take the prize for their long-term relationships with the same woman, Alejandra Oaziaza. First, Oaziaza lived with Randy and had three children with him (one while he was still married). After they split in 1994 she married Jermaine in 1995 and they had two children together. This must have made family gatherings awkward, not to mention difficult for their children. How do you explain that they're both cousins *and* half-siblings? Jermaine and Oaziaza filed for a divorce in 2004, which was finalized in 2008. The dissolution of the marriage must have helped relations between the brothers, but if I were Randy, I wouldn't leave my girlfriend or wife alone with Jermaine!

4. MARILYN MANSON AND EVAN RACHEL WOOD

So, the idea of Goth rocker Marilyn Manson hooking up in general would give anyone the creeps; but when the thirty-eight-year-old Manson went public with nineteen-year-old actress Evan Rachel Wood, the creep factor skyrocketed. The relationship was even more uncomfortable because his relationship with Wood had contributed to the end of his marriage to Dita Von Teese, who filed for divorce from Manson in December 2006.

Manson and Wood met when he asked her to be in *Phantasmagoria*, a horror film he was making. Upon dating Manson, Woods began to morph into an extension of Manson. She claimed he helped her to get in touch with her Goth side. According to the April 16, 2007 issue of *People* magazine, Manson claimed had found his twin in Wood. Everyone was just waiting to see them wearing vials of each other's blood around their necks. The couple seemed inseparable, so when they split in fall 2008 fans were stunned. Maybe Wood had come to her senses. Despite rumors otherwise, Wood claimed that her need to concentrate on work led to the break. In February 2009 the couple reconnected briefly, only to split the following month. In June 2009 Manson gave a very detailed interview to *Spin* magazine, during which he detailed his reaction to their breakup. Manson claimed he called Wood 158 times the day after their initial split, cutting himself after each one. He also admitted that for a period of time he fantasized about killing her. *Very* creepy.

5. CHER AND TOM CRUISE

Until recently neither Tom Cruise nor Cher had ever spoken publicly about their brief romance in the late 1980s. However, since Cruise was no longer the shy, private man Cher had dated, she openly told her side of the story online, in a *Huffington Post* interview and in a televised interview on *Oprah*. The unlikely duo dated for just a few months, around the time Cruise filmed *Risky Business* and his career took off. Cher said that distance was the cause of their split—she couldn't move to Chicago where he was filming *The Color of Money*—not the sixteen-year age gap. Other sources claim the affair ended because Cruise met Mimi Rogers. It was probably a combination of both. Cruise has never commented on his youthful tryst with the legendary singer/actress, so I guess we'll have to wait for his memoir to hear his side of the story.

6. ANNA NICOLE SMITH AND J. HOWARD MARSHALL

In 1991 Anna Nicole Smith hit the jackpot when oil billionaire Howard Marshall walked into the club where she worked as an exotic dancer. She was twenty-six, he eighty-nine, but I'm sure everyone in the room could feel their immediate connection. Smith and Marshall dated, and he allegedly proposed to her multiple times, until they finally wed in June 1994, just a few months after Smith's divorce from her first husband was finalized. The couple lived in wedded bliss until Marshall died on August 4, 1995. Well, they actually never *lived* together, and Smith was rumored to have entertained other men on the side, but she denied this, claiming in an interview on *Larry King Live* May 29, 2002, that she truly loved Marshall. However, she wasted no time claiming what she believed to be her fair share of his $1.6 billion fortune. So began a lengthy, and complex court case against Marshall's son. For though Marshall altered his will after his marriage to Smith, he failed to include her in the updated will. Smith argued that Marshall verbally promised her half of his fortune. This court battle continued on even after Smith's 2007 death from an overdose of prescription drugs.

7. JERRY SEINFELD AND SHOSHANNA LONSTEIN

Thanks to the little sitcom *Seinfeld* Jerry Seinfeld became one of the most famous comedians in the world. His iconic status led to intense media scrutiny when he began a relationship with seventeen-year-old Shoshanna Lonstein. The then-thirty-eight-year-old Seinfeld met the high school student at a park in New York City, though he insists they were merely friends who went to dinner. Their relationship continued throughout Lonstein's college years with Seinfeld flying across the country to visit her first, at The George Washington University in Washington, D.C., and then, at UCLA, where she transferred after her freshman year. After four years the two parted ways and Seinfeld went on to marry someone a bit more age appropriate—only seventeen years his junior.

8. LISA MARIE PRESLEY AND MICHAEL JACKSON

Two of music's most famous families united in May 1994 when Lisa Marie Presley and Michael Jackson wed. People were understandably shocked, for Jackson's sexuality had recently been under speculation, and since shortly before the nuptials Jackson had been on trial for child molestation. Though he was found innocent his image was in need of improvement. Many people felt this marriage was simply a publicity stunt. Presley and Jackson vehemently claimed their marriage was real, but this "real love" marriage lasted only two years. In a 2005 interview on *Oprah* Presley said she fell in love with Jackson because she wanted to help him with his problems. She said she believed he loved her as much as he was able. Looking back on the situation though, she thinks he used her for publicity, but she never confronted him about it.

9. MADONNA AND VANILLA ICE

The Queen of Pop and One-Hit-Wonder Vanilla Ice had a short-lived affair in 1992. Two years later Vanilla Ice told *USA*

Today that the singers did indeed had a brief relationship, but claimed that while Madonna had a good body for her age, she was obsessive—calling him at weird hours and asking whom he was with. Not surprisingly, this coupling only lasted eight months. Vanilla Ice faded into obscurity, while Madonna moved on to her next conquest.

10. LANCE ARMSTRONG AND ASHLEY OLSEN

Despite the rumors swirling in 2007, the seven-time *Tour de France* champion Lance Armstrong denies that he and former 'tween idol Ashley Olsen were ever more than friends. There were sightings of the two getting cozy in a New York restaurant—some of the rumors claim Olsen even sat on his lap. *Very* friendly behavior.

Not only did this possible affair garner attention because of the age difference—Olsen was twenty-one, Armstrong was thirty-six—but the two come from vastly different celebrity circles, plus Armstrong was a divorced father of three. What could they have in common? Armstrong protested that he and Olsen were strictly friends, claiming she was "a nice, smart lady." Really. Who refers to their twenty-one-year-old *friend* as a "lady"? Methinks he doth protest too much.

Bring on the Bling

Before you look down at your own ring finger and begin comparing your (comparatively speaking) measly engagement ring to the ones on this list, just remember that your partner probably spent a larger percentage of their income on your ring than anyone on this list did for their betrothed. Furthermore, your marriage will probably last longer than most on this list—that is, longer than those that were actually consummated. That said, you have permission to drool.

1. BEYONCÉ KNOWLES FROM JAY-Z—18 CARATS, $5 MILLION

This couple is so hush-hush about their relationship that it's hard to uncover the truth. But according to *People* magazine, Jay-Z gave Beyoncé an 18-carat flawless diamond engagement ring by jeweler Lorraine Schwartz, which is valued at more than $5 million dollars. Beyoncé first displayed the ring publicly on the red carpet for the Fashion Rocks event at Radio City Music Hall in September 2008. It wasn't until October, however that Beyoncé confirmed the couple's marriage in an *Essence* magazine interview, admitting that they had married the previous April at Jay-Z's New York City apartment.

2. PARIS HILTON FROM PARIS LATSIS—24 CARATS, $4.7 MILLION

It's no surprise that Paris Hilton received the most expensive engagement ring around the time of her engagement. How could she accept anything less than the best? In May 2007 Latsis presented Hilton with a 24-carat emerald cut diamond ring, for which he paid an estimated $4.7 million. Unfortunately, poor Miss Hilton had a major problem with her ring: it was so heavy that it hurt her finger! According to a July 2005 issue of *US Weekly*, Latsis, in order to make his fiancée comfortable, made up for his inconsiderate purchase and bought her a "more manageable diamond-less platinum Cartier band for everyday wear." Wow. I guess if you look hard enough you can find a downside to any situation. Nonetheless, two engagement rings cannot a relationship save: Hilton and Latsis broke off their engagement five months later. Some good did come of the ring, however: Hilton auctioned it off and the proceeds were donated to the victims of Hurricane Katrina. (The winning bidder got a real bargain at $2 million.)

3. ANNA KOURNIKOVA FROM ENRIQUE IGLESIAS—11 CARATS, $2.5 MILLION

The tennis star and the Latin crooner have kept the status of their relationship very mysterious: claiming to have broken up, then claiming to not be married and having no plans to ever marry. However, in late 2007 Anna Kournikova was spotted wearing an 11-carat natural pink pear shaped ring with diamond accents on the ring finger of her left hand, and the rumors that the duo was engaged began. Speculation as to this couple's status continues. In April 2008 Kournikova told *People* magazine that she was never getting married, while in June 2008 the *Daily Star* quoted Iglesias as saying he had been married. In September 2009 rumors reignited when Kournikova and Iglesias were spotted in a Cartier store in Paris. Only Kournikova and Iglesias know the true status of their relationship, but why would a couple who has been hell-bent on keeping the public out of their lives show off such a pricey stone on a tell-tale finger? Maybe it's all a game. Either way, Iglesias dropped a lot of cash for Kournikova: the ring is valued at $2.5 million dollars.

4. MARIAH CAREY FROM NICK CANNON—17 CARATS, $2.5 MILLION

Mariah Carey and Nick Cannon, eleven years Carey's junior, met on the set of the video for her single "Bye Bye" in March 2008. By May they were husband and wife. Cannon commissioned jeweler Jacob & Co. to make the ring, which cost a reported $2.5 million dollars. *In Touch* magazine reported that the jewelers confirmed that the ring was new (there had been some speculation that Cannon had recycled it from his previous fiancée Selita Ebanks, since the rings look very similar) and consisted of a 17-carat square emerald-cut, light pink center stone surrounded by fifty-eight intense pink diamonds and one half-moon diamond on either side. Carey first showed off the ring in late April, mere days before they married amid speculation that their relationship had ended because of Cannon's seemingly impersonal engagement ring. While the couple did indeed marry, it does caution men to put some thought into your girl's ring. The perfect ring doesn't ensure a blissful relationship, but the wrong ring could end a relationship.

5. CATHERINE ZETA-JONES FROM MICHAEL DOUGLAS—10 CARATS, $2 MILLION

Michael Douglas spared no expense for his future wife's engagement ring. The ring cost a reported $2 million, which is more than they spent on their wedding. What did Douglas get for his money? A 1920 Fred Leighton design antique ring with a 10-carat marquise-cut center diamond surrounded by twenty-eight smaller diamonds. So far this couple has been happily married since 2000 and have two children.

6. KATIE HOLMES FROM TOM CRUISE—5 CARATS, $1.5 MILLION

It comes as no shock that Tom Cruise spared no expense for Katie Holmes's engagement ring. If a woman can make a man want to jump on a couch like a crazy person on national TV, she can definitely get him to buy her a nice piece of jewelry. Ok, so maybe a $1.5 million dollar ring is a little more than nice, but he's Tom Cruise, he can afford it. The ring is a 5-carat oval shaped Edwardian style ring set in platinum and rose gold. After dating for only a little over two months, Cruise proposed atop the Eiffel Tower. It might sound a little cliché, but Cruise explained that he had never been to the Tower and thought it was a very romantic setting. The happy couple has been married since November 2006.

7. JENNIFER LOPEZ FROM BEN AFFLECK (AKA BENNIFER 1.0)—6.1 CARATS, $1.2 MILLION

Here is another case to show that bigger and more expensive does not ensure that a relationship thrives, or that a wedding even takes place. If Paris and Paris didn't convince you, just consider Bennifer. *People* magazine reported in November 2002 that Ben Affleck had proposed to his then-girlfriend with a stunning 6.1-carat pink diamond, from jeweler Harry Winston, valued at $1.2 million. Though the couple came closer to getting married than the Parises, the wedding was called off at the last minute and in January 2003 Lopez and Affleck went their separate ways. Harry Winston reacquired the ring and put it up for sale, though the price was available to serious buyers only. Lopez married Latin singer Mark Anthony in 2004, while Affleck took a little longer before wedding Jennifer Garner in 2005 and creating Bennifer 2.0, which many agreed was an upgraded model. Apparently

Affleck learned his lesson and bought his new love a more modest ring for only half a million dollars.

8. MELANIA KNAUSS FROM DONALD TRUMP—12 CARATS, $1 MILLION

Would The Donald ever buy anything but perfection? Of course not, he even has gold faucets in his bathroom and few people ever see that. Something so public and defining as an engagement ring is going to be top of the line, right? Knauss is Trump's third wife, but her ring is first-rate. Trump proposed to her with a 12-carat emerald cut diamond in a platinum basket setting with channel set tapered baguettes flanking each side. The ring is valued at $1.5 million dollars, but reportedly he paid only about $1 million for it. Maybe after all his marriage misfortunes he was trying to cut his losses, or show good taste and class.

9. JENNIFER LOPEZ FROM MARK ANTHONY—8.5 CARATS, $1 MILLION

Jennifer Lopez seemingly ran from Ben Affleck into the arms of one time boyfriend and recent divorcé Marc Anthony. The couple married in June 2004, a mere six months after Lopez's split from Affleck. However, Anthony said the couple married so quickly that he didn't have a chance to get Lopez an engagement ring at the time, so he presented her with one a year later. Though not as expensive as Affleck's, Anthony's million dollar ring is larger. The Neil Lane square cut 8-carat rose diamond rivals Lopez's three other engagement rings, which each represent an "unhappily" ever after. Though rumors have been swirling that the marriage is already on the rocks, let's hope the fourth ring is the charm.

10. BRANDY FROM QUENTIN RICHARDSON—11.5 CARATS, $1 MILLION

New York Knick Quentin Richardson proposed to pop star

Brandy with a million-dollar, 11.5-carat diamond ring designed by Hollywood jeweler Jason Arasheben. After becoming engaged, Brandy had Quentin's face tattooed on her back. However, like many people who get tattoos as symbols of their undying love, the engagement was called off fifteen months later. Poor Brandy had to undergo multiple tattoo sessions to make Quentin's face resemble a cat.

Money Was No Object

Weddings can be expensive for ordinary couples with dress, food, flowers, and music costing tens of thousands of dollars. For the celebrities on this list, a marriage celebration is raised to another level entirely. Perhaps it's an attempt to compensate for the lack of true affection. Or maybe they just don't have anything better to spend their money on. The extravagant weddings on this list are just the ones we know about; but there are likely even more expensive weddings than the ones included here.

1. LIZA MINELLI AND DAVID GEST—$3.5 MILLION

On March 16, 2002, at the Marble Collegiate Church in New York City, Liza Minelli, 58, put on the biggest show of her life: her wedding to TV producer David Gest, 46. This much money can create a true spectacle—even in the Big Apple, and even on a tight schedule (the couple had only started dating in September). With Elizabeth Taylor as Maid of Honor and Michael Jackson giving the bride away and acting as Best Man, the marriage might have been doomed from the start. As Jackson escorted the four-time bride down the aisle, Whitney Houston performed. Not necessarily a good omen, considering the state of her marriage.

Five hundred guests, including many current and former celebrities, witnessed Minelli and Guest's nuptials. Some of those present speculated that the blessed event occured while the bride was under the influence of drugs. Fifty-five singers, such as Tony Bennett and Natalie Cole, performed at the reception accompanied by a sixty-piece orchestra. While the wedding tops the list of most expensive, their marriage is not counted among the longest, ending only sixteen months after they vowed to spend the rest of their lives together.

2. PAUL MCCARTNEY AND HEATHER MILLS—$3 MILLION

McCartney and Mills persevered through two and a half years of dating under intense scrutiny—from the public and from McCartney's children—and finally wed in the presence of three hundred guests at Castle Leslie in Glaslough, Ireland, in 2002. For the affair, Mills designed her own dress with Eavis and Brown of London and carried a bouquet of McCartney roses (which are also known as "Paul McCartney" roses). At the reception guests dined on vegetarian Indian cusine, and were surrounded by Dutch flowers. Later in the evening they watched as the newlyweds floated on a lily-covered cabin cruiser under the light of fireworks.

3. ELIZABETH HURLEY AND ARUN NAYER—$2.5 MILLION

Elizabeth Hurley got not just one ceremony but two. On March 3, 2007, she wed her boyfriend of five years Arun Nayer, textile heir and cofounder of Software Solutions, in a lavish ceremony in front of three hundred guests at Sudeley Castle in England. Then, on March 9, the newlyweds traveled to India where a traditional Hindu ceremony was performed as part of an entire week of parties. The Hindu ceremony took place at Umaid Bhawan Palace, which the couple rented out in its entirety (normally, rooms in the palace run ten thousand dollars a night!). According to *People* magazine, there were approximately two hundred guests in attendance at the celebration in India who witnessed such spectacles as dancing white horses and walkways lined with millions of red chili peppers. Talk about a hot couple!

4. CHRISTINA AGUILERA AND JORDAN BRATMAN—$2 MILLION

Christina Aguilera pulled out all the stops for her Spanish-themed wedding to music executive Jordan Bratman in November 2002. The duo took their vows at the Staglin Family Vineyard in Napa Valley, inside the stained glass Castilian castle, which was constructed on top of a swimming pool. To complete the Spanish theme, Aguilera walked down the aisle wearing a flamenco-style wedding dress designed by Christian Lacroix and carried a diamond rosary instead of flowers. It may have been Catholic in ritual, but more extravagant than anything the Pope would approve. After the ceremony, Mrs. Bratman had two wardrobe changes, donning a Les Habitudes gown and then, later, a Simone Harouche halter dress. After leaving the party in Aguilera's $350,000 vintage white Rolls Royce Phantom, they retired to a $3,500 per night cottage at the Auberge du Soleil resort.

5. ELIZABETH TAYLOR AND LARRY FORTENSKY—$2 MILLION

Larry who? That's exactly what everyone was thinking when legendary screen siren Elizabeth Taylor, 59, announced her marriage to construction worker Larry Fortensky, 39. Where would a screen legend meet a blue-collar prince? Their relationship began while both were staying at the Betty Ford Center battling their addictions.

Though the groom may have been blue collar, their wedding was anything but. Though this was Taylor's eighth wedding, and she didn't cut any corners. Michael Jackson hosted the affair at his famous Neverland Ranch and also gave the bride away. While the pre-wedding buzz predicted a crazier spectacle than actually occured, it definitely wasn't an ordinary affair (if you hadn't already guessed that from the Neverland Ranch setting). Guests jumped on huge trampolines and were entertained in Jackson's amusement park. So much hype surrounded these nuptials that a security force of one hundred was hired. Of course, that didn't stop a parachuting photographer from landing twenty feet from the ceremony.

6. TOM CRUISE AND KATIE HOLMES—$2 MILLION

After a whirlwind romance of only two months, Tom Cruise, 44, popped the question to Katie Holmes, 27, atop the Eiffel Tower in April 2005. Though they wasted no time getting to the proposal, the pair did not wed until November 2006. During that time Holmes and Cruise welcomed baby Suri and took time to plan her dream wedding to her dream man. The result was an elegant Italian affair at Odescalchi Castle in Lake Gracciano. A Scientology ceremony was performed in front of one hundred and fifty guests, but was not recognized by Italian law. This was expected, and the couple completed the necessary paperwork in Los Angeles to legalize their union. Thank goodness, what would we do if TomKat weren't legal?

7. ELTON JOHN AND DAVID FURNISH—$1.5 MILLION

Technically, Elton John, 58, spent this small fortune celebrating a civil union, not a marriage. There was still great cause for celebration however after he and partner David Furnish, 43, were united in a private ceremony at Windsor's Guildhall: the couple had waited thirteen years to legalize their partnership! The December 2005 event, occurred during the very week that same-sex unions were legalized in England under the Civil Partnership Act.

Though their ceremony was intimate, consisting of only a few close friends, everyone was invited to the celebrations surrounding the main event. *People* magazine reported that

John and Furnish began celebrating their union two days before the ceremony with a joint bachelor party at a trendy Soho nightclub, which included a video message of support and congratulations from President Bill Clinton. Six hundred guests from around the world, including the Beckhams, Donatella Versace, Claudia Schiffer, and Sharon Stone, attended the lavish reception at the couple's Windsor mansion, where pink champagne was served and John serenaded Furnish.

8. MICHAEL DOUGLAS AND CATHERINE ZETA-JONES—$1.5 MILLION

In November 1997, Michael Douglas, 56, wed Catherine Zeta-Jones, 31, in a lavish affair at the The Plaza Hotel in New York City. Zeta-Jones allegedly wanted a dramatic yet intimate wedding, but according to *People* Magazine, three hundred fifty guests attended the ceremony, including actors Goldie Hawn, Jack Nicholson, and Meg Ryan, as well as U.N. Secretary General Kofi Annan. The guests admired Zeta-Jones as her father (who is two years Douglas's junior) walked her down the aisle, carefully avoiding her six-foot-long train.

The large, yet "intimate" group, dined on lobster and lamb, followed by the couple's wedding cake. The six-foot, ten-tier creation was covered with thousands of sugar flowers and was disassembled and reconstructed to fit into the ballroom. There were twenty-eight types of roses used to adorn the festivities and a wide variety of musical entertainment. Favorites of Douglas, Art Garfunkel and Gladys Knight sang, and to honor Zeta-Jones's heritage, a Welsh choir performed as well. One fun fact, Zeta-Jones's official last name is actually Zeta-Douglas. She only retains her maiden name for professional purposes.

9. TIGER WOODS AND ELIN NORDEGREN—$1.5 MILLION

While some might think that the theme of Woods's wedding would be golf, since he is a legend in the sport, or the beach,

because the ceremony was at Sandy Lane Beach Resort in
Barbados, the theme of the wedding seemed to be privacy.
Extreme measures were taken to make sure that the wedding of the most famous athlete in the world was kept out of
the media's view. Not even Owen Wilson and Vince Vaughn
could have crashed this wedding! Woods booked the only
helicopter company on the island so TV crews could not
fly overhead. He also rented out the entire resort—where
rooms range from $700-$8,000 per night—in order to ensure their seclusion. The sunset ceremony was a success
with an intimate gathering of only their one hundred twenty
invited guests and musical entertainment by Hootie and the
Blowfish.

10. MADONNA AND GUY RITCHIE—$1.5 MILLION

Everything Madonna does is extreme, so it was no surprise
that her wedding to film director Guy Ritchie would be as
well. There were many unfounded rumors surrounding the
nuptials, but the Material Girl did not disappoint. The December 2000 wedding, for which the couple rented out the
fifty-one bedroom Skibo Castle in Scotland, followed Scottish
traditions. The groom, a native Scot, and their four-month old
son, Rocco, both wore kilts. A Scottish tartan sash supposedly accented even Madonna's ivory silk, princess-inspired,
strapless Stella McCartney gown. The bride accessorized with
a $250,000 diamond tiara on loan from Asprey & Garrard of
London; a 37-carat, 2.5-inch diamond cross pendant from
Harry Winston of New York; and pearl and diamond bracelets
on loan from Adler of London. Which is probably more bling
than many actual princesses wear.

Living up to her Material Girl nickname, Madonna made
two wardrobe changes that evening. She wore a Jean-Paul
Gaultier dress to dinner and for dancing she dressed in a
Versace gown designed especially for her by her good friend
and wedding guest, Donatella Versace.

Cashing In

This is a list of divorce settlements that are part of the public record. Others that would probably make the list if known include: Tom Cruise and Nicole Kidman (*People* estimates she received $85 million) and Bruce Willis and Demi Moore (*People* estimates she received $70 million). Divorce proceedings between Mel Gibson and Robyn Gibson are ongoing at the time of publication, but most likely will top this list once the divorce is final.

1. MICHAEL AND JUANITA JORDAN—$168 MILLION

It is fitting that basketball icon Michael Jordan, who is probably worth more than anyone else on this list (aside from Paul McCartney), is at the top of this list. Michael and Juanita met on a blind date and married five years later. Their marriage lasted seventeen years, but not without its ups and downs. Juanita first filed for divorce in 2002, but withdrew the petition. However, in 2006 Juanita filed for divorce again and followed through with it. The couple had been living apart for almost a year of their seventeen-year marriage, so it came as no surprise to family and friends. It is alleged that Juanita had signed a post-nuptial agreement a year and a half after their marriage, which entitled her to half his fortune.

41

The final settlement, however, only gave her one-third of his total estate, approximately $168 million.

2. NEIL DIAMOND AND MARCIA MURPHY—$150 MILLION

The story goes that legendary crooner Neil Diamond went out for cigarettes in 1969 and never returned. Three weeks later he divorced his first wife, Jaye Posnerr, and married Marcia Murphy just before he became famous with his album *Touching You, Touching Me*. Over the years, Diamond has sold over 100 million albums and he continues to have devoted fans.

Diamond's second marriage lasted twenty-five years until they divorced in 1995. Murphy was awarded $150 million dollars, half his net worth and the largest divorce settlement at that time. About the settlement numerous media outlets have quoted Diamond as saying that his ex-wife was "worth every penny."

3. STEVEN SPIELBERG AND AMY IRVING—$100 MILLION

Who would have thought that a prenuptial agreement written on a restaurant napkin wouldn't be valid in court? Obviously not Steven Spielberg, one of the most famous and successful directors of all time. During divorce proceedings against his wife of four years, actress Amy Irving, he argued that the couple had a prenup . . . written on a napkin. The judge quickly dismissed the document as invalid, since Irving did not have legal representation when she signed the "contract." Instead, Irving was awarded $100 million dollars—half of Spielberg's fortune at the time. Not bad for four years of marriage. Though if she'd stuck around, she could have received half of his current net worth, an estimated $3 billion.

4. HARRISON FORD AND MELISSA MATHISON—$85 MILLION +

"The divorce that keeps on giving" perfectly describes screenwriter Melissa Mathison's divorce settlement from Harrison Ford. The couple, who met on the set of *Apoca-*

lypse Now in 1976 and married in 1983, were married for approximately eighteen years, have two children together, and had no prenuptial agreement. In the divorce Mathison was awarded $85 million dollars in addition to a percentage of future profits of all movies made during the couple's marriage, which includes the lucrative *Indiana Jones* trilogy.

5. KEVIN COSTNER AND CINDY SILVA—$80 MILLION

It was a romantic tale of young love persevering through thick and thin, one person pursuing a dream while the other stood faithfully by being supportive. Ok, so Kevin Costner and Cindy Silva's relationship was like that until she filed for divorce in 1994. The couple was much admired, for they were college sweethearts whose marriage had lasted sixteen years. However, Silva filed for divorce amidst rumors of Costner's infidelity. Silva was rewarded with $80 million dollars, which should allow her to live comfortably.

6. MADONNA AND GUY RITCHIE—BETWEEN $76–$92 MILLION

Madonna's divorce from director Guy Ritchie was the most publicized divorce of 2008. Rumors had been swirling for over a year that the marriage was on the rocks, so when rumor became reality it was no great shock. The public was curious to know why, and how much Ritchie's settlement would be, since the couple had married without a prenup. Only Madonna and Ritchie know what drove them apart after seven years of marriage, but some speculate that Madonna's obsession with Kabbalah, her constant exercising, and her supposed controlling nature caused the split. Others blame Ritchie, claiming he spent too much time at their London pub and with his friends and was not emotionally available to Madonna. Whatever the reason, this couple divorced quickly. Upon filing for divorce in London, Madonna cited Ritchie's "unreasonable behavior" as a cause and was allowed a preliminary "quickie divorce."

No matter the reason, *People* magazine reported that Ritchie walked away with between $76 million and $92 million, which includes the value of their home in western England and their London pub. This is a small percentage of Madonna's estimated $500 million dollar net worth. It seemed that both parties just wanted the divorce completed.

7. KENNY AND MARIANNE ROGERS—$60 MILLION
Country singer Kenny Rogers forked over $60 million dollars upon divorcing his fourth wife Marianne. The couple met on the set of the television show *Hee Haw* where Kenny sang and Marianne was a presenter. Though Kenny had been married three times before, his marriage to Marianne lasted almost sixteen years. They filed for divorce in 1993.

Whatever negative feelings Kenny may have had about the final settlement, he didn't let on to the public, telling the press she deserved it for putting up with him. Considering that Kenny's net worth was estimated to be $250 million, maybe he thought the outcome could have been worse.

8. JAMES CAMERON AND LINDA HAMILTON—$50 MILLION
Though actress Linda Hamilton, of *Terminator* fame, did not find lasting love and fidelity with director James Cameron, she picked a good seventeen months (eight of which they were separated) to be married to him. During that period, Cameron's hit *Titanic* was released, earning him $100 million, of which Hamilton received half in their divorce settlement. What went wrong so quickly in this marriage? The couple dated for six years before marrying, but Cameron had a wandering eye and reportedly began an affair with Suzi Amis. He later married Amis . . . probably with a rock solid prenup.

9. PAUL MCCARTNEY AND HEATHER MILLS—$48.6 MILLION
Paul McCartney's children were probably ecstatic when they found out their father had filed for divorce: reportedly they

never approved of their father's marriage to former model Heather Mills. Mills was also never beloved by the public and attitudes towards her spiraled downwards once McCartney filed for divorce. Mills complained in an interview with GMTV in October 31, 2007 that she had been "treated worse than a murderer or a pedophile."

Mills reportedly sought over $200 million dollars, but according to People.com and Fox News, received a mere $48.6 million, which includes a $33 million dollar lump sum from McCartney plus her existing assets, which were valued at $15.6 million. Additionally, McCartney will pay $70,000 per year to their child, Beatrice, plus pay for her education and her nanny.

So how did the former Beatle get off so easily when there was no prenup and when his estimated net worth was $800 million? The marriage was brief, lasting fewer than four years, and most of McCartney's fortune was earned before they wed. Furthermore, after the divorce ruling, the *Telegraph* reported that the judge said that throughout the case Mills was "inconsistent, inaccurate, and less than candid" while he found McCartney to be "honest." Perhaps the judge's feelings about the characters of McCartney and Mills worked in McCartney's favor.

10. MICHAEL AND DIANDRA DOUGLAS—$45 MILLION

Michael and Diandra's nineteen-year marriage preceded his rise to fame; they met at a party in 1977 when she was a nineteen-year-old university student and he was a 32-year-old TV actor. They married nine weeks after meeting and their union lasted for almost twenty years, which is a few lifetimes in Hollywood. In 1997, amidst allegations of Michael's infidelity and alcohol abuse, Diandra filed for divorce. The proceedings dragged on over two years. Ultimately she received $45 million, which was about one-third Michael's total worth, plus property in Majorca and in Beverly Hills.

They Can't Pick Just One

It may be true that celebrities date more than average people, but the stars on this list have gone above and beyond the call of dating duty. Not only are they frequent daters, it also doesn't seem like they will be settling down any time soon.

1. HUGH GRANT

At almost fifty years old, Hugh Grant seems committed to being a singleton for life. Of course stranger things have happened, but if Hugh Grant's track record is any indication it is very unlikely he'll ever settle down.

Grant, who has stated that he hates acting, especially movie acting, dated model/actress Elizabeth Hurley for thirteen years (1987–2000) without a ring or commitment. She even stood by him in 1995 when he was arrested on Sunset Boulevard for lewd conduct in a public place . . . with prostitute Divine Brown. It's unlikely that Brown was the first person with whom Grant cheated and probably was not the last.

Since Hurley and Grant split in 2000, Grant has been linked to numerous women, including Sandra Bullock, Helena Bonham Carter, Eimeau Montgomery (wife of golfer Colin Montgomery), and Kasia Komorowciz, his *Love Actu-*

ally costar. It was rumored that Grant and Komorowcz dated for three years immediately following his break with Hurley. From 2004–2007 Grant dated Jemima Kahn who split with her husband after meeting Grant. While he seems to be taking a break from the romantic and acting spotlight, only appearing in roles every few years, perhaps to replenish his bank account or to keep himself in the Hollywood game, his charm, charisma, and wit will guarantee that he is only ever alone by choice.

2. MARIO LOPEZ

Most of us remember Mario Lopez as the hot jock on the sitcom *Saved by the Bell*. Those dimples make him seem very lovable and datable, an all-around good guy. However, his sweet demeanor and innocent appearance has fooled many girls. Though Lopez looks like he would be a devoted boyfriend and husband, Lopez's tragic flaw is that his is a commitment phobe. He likes the appearance of being in a committed, monogamous relationship but the reality of such a relationship is just too much for him.

Example number one: he dated Miss USA, Ali Landry from 1998 until they married in April 2004. However, just two weeks later Landry had their marriage annulled after discovering Lopez's numerous infidelities throughout their relationship.

Example number two: Lopez dated *Dancing with the Stars* partner Karina Smirnoff for two years—they even lived together—until they broke up in 2008. According to *People* magazine Smirnoff's spokesperson claimed "the relationship wasn't heading in the right direction." Would that be the direction of the aisle and wedded bliss? Additionally, rumors swirled that Lopez was simultaneously dating another girl for a year of his relationship with Smirnoff. Meagan Cooper (a twenty-two year old former Hooters girl and contestant on the reality show *I Survived A Japanese Game Show*) alleged that she dated Lopez for a year and he told her he and Karina had broken up. Lopez has neither confirmed nor denied this allegation. Named *People* magazine's Hottest Bachelor in June 2008, he seems happy to be single and just keeps smiling.

3. SEAN COMBS (AKA PUFF DADDY, P. DIDDY, DIDDY)

With a net worth of approximately $358 million as of 2007 (according to panachereport.com), a successful record label (Bad Boy Records), two clothing lines, a movie production company, two restaurants, and his work as an actor, Sean Combs seems to have the world at his fingertips. While Combs has been busy creating his empire, he has not neglected his personal life. He has had numerous relationships, fathering six children with four different women. With all these options he hasn't been able to commit to just one woman. The closest he's come to commitment is with on-and-off girlfriend Kim Porter, with whom he has a son and twin daughters. When Combs and Porter announced that they were expecting twins, rumors ran rampant that a wedding would soon follow. But news that Diddy fathered a child who was only six months older than his twin girls halted any of Porter's wedding plans. Porter claimed in an interview with *Essence* magazine that she found out about Combs's infidelity while she was pregnant but waited for him to confront her. Combs failed to discuss it with her until after the twins were born in December 2007. Porter moved out of Combs's house in July 2007, though the couple has remained close, Combs even throwing Porter a birthday party in 2008. Aside from relationships with the mothers of his children, Combs enjoyed a high profile relationship with actress/singer Jennifer Lopez for two and a half years in the late 1990s, and more recently he was seen with actresses Cameron Diaz and Sienna Miller. Though he claims that he wants to marry and have ten kids, it seems likely that only the latter is probable.

Sean Combs attending the *Spider-Man 3* premier with sons, Justin and Christian. *David Shankbone*

4. PARIS HILTON

Even at the tender age of twenty-nine, Paris Hilton's list of male conquests is already longer than most people twice her age—that's with a year of proclaimed celibacy and "self-discovery" from mid-2006 to mid-2007. Hilton has allegedly dated or at least hooked up with the following notables: Edward Furlong, Rick Salomon, Oscar de la Hoya, Nick Carter, Travis Barker, Cisco Adler, Adrian Grenier, Jared Leto, Fred Durst, Val Kilmer, Brandon Davis, Jamie Kennedy, Stavros Niarchos, and Benji Madden.

Since her split from Madden in 2008, Hilton has been dating Doug Reinhardt on-and-off and the two claim that marriage plans are in the works. However, Paris has been here before. She was engaged to model Jason Shaw from 2002-2003 and Greek shipping heir Paris Latsis in 2005. Many times Paris has proclaimed: to be happier than she's ever been; to be so over the club scene; and to want to "settle down" with her beau of the moment and have children. Admittedly, Hilton and Reinhardt do share at least one common interest: they crave attention. Maybe Paris has just been looking for her Spencer Pratt. . . . No, not Paris!

5. WILMER VALDERRAMA

Wilmer Valderrama is the male version of Paris Hilton, yet while Hilton constantly proclaims her desire spend her life with her boyfriend of the moment, thirty-year-old Valederrama does not disclose such thoughts. He prefers going on Howard Stern and talking about his sex life with past girlfriends, justifying the interview merely "playful." Valderrama has been linked to Mandy Moore, Jessica Alba, Jennifer Love Hewitt, Lindsay Lohan, Ashley Simpson, Mila Kunis, Rosario Dawson, Erika Christensen, Ashley Olsen, Mischa Barton, Jaime Pressly, Christina Milian, and Rihanna. On Stern's radio show Valderrama candidly spoke about his sexual encounters with Moore, Hewitt, Lohan, and Simpson. He spoke positively about his experiences with each girl, such as claiming he took Moore's virginity, rating Hewitt an 8 on a scale of 10, informing the world that Simpson was a screamer, and that Lohan liked to wax. It is no surprise that none of the girls were pleased with his lack of discretion. He did nobly claim that he never slept with Alba, Dawson, or Pressly.

Though Valderrama's acting career has cooled since *That '70s Show* went off the air, he continues to be a staple on the Hollywood club circuit with no sign of settling down.

6. **CAMERON DIAZ**

Ranked as the highest paid actress of 2008 by *Forbes*, model-turned-actress Cameron Diaz feels no need to settle down as she creeps closer to the big 4-0. Diaz seems to live a carefree life outside of work, surfing, spending time with her girlfriends, and dating any guy she wants. Why settle down when she has every man at her fingertips? Since appearing on the Hollywood radar with her breakout role in *The Mask* (1994), Diaz has racked up an impressive black book including long term relationships with Matt Dillon, Jared Leto (to whom she was engaged), and Justin Timberlake, as well as shorter alleged hookups with Sean Combs, Scott Speedman, Robbie Williams, John Mayer, Paul Sculfor, Criss Angel, Gerard Butler, Edward Norton, Bradley Cooper, and Vince Vaughn.

7. **DREW BARRYMORE**

Drew Barrymore seems to be open to love and marriage but just doesn't seem to know how to sustain a relationship. She has actually married twice: her first marriage to bar owner Jeremy Thomas lasted only just over a month; her second marriage to Tom Green lasted under six months.

An actress from a very young age, she broke out at age seven in the role of Gertie in *E.T.* At age thirteen Barrymore entered rehab for drug and alcohol abuse and at age fourteen she attempted suicide. Her teenage years were wild and crazy, flashing David Letterman, and posing nude for *Playboy* and *Interview* magazines. Upon entering her twenties Barrymore went to great lengths to change her image and has become one of Hollywood's sweethearts. Barrymore reportedly dated Corey Feldman, Jack Nicholson, Leonardo DiCaprio, Balthazar Getty, Rick Salomon, David Arquette, Chris O'Donnell, Val Kilmer, Luke Wilson, Edward Norton, Brandon Davis, Spike Jonze, Zack Braff, Justin Long, and *Gossip Girl* actors Chase Crawford and Ed Westwick. She was engaged to actor/singer Jamie Walters and to singer Fabrizio Moretti. Barrymore seems to have her professional life together and is now working on her personal life. In the April 2009 issue of *W* magazine, Barrymore confessed, "I'm just learning who I am and how relationships work and how to make them function." I'm sure Barrymore will walk down the aisle again, lets hope the third time is the charm.

8. GEORGE CLOONEY

George Clooney is a staple on "sexiest men" and "hottest bachelor" lists, including being honored as *People* magazine's Sexiest Man Alive twice: in 1997 and 2006. His dry sense of humor and ability to laugh at himself, in addition to his good looks, draw women to him. However, since his brief marriage to Talia Balsam (1989–1993) he has adamantly stated that he will never marry again. *The Boston Globe* reported on January 20, 2010 that Clooney told the British magazine *Reveal*, "I tried marriage and it didn't work. . . . My fear is that I would make a lousy husband." Clooney's feelings about marriage have not kept women from pursuing him—perhaps it makes him even more desirable.

He is an equal opportunity serial dater, being linked to both famous and non-famous women. He has dated such actresses as Renée Zellweger, Teri Hatcher, Lucy Liu, Charlize Theron, Ellen Barkin, Krista Allen, and Kelly Preston. He has also been linked to British model Lisa Snowdon; cocktail waitress and model Sarah Larson; and is currently dating Italian TV personality, model, and actress Elisabetta Canalis. Dating Clooney gives unknown women visibility, which ultimately leads to a career boost. For example, Sarah Larson is no longer a Las Vegas cocktail waitress, but works as a private yoga instructor in Los Angeles, where she moved while she was dating Clooney, and currently developing her own yoga-inspired clothing line. Dating Clooney has opened doors and may make her a household name. He is not shy about his dating life, having his girlfriend of the moment walk red carpets with him, join him at film festivals, and be photographed on vacations with him. While Clooney might not be life partner material, the benefits seem to outweigh the costs. And who knows, maybe one day Clooney will meet a woman who makes him want to take a chance on marriage again.

9. JENNIFER LOVE HEWITT

Ever since audiences fell in love with Jennifer Love Hewitt as Sarah on the family TV drama *Party of Five*, Hewitt has been seen as the lovable yet sexy girl next door. How could she have hit thirty without being married, especially with the numerous guys she's dated? She appears to be on the lookout for a long-term mate, so is it her? or is it them?

She dated Will Friedle, Joey Lawrence, Andrew Keegan, Carson Daly, Antonio Sabato Jr., John Mayer, Wilmer Valderrama, Enrique Iglesias, Alec Baldwin, Jimmy Fallon, John Cusack, and Rich Cronin. She was engaged to Ross McCall for a year before calling off their engagement in January 2009. Soon after the split, she began dating her *Ghost Whisperer* costar Jamie Kennedy, which he confirmed on Ryan Seacrest's radio show March 13, 2009, stating that their bond was "more than love." *Us Weekly* reported that Hewitt and McCall's engagement was broken because Hewitt's "jealousy, fights, and insecurities exploded." Could this be a serial problem? Former boyfriend Rich Cronin commented on his relationship with Hewitt, saying that she gave him a Cartier ring signifying she wanted to marry him. However, he said he later found out that she gave the same ring to former boyfriend Jeff Timmons, whom she denied dating. Cronin went on to explain that their relationship ended abruptly when he confronted her about rumors that she was cheating on him.

10. JACK NICHOLSON

Labeled "The Great Seducer" by *Rolling Stone*, Jack Nicholson embodies the ultimate playboy. Married to Sandra Knight from 1962 to 1968, Nicholson realized that he wanted nothing to do with marriage thereafter. Whether or not Nicholson was monogamous throughout his marriage is questionable, for he once told *Men's Journal* that the lifestyle he led in the 1960s could have resulted in his fathering as many as 9,000 children. I'm not sure how he made this calculation, but it is an astounding number, especially considering he was married for half of that decade.

His longest relationship was with Anjelica Huston and it lasted almost sixteen years, ending abruptly when Huston discovered that Nicholson had impregnated Rebecca Broussard. He has been linked to such celebrities as Shirley MacLaine, Janice Dickinson, Candice Bergen, Joni Mitchell, Cher, Kate Moss, Lara Flynn Boyle, and Diane Keaton. And though he is seventy-seven years old, young, beautiful women always flock to him. He is quite candid when discussing his life, which he describes as having been "one long sexual fantasy." Though he does not go into detail, he is quite philosophical saying, "all guys forget about women one hour after having sex with them." He admits that his body isn't what it once was, and openly discusses his need for Viagra when pleasuring more than one woman at a time. He also realizes that it doesn't look right for him to approach young women anymore; however, he considers himself fortunate that plenty of girls approach him, thus allowing him to date a nice range of girls each year, just as he prefers.

What's in a Name?

No traditional baby name books for the celebrity parents of the children on this list. The names below are so unique they make names like Apple, Suri, and Rumer seem unimaginative and common in comparison. While celebrities choosing distinctive names are not surprising, the following names are beyond eccentric.

1. MOON UNIT, DWEEZIL, AHMET EMUUKHA RODAN, AND DIVA THIN MUFFIN PIGEEN—FRANK ZAPPA AND ADELAIDE GAIL SLOATMAN ZAPPA

Frank Zappa once said, "My job is extrapolating everything to its most absurd extreme." He certainly took his job very seriously when it came to naming his children. With the exception of Ahmet, their names are so unusual that I couldn't pick just one, so the Zappa children have landed at the top of our list.

Gail explained that her husband Frank gave her a Sophie's choice between Star and Moon as the first name of their firstborn. Unit apparently made sense as the middle name because upon her arrival Moon made them into a family unit.

Dweezil was not actually the name on Frank Zappa's

eldest son's birth certificate, but only because the hospital refused to register the newborn under such a name. His legal name was Ian Donald Calvin Euclid Zappa, but he was always called Dweezil, which was Frank's nickname for one of Gail's toes. Allegedly, upon finding out at age five that it was not his real name, he insisted that Frank legally change his son's name to Dweezil. That's right, he actually wanted to be named after a toe. Or maybe he was just worried about being teased by his siblings.

Frank's youngest daughter was named Diva because apparently, she was the loudest baby in the hospital nursery. He made no mention of the reasons behind her middle names, Thin, Muffin, and Pigeen, which might have been even more interesting.

2. FIFI TRIXIBELL, PEACHES HONEYBLOSSOM, LITTLE PIXIE, AND HEAVENLY HIRANNI TIGER LILY—BOB GELDOF AND PAULA YATES

Again, we have a family that comes in at number two. Paula Yates was a British TV personality who hosted such shows as *The Tube* and *The Big Breakfast*. Bob Geldof, an Irish musician (a member of the group Boomtown Rats), actor, and founder of Live Aid, fathered Yates's first three daughters: Fifi, Peaches, and Pixie. In 1994, Yates left Geldof for INXS front man Michael Hutchence with whom she had Tiger Lily in 1996. In 1997, Hutchence was found dead in his hotel room of a suspected suicide. In 2000, Yates was also found dead, of an apparent drug overdose. Geldof took Tiger Lily in and later adopted her.

Cracked.com reported that Yates said she chose ethereal names for her daughters to give them part of the fairytale upbringing she craved as a child. Sadly, the aforementioned events shattered the chances of such a fairytale childhood for her daughters.

Yates only explained her eldest daughter's name. She

said that Fifi was the name of Geldof's aunt and "belle" came from her obsession with the southern belle lifestyle. The "Trixi" part of her name remains a mystery. While Fifi's name is highly unusual, she is reportedly the most down-to-earth of the Geldof girls, while her sisters Peaches and Pixie are regulars on the British club scene in typical socialite fashion. Peaches has also been targeted in the media for speculation of a drug overdose, as well as for her elopement with Max Drummey in August 2008. Pixie regularly appears in the British papers, àla Mary-Kate Olsen, for her fashion statements.

3. MOXIE CRIMEFIGHTER AND ZOLTEN—PENN JILLETTE AND EMILY ZOLTEN

Moxie and Zolten are children of the famous comedian, magician, and *Dancing with the Stars* contestant, Penn Jillette. Upon explanation of his daughter's middle name, Crime-Fighter, Jillette stated that middle names are rarely used, so he wanted to have some fun with it. He also thought it would be an asset to her if she were pulled over for speeding, because the officer might let her off the hook if he thought they were on the same side. Maybe he would let her off regardless, just for being saddled with such a name.

Though it sounds like a superhero's name, Zolten is Jillette's wife's maiden name. However, he further explained that, more importantly, it is just one letter off from the spelling of the name of Dracula's dog (Zoltan). Wait, Dracula had a dog?

4. AUDIO SCIENCE—SHANNYN SOSSAMON

Audio Science isn't just a college course. As of May 29, 2003, it is also a child's name thanks to actress Sossamon, who is best known for her roles in *A Knight's Tale* and *40 Days and 40 Nights*.

Sossamon explained that she wanted her child's name to be a word that was special to her, not a name, so her boyfriend read through the dictionary a few times to find suitable candidates. They were going to name him Science, but were afraid that he might get a nickname like "Sci" and people would assume it was short for Simon . . . heaven forbid!

5. ZUMA NESTA ROCK—GWEN STEFANI AND GAVIN ROSSDALE

The name given to Gwen Stefani and Gavin Rossdale's second child makes their first child's name, Kingston, sound conservative by comparison. In trying to decipher the meaning behind the unusual name choices, *Us Weekly* suggests that Zuma is inspired by Zuma Beach in Malibu, California. This location is not only where the family likes to spend time, but is also where Rossdale had an epiphany that began his career. Nesta was Bob Marley's first name until an immigration officer switched it with his middle name, Robert. Both Stefani and Rossdale are major Marley fans; Stefani and her group No Doubt even recorded an album, *Rock Steady*, primarily in Jamaica that has a reggae influence. Some say this album title was the inspiration for Zuma's third name, Rock, while others speculate that Rock comes from the fact that both his parents are rock stars.

6. JERMAJESTY—JERMAINE JACKSON

It's not surprising that a member of the Jackson clan bestows their child with an odd name, but for once it's Jermaine Jackson and not his little brother Michael (who has also landed on this outlandish list). Jermaine combined his own name with a royal title: Jermaine + Majesty=Jermajesty. I'd hate to think what kind of ego this name might give a child. The sad thing is that not only is the kid stuck with this name, but also everyone is asking themselves, "Which one's Jermaine?"

7. QUEEN ELIZABETH AND PRINCESS—MANNY PACQUIAO

Manny Pacquiao, WBC super featherweight world champion, one-upped Jermaine by giving his new daughter an actual royal title as a name. While this is not unusual in some cultures, naming a child after one of the most famous monarchs of our time is more than atypical in a country with no monarchy. I'll give him the Queen part, but why this Filipino boxing champion, with no known ties to England, would choose such a famous middle name is beyond me. Furthermore, this could give Pacquiao's daughter, Princess, an inferiority complex.

8. TU MORROW—ROB MORROW AND DEBBON AYER

Why would any couple make their child's name a pun? To carry on a family tradition! Morrow, best known for his role as Dr. Joel Fleishmann in the TV series *Northern Exposure*, explained that his wife's name, Debbon Ayer, is also a pun. Morrow didn't say whether the tradition went further back in Ayer's family, but hopefully it went so far back that they felt too guilty to break it. Maybe Debbon argued that having a funny name is character-building or something. But really, if people breaking out into *Annie* songs don't drive her insane, the fact that her name is merely Tu just might.

9. PILOT INSPEKTOR—JASON LEE AND CEREN ALKAC

Even Earl on the zany sitcom *My Name is Earl* probably would not name his child Pilot Inspektor, and he does a lot of crazy things. However, it seems that Jason Lee, the actor who plays Earl, has gone beyond the wackiness of his TV show. How was the name Pilot Inspektor created? Lee's agent explained that they liked the name Pilot, which they heard in the song "He's Simple, He's Dumb, He's the Pilot" by the group Grandaddy. It's said that Danny Masterson suggested the name Inspektor, which both Lee and his girlfriend liked. I guess they just felt that Pilot and Inspektor went together. I wonder why.

10. PRINCE MICHAEL, PRINCE MICHAEL II "BLANKET," AND PARIS MICHAEL KATHERINE—MICHAEL JACKSON

Michael Jackson stuck with fairly obvious and repetitive names, but admit it, you expected worse. Jackson never specified the reasoning behind his children's names, but obviously he wanted people to know they were *his* children since Michael is a part of each child's name. How can one *not* feel sorry for Prince Michael II, who was given the same name as his older brother. Talk about living in someone's shadow. Jackson's children have faced many hardships since their father's passing, but they are the late King of Pop's children, so it's not likely that their names will hinder them in the future.

HONORABLE MENTION: GEORGE—GEORGE FOREMAN

Ok, so George isn't outrageous; it's actually quite conservative. However, naming *all five* of your sons George is highly unusual, thus landing it a spot on this list. Who would do such a thing? Why Olympic gold medalist, two-time Heavyweight Champion of the World, grill master, rancher, and minister (he's ordained and actively preaches in Houston, Texas), George Foreman—that's who. Foreman has ten children, five boys and five girls. His boys are affectionately named George Jr., George III, George IV, George V, and George VI, and when I say affectionately I'm referring to Foreman's affection for himself. Foreman says on his website that he almost named all his daughters George as well, but felt it might be a bit much. What modesty. Instead, only two daughters, Georgetta and Freeda George, have George as part of their names. I guess we know who the black sheep in this family are. Sorry Michi, Natalie, and Leola, but at least your name isn't a constant reminder of your highly accomplished parent.

Celebrity by Birth

From even before their births these babies have been in the media spotlight. Though they have not done anything to warrant the media frenzy surrounding them, these offspring garner as much—if not more—attention than their famous parents, simply for being alive.

1. SURI CRUISE—TOM CRUISE AND KATIE HOLMES

Suri Cruise, aka Tomkitten, was one of the most anticipated babies ever, and in 2008 she was the most-referenced celebrity child in the media. There was much speculation surrounding her parents' relationship (they dated for a little more than three months before she was conceived), whether Cruise was really Suri's biological father, and there were even some who doubted that Katie Holmes was actually pregnant. Suri was born April 18, 2006, just over a year after her parents' first public appearance together. The baby was kept secluded, the first pictures of her not surfacing until almost six months later when the September issue of *Vanity Fair* magazine published the exclusive first photos.

Since then, Suri has become the most photographed Hollywood spawn, seemingly leading a fairytale life. She is already a fashion icon. Anything she is photographed wearing—and usually it's a designer dress—sells out shortly thereafter. Donatella Versace reportedly joked that Holmes was the first celebrity to order couture "mommy and me" outfits.

Suri's birth has also managed to improve Cruise's image in the public. Before her birth his most remembered TV appearances included his couch-jumping episode on *Oprah* and his rudeness to Matt Lauer during an interview on the *Today* show. Pictures of Cruise with Suri show him as a caring, hands-on father, which has made people think twice about writing him off as a madman. As she ages, can Suri maintain or increase her power? Or will a younger tot take her place as Hollywood's mini media darling?

2. SHILOH JOLIE-PITT—BRAD PITT AND ANGELINA JOLIE

In 2007 *Forbes* ranked Shiloh Jolie-Pitt number one on their Hottest Tots in Hollywood list. In her first year she was mentioned in over two thousand articles. Like Suri, controversy surrounded her parents' relationship, which is alleged to have stemmed from an affair between Pitt and Jolie while on the set of *Mr. and Mrs. Smith*. Pitt was still married to Jennifer Aniston at the time. Whether one was a "Team Jolie" or "Team Aniston" supporter, everyone was curious to see what the biological child of two of the most beautiful people on the planet would look like. Would it be an über-beautiful baby or a fugly combination of the two? Fortunately for Shiloh she is proving to be a beautiful little girl, looking much like her father with her mother's sensuous lips.

Unlike Suri, Shiloh appears much more down-to-earth, and definitely does not seem to receive any princess-like treatment. Though the first biological child for the couple, Shiloh has three older adopted siblings and younger biological twin siblings. People constantly want to know how she is treated, and how the whole gang gets along. There continues to be interest in this family, for though Angelina and Brad received over $4.1 million from *People* magazine to publish the first pictures of Shiloh in the United States in 2006 (the most money paid for any celebrity baby picture at the time), they received $11 million for pictures of their twins born in 2008. (The couple donated all of the money to charity.) Though the twins are not out enough to be photographed often, Shiloh may have a run for her place on this list. Two are better than one, right?

3. PRINCE WILLIAM OF WALES—PRINCE CHARLES AND PRINCESS DIANA OF WALES

While Suri Cruise might be the closest thing Americans have to a princess, the British have real royal children. Prince William's birth on June 21, 1982, was an important day in England, for this baby was second in line for the British throne. Though William was the future king, his mother, Princess Diana wanted him to be well-rounded, and brought him out among the British subjects to participate in her beloved charity projects.

As a royal, the British press documents William's every move. When he enrolled at Eton, however the royal family made a deal with the press: the royals promised to provide periodic updates about William, and in return the press agreed to let William study camera-free. Since graduating from university William's movements have been closely followed, as has his love life—primarily his relationship with on-again off-again girlfriend Kate Middleton. With William's majestic future, there is little doubt that he will make headlines throughout his life.

4. DANNIELYNN BIRKHEAD—ANNA NICOLE SMITH AND LARRY BIRKHEAD

Dannielynn Birkhead has been in the news since birth for very unfortunate reasons. First, there was the question of paternity. Facing claims from former boyfriend, Larry Birkhead, that he was the baby's biological father, a pregnant Anna

Nicole Smith, was adamant that attorney-turned-boyfriend Howard K. Stern was the baby daddy. Smith fled to Nassau, Bahamas, where Dannielynn was later born, in order to avoid paternity testing.

The second incident that put Dannielynn in the news was Smith's death February 8, 2007. Not only was there contention over where Smith's body would be buried, but the custody of Dannielynn came into question. Ultimately DNA testing of Stern and Birkhead became necessary. After DNA confirmed Larry Birkhead as the baby girl's father, he was awarded custody of the child on April 10, 2007.

Though the controversy surrounding Dannielynn has concluded, and she and Birkhead live a seemingly quiet life, a good deal of media attention is still focused on her. *OK! Magazine* bought the rights to publish the first pictures of Dannielynn and Birkhead for $2.1 million. Her birthdays continue to be covered by the tabloid press, and updates surface periodically of this poor little girl growing up without a mother and a single father doing his best to raise her. There was talk of a reality show, but to date nothing has surfaced. If Dannielynn is anything like her mom, she won't stay out of the spotlight for long.

5. PARIS MICHAEL KATHERINE JACKSON, PRINCE MICHAEL JACKSON JR., PRINCE MICHAEL JACKSON II—MICHAEL JACKSON AND DEBORAH ROWE

Until recently, Michael Jackson's three children, Paris, Prince Michael Jr., and Prince Michael II, were rarely seen in public. When they were, their faces were usually covered. Michael Jackson was such an eccentric character, and there is so much secrecy surrounding his children's births and lives that they incited media frenzy whenever they were spotted. Any clue about their existence or personality led to media attention. Not only have the children been raised without a mother—Debbie Rowe, the mother of Jackson's eldest two children gave up all rights to them, and the third child was carried by a surrogate—but they've also lived in almost complete isolation. They never attended regular school and don't seem to have any friends. It was just them and their father.

Since Jackson's death the children have been in the media spotlight more than ever. Who will raise the children now? How will they adjust to a more traditional lifestyle? Needless to say, it would be impossible for anyone to even attempt to replicate the life Jackson would have made for them. A childhood memoir from any of Jackson's offspring would be an instant best-seller, but even without a book contract, these children of the King of Pop will always generate media attention.

6. SEAN PRESTON FEDERLINE AND JAYDEN JAMES FEDERLINE—BRITNEY SPEARS AND KEVIN FEDERLINE

Spears and Federline's announcement that they were expecting came on the heels of their impromptu marriage, surprising family, fans, and media. When they married in October 2004, Spears was only twenty-two years old and Federline already had two children with his ex-girlfriend, Shar Jackson. Sean Preston was born eleven months later on September 14, 2005. His birth received intense media attention, and Spears's mothering skills were highly scrutinized by the public. Most memorably, Britney was photographed driving with Sean sitting in her lap, as opposed to in his car seat. Spears blamed the presence of the mass of paparazzi for forcing her to hurriedly get into her car without taking time to buckle up her baby. Sean Preston was followed one year later, almost to the day, by baby brother Jayden James on September 12, 2006. Only months later Spears filed for divorce from Federline and so began the fight for the boys. Her January 2008 breakdown put Spears and her children's questionable future front and center in the media. She and Federline have had an extensive custody battle throughout their divorce proceedings and Britney's journey back to stability. The media has had a field day speculating about the children's life with their father, monitored visits with their mother, and finally their life with mom on tour under the conservatorship of Spears's father, Jamie. In the documentary *For the Record* Spears claims her life under conservatorship is like *Groundhog Day*. Though she may live a totally planned existence now, the media will continue to document Sean and Jayden's family life throughout their youth because one never knows what Spears will do next.

7. BROOKLYN BECKHAM, ROMEO BECKHAM, AND CRUZ BECKHAM—DAVID AND VICTORIA (ADAMS) BECKHAM

As the offspring of England's most famous footballer (soccer player here in the U.S.), David Beckham, Brooklyn, Romeo, and Cruz are probably the three most famous British children, after Princes William and Harry. The fact that Victoria Beckham, aka Posh Spice, is their mother only makes them more famous. Paparazzi staked out the hospital while Victoria was in labor, waiting for any news of the newest addition. Bets were placed on what each boy would be named and odds have been made over the likelihood that each boy will play for England, as well as a 1000/1 odd that all three will play for England.

The Beckhams' move to the U.S. has made them regulars on the Hollywood scene. Even their boys have become A-listers on the playground, having been spotted in the company of numerous other famous tots, including Leni Briatore (Heidi Klum's daughter), Harlow Madden (Nicole Richie's daughter), Kingston Rossdale, and Suri Cruise.

8. FRANCES BEAN COBAIN—KURT COBAIN AND COURTNEY LOVE

Public interest in Frances stems from her parents fame and controversy. In April 1994, Kurt, a known drug addict, committed suicide by shooting himself in the head when Frances was only one-and-a-half-years-old.

Love has continued to appear in the public eye, primarily for drug-, weight-, and money-related issues. Though Love claims her words were reported out of context, a *Vanity Fair* article quoted her as admitting to knowingly taking heroin during her pregnancy. This caused uproar among many parenting groups, leading many people to advocate for Frances's removal from her parents care upon her birth. Over the past sixteen years Courtney has also been arrested multiple times for drug possession. On one such occasion the California Child and Family Services Department removed Frances from Love's care and placed her in the care of Cobain's mother. After Love completed a drug rehab program she won back custody of her then-twelve-year-old daughter.

Though many have questioned the environment in which Frances was raised, in public she is seemingly quite a stable girl. Her grounded attitude has come out in the four interviews she has given, the most recent of which was to *Harper's Bazaar*. In it she acknowledged, "I'm famous by default. I came out of the womb and people wanted to know who I was because of my parents. . . . I understand why you would want to get to know me, but I'm not my parents. People need to wait until I've done something valid with my life." With all the doors open to her, Frances will more than likely find her calling, and no doubt the media will let us know what happens.

9. LISA MARIE PRESLEY—ELVIS PRESLEY AND PRISCILLA (WAGNER) PRESLEY

Though Lisa Marie Presley was born prior to 1980, she makes this list because she is the sole progeny of the legendary Elvis Presley. Furthermore, Lisa Marie is living proof that interest in celebrity children does not necessarily wane as they become adults and parents themselves.

When Lisa Marie was born on February 1, 1968, she became the Princess of Rock 'n Roll. She admits to being pampered by her father, who showered her with jewels, fur coats, and made his staff at Graceland cater to her every whim. Elvis even named his private jet "Lisa Marie."

Elvis died when Lisa Marie was only nine, and she became the sole heir of his estate when she turned twenty-five. Along with her responsibilities to the Elvis estate, Lisa Marie tried her hand at singing. In 2003 she released her debut album *To Whom it May Concern*, and in 2005 she released her sophomore album *Now What*, both of which have gone platinum. Though Lisa Marie had a few hits off her albums, her career never took off.

Aside from media interest in her music career, Lisa Marie's love life has merited attention as well. Most famously, Lisa Marie was married to Michael Jackson from 1994–1996. Several years later she had a brief marriage (August–November 2002) to actor Nicolas Cage, which was also closely followed and examined.

For the last several years Lisa Marie has chosen to live her life out of the spotlight. In 2006 she wed Michael Lockwood, her music producer and director, and in October 2008 the couple celebrated the birth of twin daughters.

10. SAM ALEXIS WOODS AND CHARLIE AXEL WOODS— TIGER WOODS AND ELIN NORDEGREN

Sam and Charlie have big golf shoes to fill. Tiger Woods is certainly the most famous golfer—perhaps even sportsman—today, and arguably the greatest golfer of all time. Woods has also become a celebrity outside the golf world, raking in hundreds of millions of dollars in endorsement deals with companies like Buick, Nike, and Gatorade, and becoming a household name in the process. Naturally, the whole world looks on with anticipation when Woods announces that he and his wife are expecting. The world will have to wait a few years before finding out if Sam or Charlie has inherited Woods's golfing skill and will follow his footsteps. In the meantime, Sam is certainly taking the toddler world by storm, coming in fifth on *Forbes* magazine's 2008 "Hollywood's Hottest Tots" list; she was mentioned in over one thousand news articles in 2008 alone. I wonder how many endorsement deals she's been offered already?

All in the Family

All parent–child relationships can be tenuous at times, but the family dynamics on this list far surpass normal disagreements and teen angst. Reading this chapter will show you that, in fact, celebrities do not have it all.

1. RYAN O'NEAL AND HIS CHILDREN

It's hard to believe that Ryan O'Neal, the leading man of one of the most romantic films of all time, *Love Story* (1970), and the man who sat by Farrah Fawcett's bedside in her final days, has been called the worst father in Hollywood. According to *A Paper Life*, his daughter, actress Tatum O'Neal's 2004 memoir, he has spent over forty years earning this title. She discusses O'Neal's battles with anger management issues and substance abuse problems, and describes how he took out on her and her brothers Griffin and Patrick. Physical abuse was commonplace in the O'Neal household. Tatum recalled, "My father terrorized me, but Griffin was his real whipping boy." She revealed that her Oscar win at age ten for her role in *Paper Moon* led her father to beat her out of jealousy: O'Neal played the role of her father in the film and did not receive an Oscar nomination. She continues on stating that Ryan once knocked out Griffith's teeth when he was fourteen-years-old and that he encouraged his teenage daughter to snort cocaine to lose weight.

Eventually Tatum cut all ties with her father, and has tried to stay on the straight and narrow. O'Neal, on the other hand, seems to have remained the same. In early 2007 police were called to a house where gunshots had been reported. The story goes that Griffin had swung a fireplace poker at O'Neal, and in response his father had grabbed a gun, waved it in his son's direction, and the gun accidentally fired. While the details surrounding this incident remain in question, Tatum believes her brother. There does not seem to be any resolution to this family fued. In 2009 Tatum attempted to put their differences aside and attended Farrah Fawcett's funeral; she had been her father's long-time love. O'Neal not only failed to recognize his own daughter, he started hitting on her. It's debatable which is more upsetting: the fact that he hit on his daughter or the idea that he was hitting on anyone at the funeral of the supposed "love of his life." When asked to comment about the incident, Tatum told *Vanity Fair* "That's our relationship in a nutshell. You make of it what you will."

2. MACAULAY CULKIN AND KIT CULKIN

Macaulay Culkin and his father, Kit, have one of the most famous feuds in Hollywood. Audiences fell in love with Mac when he starred in *Home Alone* in 1990. After that initial success the offers rolled in, such as *My Girl* (1991) and *Richie Rich* (1994). However, life was not so rosy behind the scenes for this child star. In an interview with *New York Magazine* (March 5, 2006), Mac claims that Kit ruled "his kingdom," the family, by humiliation and physical abuse. His father and manager was reportedly a nightmare on set as well, making many enemies. He was known as "the dad from hell" on set and as well as off the set during salary negotiations—sometimes for roles Mac hadn't even approved. Because many executives did not like dealing with Kit, ultimately Mac received fewer job offers.

When Mac was fifteen his parents divorced, and a nasty custody battle ensued. Both parents wanted custody and the right to manage their children's careers—Mac's younger siblings Kieran, Christian, Rory, and Quinn also act. This bickering led Mac to file for emancipation from his parents, blocking both parents from controlling his seventeen-million-dollar fortune.

In 2000 Kit tried to make amends with his son, but Mac wanted nothing to do with his father.

3. TORI SPELLING AND CANDY SPELLING

The feud between Candy Spelling and her daughter Tori is complex. The exact source of the conflict is difficult to pinpoint, since many have said that mother and daughter had a strained relationship for many years before the animosity became public. Upon the death of producer Aaron Spelling, his wife, Candy was named as the executor of his will. According to Spelling's last will and testament, his daughter, Tori, was given only $800,000 of his over half-billion-dollar estate.

By this time, Candy and Tori had already been at odds for a while, allegedly bickering while planning Tori's 2004 million-dollar wedding to Charlie Shanian. Reportedly, Tori was upset because she did not think the wedding was big enough, and Candy was upset because not all of her friends were included on the guest list. Tensions increased between Tori and her mother when she divorced Shanian in April 2006 and eloped the following month to Fiji with fellow actor Dean McDermott, whom she'd met on the set of a Lifetime movie. Her family was not happy about the divorce, the elopement—of which they were not informed—or her choice of husband. Candy was also not pleased about how her character was portrayed in Tori's 2006 docu-comedy TV show, *So NoTORIous*.

Tori claims that she stopped seeing her parents because her mother was "spending time" with a family friend, while her husband's health deteriorated. Tori explained, "My mom's behavior simply made me uncomfortable to be around my family," *Us Weekly* reported. Candy has denied these claims.

Though there has been no resolution to the conflict between mother and daughter, there was a brief reconciliation upon the birth of Tori's first child Liam. Candy claims to have tried to contact her daughter by pleading to her on TV and the Internet. Tori denies these attempts have been made; she says her mother knows her phone number and knows where she lives if she wants to get in touch with her. So does either party truly care about reconciling, or is this just a stunt to gain media attention? Only time will tell—who knows, maybe there's a mother–daughter reality show in their future.

4. ANGELINA JOLIE AND JON VOIGHT

Jolie's relationship with her father, Jon Voight, has always been strained, stemming from the events surrounding her parents' divorce in 1978. Though father and daughter were on relatively good terms when they costarred in the 2001 film *Lara Croft: Tomb Raider*, their relationship quickly deteriorated the following year. Voight blamed their rift on Jolie's "serious emotional problems" during a TV interview with *Access Hollywood*. Jolie responded by issuing a statement saying, "I have determined that it is not healthy for me to be around my father." Jolie's brother, James Haven, further fueled the fire by accusing Voight of mentally abusing their mother. Voight insists that his children paint him as a bad guy, but that the problem lies with them. He explains that their feelings towards him stem from their "inability to let go of years of programmed anger from their mom." He is adamant that he has tried to mend his relationship with his children, and that he's always there if they want to talk. Since Jolie and Pitt have become a couple and the parents of six children, rumors have circulated that Pitt is urging Jolie to reconcile with her father for the sake of their children. According to the November 11, 2009 issue of *Us Weekly*, Voight told them that, largely thanks to Pitt's urging, Jolie has reached out to him and father and daughter are slowly rebuilding their relationship.

5. DREW BARRYMORE AND JAID BARRYMORE

Everyone in Hollywood knows about the little girl who began frequenting clubs with her mom at age nine and by age thirteen was in rehab for drug and alcohol abuse. That little girl was Drew Barrymore, and her mother was Jaid Barrymore. Jaid was a B-list actress and Drew's manager. She was also very jealous of her little girl who shot to stardom at age seven with a role in *E.T.* According to the United Kingdom's *Express* online, when asked about her daughter's success, Jaid exclaimed, "At two, she was perfect. It was disgusting. I was going to be the star, not her!"

After completing rehab twice, Drew sought emancipation from her mother at age fifteen. Though Jaid no longer controlled Drew's money, she sought to capitalize on her daughter's fame by auctioning Drew's baby clothes and possessions on the Internet.

Jaid walked Drew down the aisle when she wed Tom Green in 2001, but in the March 2009 issue of *W* magazine, Drew admitted that she and her mother "split ways when [Drew] was very young and have never really reconciled."

6. LINDSAY LOHAN AND MICHAEL LOHAN

This war is basically the entire Lohan clan vs. Michael Lohan, for none of Michael's children have a relationship with their father, now an ordained minister after finding God in prison. In the late 1980s, Michael was a Wall Street trader who first served four years in jail for stock fraud. In 1998 he spent time behind bars again for violating probation, and in 2000 violating an order of protection that prevented him from seeing his children sent him back a third time.

When Michael was released from jail in 2007 he and Lindsay's relationship was tenuous at first and quickly deteriorated. In 2007 she said she was no longer in contact with him, because dealing with him was too difficult. She couldn't forgive his infidelity to her mother, Dina, during their marriage. In 2008 claims also surfaced that Michael fathered a child with another woman while still married to Dina. In December of the same year, *The Insider* reported that Lindsay blogged on her MySpace page, "My father just let my family and I know . . . that he had another child. . . . [H]e cheated on my mother and that really sucks." Thus confirming the rumors.

Michael has repeatedly disapproved of Lindsay's lifestyle, reaching out to her through the media. He vocally disapproved of her relationship with Samantha Ronson, and even wrote a short-lived blog (it lasted about three months) about Lindsay in early 2009. In an August 2009 interview with RadarOnline, Michael claims to have patched up his relationship with Lindsay, claiming he chatted with Ronson and realized the rumors he'd heard were untrue. Though he claims to care about Lindsay and her well being, his continual public hashing-out of their personal issues puts his motives into question.

7. MADONNA AND CHRISTOPHER CICCONE

Madonna and her brother, Christopher Ciccone, were close for many years, while he acted as her choreographer, director, designer, and stylist for twenty years. However, when Christopher published an unflattering tell-all about the pop icon, *Life With My Sister Madonna* (2008), their soured relationship went public. In an interview on *Good Morning America* Christopher said the purpose of his book was to deflate Madonna's ego by "[putting] a nice little staircase up and help her walk back down to earth with the rest of us," and to dispel the myths surrounding her childhood and early career.

There were numerous incidents that served to weaken Christopher and Madonna's tight relationship. One episode Christopher detailed was the taping of Madonna's *Truth or Dare* (1991) documentary, during which she rolled around on her mother's grave. Another was her lack of financial support to aid their blind ninety-seven-year-old grandmother. Allegedly Madonna gave her five hundred dollars a month and paid her medical bills, but Christopher thought she should have paid for a car and driver for their grandmother as well. However, the nail in the coffin of their relationship was Madonna's marriage to Guy Ritchie, whom Christopher claims is a homophobe.

Christopher says he still loves his sister, more than he likes her, and hopes they will reconcile one day as equals.

8. AARON CARTER AND JANE CARTER

There have been numerous feuds within the Carter family, but the most famous was between Aaron Carter and his mom, Jane. In December 2003 sixteen-year-old Aaron discovered financial discrepancies, fired his manager, Jane, and sought emancipation. In a December 2003 *Teen People* interview he stated, "I am more of a cash cow than a son to her." Only a few months later though, Aaron announced that he and his mother had worked out their differences, and that he was reinstating her as his manager. All was not forgiven though, because once Aaron's parents' divorce was finalized in 2004 he moved in with his father.

In 2006 the Carter children starred in a Reality TV show, *House of Carters*, for E! Networks. The show portrayed their dysfunctional home life. Though Aaron Carter's personal issues and 2008 arrest for possession of marijuana have somewhat overshadowed his career, his Fall 2009 appearance on *Dancing with the Stars* gave his career a much-needed restart.

9. JENNIFER ANISTON AND NANCY DOW

Jennifer Aniston broke off all communication with her mother, Nancy Dow, after Dow gave an interview on a tabloid TV show, and subsequently published a book about their relationship, *From Mother and Daughter to Friends: A Memoir* (1999). Her mother's desire to cash in on her daughter's fame rightly irked Aniston, who refused to invite her mother to her 2000 wedding to Brad Pitt. In an interview on ABC's *Prime Time Thursday*, which aired in January 2004, Aniston said she never imagined that her mother would not know her husband, but mother and daughter did not reconcile until after Aniston and Pitt's union ended in 2005. Aniston said in *Vogue's* December 2008 issue, "She's changed," and they have been slowly mending their relationship ever since.

10. EMINEM AND DEBBIE MATHERS

Rapper Eminem instigated a feud with his mother when he rapped about raping and killing her in the song "Cleanin Out My Closet." She unsuccessfully tried to sue for slander, and wrote a book in revenge, *My Son Marshall, My Son Eminem: Setting the Record Straight.* However, the feud has died down since Debbie was diagnosed with cancer, which inspired her to attempt to reconcile with her son. Though there are no reports of any meaningful reconciliation, he is reportedly paying her medical costs.

Good Genes

Though many second and third generations seek success and fame by riding on the coattails of their famous last name or connections within the entertainment industry—usually with little genuine achievement—the families on this seem to be truly gifted, generation after generation. Having a famous last name certainly doesn't hurt, but these people would have had a good chance of succeeding in the entertainment industry regardless.

1. COPPOLA FAMILY

The Coppola family has been involved in Hollywood for three generations. Today the most famous members of the family are producers, directors, and screenwriters Francis Ford Coppola and his daughter Sofia Coppola. Francis won an Oscar for writing *The Godfather* (1972) and was nominated for directing the project. He won Oscars for producing, directing, and writing for *The Godfather Part II* (1974). His father, Carmine Coppola, won both an Oscar and a Golden Globe as a composer. Francis's daughter, Sofia, made Oscar history as the first American woman nominated for the Best Director Award for her work on the film *Lost in Translation* (2003), for which she won the 2004 Best Original Screenplay Oscar.

Two actors who are members of the famous Coppola clan, yet do not share the famous surname, are Nicolas Cage and Jason Schwartzman. Cage actually changed his surname from Coppola (his father August is Francis's brother) because he wanted to make his own way in the acting business. However, his first roles were in films directed by his uncle: *Rumble Fish* (1983) and *The Cotton Club* (1984). Today, Cage is an A-list actor on his own merit. Family connections may have given him a leg up on the competition, but they can't create something out of nothing. An up-and-coming actor in the Coppola family is Jason Schwartzman. Schwartzman is known for playing quirky roles most famously in *Rushmore* (1998), but also in *I Heart Huckabees* (2004), *Shop Girl* (2005), *Marie Antoinette* (2006), and *Darjeerling Limited* (2007). Schwartzman's mother is Talia Shire (sister of Francis and August), who is most famously known for her role as Adrian in the *Rocky* movies. Many other members of this family work in Hollywood as producers, directors, or actors, ensuring that the Coppola legacy will continue.

2. BARRYMORE FAMILY

Producer-director-actor Drew Barrymore is this generation's representative in Hollywood for the Barrymore family. Often labeled the "royal family" of acting, this family has been part of the fabric of Hollywood since the beginnings of the American entertainment industry. Drew's grandfather, John Barrymore, is called "the world's greatest actor," well-known for his roles in such films as *Dr. Jekyll and Mr. Hyde* (1920), *Sherlock Holmes* (1922), and *Moby Dick* (1930).

John's siblings, Lionel and Ethel, were also very accomplished actors. Lionel acted in over two hundred films, including *You Can't Take it With You* (1938) and *It's A Wonderful Life* (1946). Ethel was a famous stage actress, and also won an Oscar for *None But the Lonely Heart* (1944). Drew's father, John Jr., was a product of his father's third marriage to famous silent screen actress Dolores Costello. John Jr. had the talent to be an actor and actually landed numerous roles, but he was unreliable and never achieved the success of the previous generation.

3. HUSTON FAMILY

Like the Barrymore clan, the Huston family has been a part of the American film industry since the earliest days of Hollywood. Walter Huston acted throughout the 1930s and 1940s, appearing in such classic films as *The Devil and Daniel Webster* (1941), *Yankee Doodle Dandy* (1942), and *The Treasure of the Sierra Madre* (1948), for which he won an Oscar. Walter's son John Huston found success in the entertainment industry as an actor, a screenwriter, and most famously as a director. He directed such projects as *The Maltese Falcon* (1941), *The Treasure of the Sierra Madre* (1948), *Key Largo* (1948), *Moulin Rouge* (1951), *The African Queen* (1951), and *Annie* (1982). His work won him two of the ten Oscars and three of the eight Golden Globes for which he was nominated. Two of his children, Danny and Anjelica have made names for themselves as actors. Danny is less well-known, though he has landed roles in several notable films, including *Leaving Las Vegas* (1995) and *X-Men Origins: Wolverine* (2009).

Anjelica's acting career has been very successful. She is most recognized for her role in *The Addams Family* (1991) and *The Addams Family Values* (1993), both of which garnered her Golden Globe nominations. Her performance in *Prizzi's Honor* (1985), a project directed by her father, earned her the 1986 Oscar for Best Supporting Actress, making the Huston family the first to have three generations of Oscar winners. More recently, Huston has appeared in such films as *The Royal Tenenbaums* (2001), *The Life Aquatic with Steve Zissou* (2004), and *The Darjeeling Limited* (2007).

4. SHEEN/ESTEVEZ FAMILY

The name Ramon Antonio Gerard Estévez might not ring a bell, but the name Martin Sheen certainly should. Ramon decided to create a stage name when he started acting and his son Charlie, aka Carlos Irwin Estévez, followed suit. Martin gained recognition for his role in *Apocalypse Now* (1979) and more recently for his role as U.S. president on the popular TV drama *The West Wing*, for which he earned six Emmy and eight Golden Globe Award nominations. Each award he won only once.

All four of Martin's children pursued acting as well, most famously his sons Charlie and Emilio. Emilio rose to stardom during the 1980s as one of the core members of the Brat Pack, starring in such movies as *The Outsiders* (1983), *The Breakfast Club* (1985), *St. Elmo's Fire* (1985), and *Young Guns* (1988). In the 1990s he was widely known for his role as Gordon Bombay in *The Mighty Ducks* films. He has since expanded his resume, focusing on writing, directing, and producing projects. He chose to retain his surname to avoid riding on his father's coattails.

Whether younger brother Charlie wanted to distance himself from Emilio, or he wanted to display close ties to his father, Charlie too adopted the surname Sheen. Charlie has experienced career highs, as a member of the Brat Pack, and personal lows in the 1990s, including assault charges and multiple trips to rehab. He seems to have come out on top though, experiencing a career resurgence upon entering the twenty-first century, which is expanded upon in the "Celebrity Comebacks" chapter.

5. FONDA FAMILY

Henry Fonda was an actor who was active from the mid-1930s through the 1970s. The American Film Institute ranked Henry sixth on its list of Greatest Male Stars of All Time, which demonstrates his influence as an actor during his career. His most famous roles were in the films *The Grapes of Wrath* (1940), *The Ox-Bow Incident* (1943), *12 Angry Men* (1957), and *On Golden Pond* (1981)—the only project he worked on with his daughter, Jane, as well as his only role to earn him an Oscar.

Jane Fonda found fame as an actress, a fitness guru, and a political activist. Between 1960 and 1990 Fonda was nominated for seven Academy Awards, and eleven Golden Globes (she won two and four respectively). Between 1982 and 1995 Jane produced twenty-three workout videos and five workout books. Her first video is the highest-selling workout video of all time, selling over seventeen million copies. Jane announced her retirement from acting in 1991, but has since appeared in two films, *Monster-in-Law* (2005) and *Georgia Rule* (2007), and worked on Broadway. She has been criticized for her political activism—she protested against the Vietnam War, even visiting Vietnam in 1972, earning her the nickname "Hanoi Jane." She has also spoken out against the Iraq War.

Jane's brother Peter and his daughter Bridget have entertained moderate success as actors as well. Peter is best known for starring and producing the film *Easy Rider* (1968) and was nominated for an Oscar for his role in *Ulee's Gold* (1997). More recently, he appeared in the film *3:10 to Yuma* (2007). Though he isn't widely known, he has worked steadily since 1963. Bridget made her film debut at age four in *Easy Rider*, but her breakout role came when she played Grace Hamilton in *The Godfather Part III* (1990). She worked steadily throughout the 1990s, receiving two Golden Globe nominations, but seems to have stepped away from acting, her last appearance onscreen being in 2002.

6. DOUGLAS FAMILY

Actor Kirk Douglas is the patriarch of the Douglas family, and has set the bar high for his sons, all of whom work in the entertainment industry. Kirk debuted in the film *The Strange Love of Martha Ivers* (1946), for which he received rave reviews and more job offers. He is best known for his roles in *Paths of Glory* (1957) and *Spartacus (1960)*. He received three Oscar nominations, yet never won. However, his acting talent has been recognized internationally: he is a recipient of the Chevalier of the Legion of Honor in France, the Golden Kamera Award from Germany, and the American Cinema Award in 1987. The Academy of Motion Picture Arts and Sciences awarded Kirk with an honorary Academy Award in 1995, and in 1999 he received the American Film Institute's Lifetime Achievement Award. Currently in his mid-nineties, Kirk continues to be active, recently appearing in the one-man stage production *Before I Forget.*

All of Kirk's sons have pursued careers in the entertainment industry, but only Michael Douglas is on track to match his father's industry achievements. Michael has won two Oscars, the first for producing *One Flew Over the Cuckoo's Nest* (1975) and the second for his performance in *Wall Street* (1987). Michael has acted in numerous memorable films including *Romancing the Stone* (1984), *Fatal Attraction (1987)*, *Basic Instinct* (1992), and *Wonder Boys* (2000). After marrying fellow A-list actress Catherine Zeta-Jones, Michael was propelled into the status of Hollywood royalty and his career doesn't appear to be slowing any time soon. His son, Cameron, seems to be following in the family business. Cameron first appeared in the film *It Runs in the Family* (2003) alongside his father and grandfather and has since landed some minor film roles.

7. PALTROW FAMILY

Actress Gwyneth Paltrow is the most well-known member of the Paltrow family, but she has inherited her film talent from her parents. Her father, Bruce Paltrow, was a TV and film director who directed the popular dramas *St. Elsewhere* and *Homicide: Life on the Street*. Gwyneth's mother, Blythe Danner, has earned both a Tony and an Emmy Award for her acting. Well-known for her film roles in *Meet the Parents* and *Meet the Fockers*, and TV roles on *Will & Grace* and *Huff* (for which she won her Emmy).

Gwyneth quickly rose to A-list status with lead roles in such films at *Emma* (1998) and *Shakespeare in Love* (1998) for which she won an Oscar and Golden Globe. Gwyneth has shown range as an actress, taking roles in romantic, serious, and offbeat films including *The Royal Tenenbaums* (2001), *Shallow Hal* (2001), *Proof* (2005), and *Running with Scissors* (2006). Since the birth of her second child, Moses, in 2006, Paltrow has worked less, choosing to focus on raising her children with Coldplay front man Chris Martin. However, Gwyneth still has the star power to attract major roles, most recently appearing in the 2008 blockbuster *Iron Man*. Only time will tell whether Gwyneth's children will follow in the family business, but they definitely come from a talented gene pool.

8. HAWN/HUDSON/RUSSELL FAMILY

Goldie Hawn was a major comedic talent primarily during the 1970s and 1980s, winning an Oscar for her first major role in the movie *Cactus Flower* (1969) and receiving an Oscar nomination for *Private Benjamin* (1980), which she also produced. Though Hawn's two children, Kate and Oliver, were fathered by her ex-husband, Bill Hudson, both claim that Hawn's longtime partner, Kurt Russell, is more of a father figure to them than their biological father. Russell is also a well-known Hollywood actor and Kate and Oliver have followed his and Hawn's footsteps, becoming players in the acting business. Kate has become an A-list actress, primarily known for roles in romantic comedies, such as *How to Lose a Guy in 10 Days* (2003) and *Bride Wars* (2009), as well as for her breakout role in the indie film *Almost Famous*

(2000), for which she won a Golden Globe Award and received an Oscar nomination. Her brother Oliver, though less well known, is also an actor. His most memorable part was a supporting role on *Dawson's Creek* from 2002–2003 before his starring role on the CBS sitcom *Rules of Engagement* (2007–2010).

9. JUDD FAMILY

The Judd family was originally known for the mother-daughter singing duo, The Judds, which consisted of Naomi and Wynonna. This duo rocked the country world during the 1980s selling twenty million albums, releasing fifteen number one hits, and earning five Grammy Awards. They also won Best Country Duo for eight years straight at all three major country music award shows. However, their career came to a halt when Naomi was diagnosed with Hepatitis C in 1990, forcing her into retirement. In 1992 Wynonna tried her hand as a solo artist and met with moderate success. She has since produced eight albums with twenty-five country hits (three of which went to number one), with sales over ten million.

Wynonna isn't Naomi's only famous daughter. Wynonna's half-sister, Ashley, commented that she always felt like the black sheep of the family because she wasn't a talented singer. However, as a teenager she discovered she had acting talent. Her first successful role was on the TV drama *Sisters*. She segued to the big screen and is known for her roles in *Double Jeopardy* (1999), *Divine Secrets of the Ya-Ya Sisterhood* (2002), and *De-Lovely* (2004), for which she received a Golden Globe nomination.

10. CURTIS FAMILY

Many people might not know that Jamie Lee Curtis comes from a family of actors. Her parents are actors Janet Leigh and Tony Curtis. Leigh is best known for her roles in *Little*

Women (1949), *Touch of Evil* (1958), and *Psycho* (1960), though she continued to appear on TV until late in her life. Tony Curtis had a long and varied career. He didn't want to be pigeonholed into playing one type of character. He appeared in over one hundred films, most memorably *The Defiant Ones* (1958) and *Some Like it Hot* (1959).

Jamie Lee has made a name for herself as a respected actress and children's book author. She received the title of "Scream Queen" early in her career, for her many appearances in horror films, including almost every installment of the *Halloween* franchise. However, she showed her comedic side in *A Fish Called Wanda* (1988) and her sexy side in *True Lies* (1994), for which she won a Golden Globe Award.

BFFs

Friendships between women are fragile in the most ordinary situations, but when you add in fame and fortune and magnify the competition by about a million, and true female friendships become even more rare. This list is a collection of women who appear to be real "best friends forever." They spend time together not just because they're thrown together for work or publicity, but because they genuinely care about each other when the cameras stop rolling.

1. OPRAH WINFREY AND GAYLE KING

Oprah Winfrey and Gayle King's friendship is one of the most famous in the entertainment industry. Periodically, rumors have surfaced that these women are "more than friends" but that can be said for every duo on this list. It seems as if two women can't be close friends without speculation that there is something more to their relationship. (Though Winfrey's comment that they are "one soul in two bodies" did not quell the rumors.)

Winfrey and King met in the 1970s when Oprah was a news anchor and King was a production assistant at Baltimore WJZ-TV. The story goes that the women became close friends after Winfrey invited King to her house, which was walking distance from the station, to wait out a snowstorm. They bonded instantly and have been close friends ever since.

Though King is now known solely because she is Winfrey's best friend, she enjoyed a successful eighteen-year career in TV, winning three Emmy Awards for newscasting. King currently works as Editor-at-Large for *O, The Oprah Magazine*, hosts her own radio show on Winfrey's XM radio channel, and frequently appears on *Oprah*. She admits that she has benefited from her friendship with Winfrey, but she maintains her own life.

2. NICOLE KIDMAN AND NAOMI WATTS

Nicole Kidman and Naomi Watts became friends under the most unlikely of circumstances: a modeling audition. Most people see their competitors as "the enemy" but Kidman and Watts shared a cab ride home after the audition and have remained best friends throughout their careers.

It couldn't have been easy for Watts, a struggling actress for many years, to see her friend quickly achieve fame and fortune, but the two remained close. Kidman called Watts right after her 2003 Oscar win, and Watts moved into Kidman's house for moral support following the breakup of Kidman's marriage to Tom Cruise. Watts, who is now an A-list Hollywood actress herself, said that Kidman's success inspired her to keep pursuing acting. They both acknowledge that it is really rare for actresses to be such close friends and they take pride in their strong friendship.

3. COURTNEY COX AND JENNIFER ANISTON

Courtney Cox and Jennifer Aniston are famous BFF's on-and off-screen. They met on the set of their hit sitcom *Friends* (1994–2004), where life imitated art as they played best friends Monica Geller and Rachel Green. Aniston and Cox claim they hit it off right away and have been best friends ever since. Aniston recalls that the first day she met Cox, Cox immediately started talking about her relationships, initially shocking Aniston.

Many actors strike up friendships on set because these are the people they're around the most, but many dim once filming ends and actors move on to other projects or break down when one actress begins to outshine the other. However, Cox and Aniston have remained very close. Cox was there for Aniston during her highly publicized divorce from Brad Pitt. Aniston showed support for her friend after Cox's father's death. Aniston is so often photographed vacationing with Cox, Cox's husband, David Arquette, and their daughter Coco (Aniston is her godmother), she seems to be an honorary member of the Cox-Arquette family.

4. BEYONCÉ KNOWLES AND KELLY ROWLAND

Beyoncé Knowles and Kelly Rowland have the rare connection of becoming friends as teens, staying friends as they became famous, and maintaining their close relationship after going their separate ways. Guys tend to have more success at these relationships than girls because it seems like girls let egos and jealousy tear them apart, but so far Knowles and Rowland are an exception.

The girls met in 1990 when they auditioned for the girl group Girl Tyme. Upon landing spots in the group Rowland moved in with the Knowles family. After a rocky start and several name changes Columbia Records signed Destiny's Child in 1997 and the group quickly rose to prominence. Originally the group was made up of four members, but after some changes the final group was comprised of Beyoncé, Rowland, and Michelle Williams.

In 2005 the group officially disbanded so the girls could pursue individual careers. As the most successful breakout of the group, Knowles more than likely favored this decision. However, even though Knowles has enjoyed much more post–Destiny's Child fame and fortune than Rowland, the two remain close friends. Rowland attended Knowles's ultra-exclusive wedding to Jay-Z in 2008, and the girls continue to support each other by showing up to one another's events. However, Rowland recently parted ways with her manager—Knowles's father—so we'll see if their friendship can survive this delicate situation.

5. PENÉLOPE CRUZ AND SALMA HAYEK

Spanish actress Penélope Cruz and Mexican actress Salma Hayek became close friends upon Cruz's arrival in Los Angeles. Cruz recalls that Hayek was the only person she knew when she came to L.A. in 1999. Hayek even picked her up from the airport and brought her to her home to stay until Cruz became acclimated to the city. The women, who are both foreign-born, bonded while living together, and they continue to support one another in good times and bad. They costarred in *Banditas* (2006), and Cruz was at Hayek's house when she heard she had been nominated for an Oscar for her role in *Vicky Cristina Barcelona* (2008). To celebrate Cruz's nomination, Hayek hosted an A-list bash. In turn, Cruz has been by Hayek's side during the pregnancy and birth of Hayek's daughter, Valentina, as well as her marriage to French billionaire François-Henri Pinault.

6. TYRA BANKS AND KIMORA LEE

Tyra Banks and Kimora Lee became friends while they were both struggling models rooming together in Paris. Their friendship grew as both women achieved great success in the competitive modeling industry. Now both women have become moguls of their own empires, all the while maintaining a strong friendship. Banks is the godmother of Lee's two daughters. Lee, president and creative director of Baby Phat fashions, was a judge on the first season of Banks's hit Reality TV show *America's Next Top Model*; her popularity on the show led to her own show *Kimora: Life in the Fab Lane*. Lee is also a frequent guest on Banks's talk show and these close friends are often seen out together. Though they both lead hectic lives, they make time for one another.

7. SHAWNTAE HARRIS, AKA "DA BRAT" AND MARIAH CAREY

No, you're not reading it wrong. Mariah Carey and Shawntae Harris, better known as Da Brat, are very close friends. Da Brat was one of the singers featured in Carey's song "Always Be My Baby" (1996) and she also contributed to remix versions of "Honey"(1997) and "Heartbreaker" (1999). And it's clear she and Carey are close since she appeared in Carey's film flop *Glitter*.

Prior to Carey's marriage to Nick Cannon, rumors surfaced that Da Brat and Carey were dating because they were often seen together in New York and Las Vegas. Though the rumors turned out to be false, Da Brat was one of the few witnesses at Carey and Cannon's wedding. Sadly their friendship has been put on hold since Da Brat was sentenced to three years in prison for aggravated assault in 2008.

8. DREW BARRYMORE AND CAMERON DIAZ

It isn't difficult to see why Drew Barrymore and Cameron Diaz are close friends. Both women are in their mid thirties, single, laid back, and both enjoy having fun. However, their bond of friendship runs much deeper then obvious similarities. Prior to costarring in the remake of *Charlie's Angels* (2000), Barrymore and Diaz were on friendly terms—they'd say "hi" when they saw each other—but did not become friends until working together. InStyle.com reported that Barrymore told Britain's *Elle* magazine that on the set "we spent every waking moment together for months and months—and years!" The relationship that formed while filming continued to solidify after the movie wrapped. Barrymore is adamant that Diaz helps keep her sane and is one of her closest confidants. Numerous media outlets reported that in an issue of Britain's *OK! Magazine* Barrymore admitted that Diaz helped her see that "you can't go through life blaming your own failure on your parents." The duo is often seen out around L.A. and has even vacationed together.

In January 2009 rumors started flying that Barrymore's and Diaz's BFF status was shaky, but this friendship seems like the real deal, so I'm sure they'll work it out. Who hasn't argued with their BFF?

9. GWYNETH PALTROW AND MADONNA

Though A-list actress Gwyneth Paltrow and shock-and-awe songstress Madonna might seem to have nothing in common aside from their blonde hair and toned bodies, these women have built a long-lasting friendship. They met in 1999 and became fast friends, Paltrow was a bridesmaid at Madonna's 2000 wedding to Guy Ritchie. Until Madonna's divorce from Ritchie, both Paltrow and Madonna were British transplants. In London Paltrow frequented Madonna's private gym, both of them working with celebrity trainer Tracy Anderson. They also bonded over their roles as mothers. Paltrow has admitted that Madonna helped her through postpartum depression, which she experienced following the birth of her son, Moses. Paltrow explained in a September 2008 appearance on *Oprah*, "[Madonna] is one of the most caring women. . . . She's given me a lot of great advice."

10. JENNIFER LOPEZ AND LEAH REMINI

These days Jennifer Lopez, aka J-Lo, is most often seen out with her children or husband, Mark Anthony, in tow, but even before she became a family girl she was rarely seen out with a girlfriend. But Leah Remini is the exception. Neither celebrity seems like a "girlie girl" so maybe that's why they click. J-Lo and Remini were often photographed shopping and lunching together. They even went out to parties together and were photographed hand-in-hand, seemingly joined at the hip. Remini also visited J-Lo at the hospital after the birth of twins Max and Emme to show her friend support.

Now that both J-Lo and Remini are working wives and mothers, it isn't surprising that their girl time has suffered.

Bromances

CNN.com defines "bromance" as: "a close, non-sexual relationship between two heterosexual males." Basically, it's the male version of BFFs. Men tend to not be as fickle in their friendships as women, but they also tend to hold back their emotions. A bromance breaks through this emotional block. The duos on this list seem to be genuine friendships, and they didn't need to go on the reality TV show *Bromance* to find each other.

1. BEN AFFLECK AND MATT DAMON

Ben Affleck and Matt Damon have one of the most famous bromances in Hollywood. They shot to fame through *Good Will Hunting* (1997), a film they wrote together and in which they costarred. Everyone must have liked these apples because the film was a success both with critics and at the box office. It received numerous Oscar nominations, and won the newly crowned power duo an Oscar for Best Original Screenplay (and Robin Williams an Oscar for Best Supporting Actor). Not only were Damon and Affleck's performances the talk of the town, but also the fact that these two friends created the vehicle that made them A-list actors led to a lot of media buzz.

Damon and Affleck met when Damon was ten and Affleck was eight, and they lived two blocks apart in Cambridge, Massachusetts. Affleck claims that without Damon's influence he probably would not have become an actor, for Damon gave him camaraderie and confidence to pursue his passion. Though fame destroys many friendships, Damon and Affleck claim that their friendship has gotten stronger over the years. Though they are now a plane ride away from each other—Damon lives in Miami and Affleck lives primarily in Boston—they still make time to see each other. They have been spotted vacationing together with their respective families, as well as together on "guys only" outings. This friendship has been tested and has endured through their rise to fame, rehab, Bennifer, and *Gigli*. It seems likely that this bromance will last a lifetime.

2. KEVIN SMITH AND JASON MEWES

Kevin Smith and Jason Mewes also grew up just two blocks apart. Though they were acquainted they did not actually know each other well until Mewes became an integral member of Smith's group of friends. Smith even says that at first he and Mewes did not gel, but as their friends drifted away, they were left together and became inseparable.

While Smith pursued screenwriting and directing, Mewes pursued black tar heroin. Smith gave Mewes some career direction by casting him in all of his movies except *Jersey Girl*—during filming Mewes was too strung out to participate. Smith has remained a steadfast friend to Mewes despite Mewes's long battle with drug addiction. In 1997 Smith assisted Mewes into his first stint in rehab. Two years later Mewes was arrested for heroin possession. In a 2006 *Entertainment Weekly* interview Smith recounted how Mewes's drug addiction got so severe that he stole Smith's ATM card and charged a delivery of heroin for $1,100.

After realizing that he was losing his career and his friends, Mewes returned to rehab and has remained clean since 2003. His acting career is flourishing, and his friendship with Smith has remained intact. These are no fair-weather friends.

3. CHRIS FARLEY AND DAVID SPADE

Chris Farley and David Spade were friends both on and off the set. They appeared on *Saturday Night Live*, where Spade worked from 1990–1996 as a writer and cast member and Farley worked as a cast member as well from 1990–1995. They also costarred in two films, *Tommy Boy* (1995) and *Black Sheep* (1996), both of which have achieved a certain amount of cult film status. While both comedians seemed to be enjoying success in the 1990s, Farley was battling a serious drug problem. Between 1993 and 1997 Farley sought treatment seventeen times. Despite his and his friends' attempts to save him, Farley died of a cocaine and heroin overdose on December 18, 1997. Spade spoke out in the April 2, 2008, *New York Post* saying that he was still taking heat for not saving his friend. Spade argued that Farley's addiction was so severe at times that instead of the friend he knew and loved, Farley turned into "a junkie who's wasted all the time and moody and angry and trying to knock you around." Spade raised eyebrows when he did not attend Farley's funeral. He stated simply, "I could not be in a room where Chris was in a box." Though this duo had their ups and downs, Spade remained a friend to Farley until the end.

4. TOBEY MAGUIRE AND LEONARDO DICAPRIO

Now famous actors, Tobey Maguire and Leonardo DiCaprio met as child actors often auditioning for the same roles. Rather than making them rivals, Maguire and DiCaprio became friends, even going so far as to help each other get work. For example, both boys auditioned for a role on the 1989 television series *Parenthood*, and when DiCaprio got the role he recommended Maguire for a guest role on the show. They also worked together in the film *This Boy's Life* (1993). The film starred DiCaprio and Maguire played one of his friends.

In 1997 DiCaprio hit superstar status when he starred in the blockbuster film *Titanic*. Though Maguire wasn't a household name yet, he wouldn't play second string for long. In a May 2007 *Men's Journal* interview Maguire admitted to having entered an underage Alcoholics Anonymous program in 1995, where he learned how to deal with his addictive and obsessive compulsive nature. During that time he changed his career path so that he and DiCaprio would not be constantly competing for roles, which led to increasing professional success for Maguire. Maguire starred in a slew of films including *The Ice Storm* (1997), *Pleasantville* (1998), and *The Cider House Rules* (1999). His superstar role came along in 2002 when he starred as Peter Parker in *Spiderman*, a role he has reprised twice.

Both Maguire and DiCaprio are now A-list actors, and still remain close friends. They are often seen together at Lakers basketball games, and even take family vacations together.

5. PAUL NEWMAN AND ROBERT REDFORD

Ok, so Paul Newman and Robert Redford would both probably cringe at hearing their friendship referred to as a bromance, but these two men enjoyed a very long, close relationship. Newman and Redford met on the set of the classic film *Butch Cassidy and the Sundance Kid* (1969). Newman was already an established actor, and he pushed for Redford to be chosen for the film even though Redford was an unknown. Redford said that as they got to know each other on the set, they discovered that they shared common interests and similar values. For example, they both felt that acting was a craft and family was their top priority. Throughout the years their friendship grew closer and they continued to act together, teaming up again for *The Sting* (1973). At one time they both lived in Connecticut, a mere mile apart, constantly playing jokes on one another. In interviews they made their friendship sound laid back and effortless. I guess it's a guy thing.

6. GEORGE CLOONEY AND BRAD PITT

George Clooney and Brad Pitt are another pair that has received much attention for their close friendship. Clooney and Pitt's relationship was first noticed upon the release of the remake of *Ocean's Eleven* in 2001. Stories of intense male bonding amid poker games and pranks ran rampant, and at the center were the dreamy film stars: Clooney and Pitt. Such pranks included Pitt telling the crew to call Clooney "Mr. Ocean" to help him stay in character and to not look him in the eye. Clooney retaliated by putting a bumper sticker on Pitt's car that referenced his miniature-sized manhood—a sticker that Pitt did not find for two days.

They appear to have bonded beyond work, hosting dinners together, supporting each other's film projects and charitable works. Though Clooney is a confirmed bachelor and Pitt is now a father of six, they seem to have similar interests—cards, philanthropy, looking good—and personalities that allow their friendship to endure.

7. SETH ROGEN AND EVAN GOLDBERG

Though Seth Rogen is the public face of this duo, he and childhood friend Evan Goldberg are writing and producing partners. They met as preteens at barmitzvah preparation class and became fast friends. As adults they worked together as writers for *Da Ali G Show*, starring Sacha Baron Cohen, and later teamed up with director Judd Apatow for their semi-autobiographical screenplay *Superbad* (2007). Goldberg has had a hand in almost every movie Rogen has appeared in: he was an executive producer on *Knocked Up*

(2007) and cowrote *Pineapple Express* (2008). Rogen and Goldberg have already become a Hollywood power duo and they've only been on the scene for a few years. Their string of successful films ensures that they will be around for many years to come.

8. ADAM SANDLER AND ROB SCHNEIDER

Rob Schneider and Adam Sandler met when both were performing on the L.A. comedy club circuit. They quickly became friends and eventually both ended up as regular cast members on *Saturday Night Live*—Sandler from 1991–1995 and Schneider from 1990–1994. After *SNL* both comedians went on to act in various films, though Sandler's films were considerably more successful. In 1999 Sandler started his own company, Happy Madison Productions. His first projects were films starring Schneider, including both *Deuce Bigalow* films and *The Hot Chick*. Sandler made cameo appearances in some of Schneider's films, and Schneider has appeared in nearly every film starring Sandler.

Though Schneider and Sandler's relationship might seem rooted in business, these two were friends before they were famous and they continue to be seen around Los Angeles together.

9. OWEN WILSON AND BEN STILLER

Owen Wilson and Ben Stiller's relationship began after Stiller offered Wilson his first film role, a small part in *The Cable Guy* (1996). Though they have opposite personalities and comedic style, the two hit it off during production and their relationship blossomed making them one of the most lucrative comedic duos today. As of 2009, Stiller and Wilson have appeared in ten films together including, *Meet the Parents* (2000), *Zoolander* (2001), and *Starsky and Hutch* (2004). Wilson was slated to play a role in *Tropic Thunder* (2008), but withdrew from the film following his suicide attempt.

10. MATTHEW MCCONAUGHEY AND LANCE ARMSTRONG

In a 2006 interview with *People* magazine Matthew McConaughey commented on his highly buzzed-about relationship
with Lance Armstrong saying, "[Lance] is one of the great
new relationships I've found in the last couple of years."
McConaughey finds Armstrong an inspiring person, considering all that he's overcome (both testicular and brain
cancer) and achieved (winning the Tour de France seven
consecutive times after beating cancer). While this friendship
has received much media attention, it isn't a very surprising
relationship. Both men enjoy physical activity, though Mc-
Conaughey asserts that he cannot keep up with Armstrong,
and both are were seemingly confirmed ladies men and now
have children with their girlfriends. Despite their new family
commitments, McConaughey and Armstrong still manage to
make time to maintain their friendship.

Fair Weather Friends

In a town where you're only as big as your last hit it's not surprising that friendships are as fleeting as fame. But it seems some celebrities go out of their way to *make* enemies. Is it to stay in the limelight? Are they bored? Whatever the reason, those included on this list have made feuding a sport.

1. PARIS HILTON

Paris Hilton feuds with so many people that it would be impossible to cover them all. Basically, if you are friends with Hilton, your friendship will likely end bitterly. And don't worry if you are a famous young celebrity who isn't her friend—she'll find a way to feud with you too. Paris doesn't see it this way though, so maybe the news stories are all wrong.

In a 2006 interview Hilton claimed she had never feuded with anyone saying, "All those stories are made up." Apparently, others simply use her to get media attention. Um . . . wasn't it Hilton who held a press conference in May 2005 to alert the media that she and Nicole Richie were no longer friends? Granted, she never used the word "feud" or stated what caused the rift between *The Simple Life* costars and former BFFs. She merely, said: "Nicole knows what she did, and that's all I'm ever going to say about it." Nicole never commented on the falling out at all, and neither has divulged the true reason for their split. The pair reconciled in 2006, and appeared in the final season of *The Simple Life* together, but they don't seem to be as close as they were pre-feud.

Though the quarrel with Richie came to an end in 2006, it was a banner year for warring with Hilton. That year Hilton allegedly got into a physical fight with Shanna Moakler. Hilton claimed Moakler hit her, while Moakler said Paris's then-boyfriend Stavros Niarchos pushed Moakler down the stairs. The reason for the dispute: Hilton apparently had a fling with Moakler's estranged husband Travis Barker. This dispute is ongoing.

Hilton also made headlines in 2006 for quarreling with actresses Mischa Barton and Lindsay Lohan. Though they were not close, Barton and Hilton's fallout came after Barton began dating Cisco Adler, an ex-fiancé of Paris's friend Kimberly Stewart. At a British Academy of Film and Television Awards after-party, London's *Daily Mirror* asked Barton about being on Hilton's hit list. Barton's reply was that, "Paris seems to hate everyone around her age who is more successful. . . . She steals people's boyfriends." Hilton responded by saying she didn't know Barton, and that it was Barton who was creating drama through her comments. Lohan and Hilton were close friends at one time, but after Lohan allegedly fooled around with Hilton's ex Niarchos, they argued, which led to numerous other quarrels and public jabs at one another.

2. SHANNEN DOHERTY

Shannen Doherty is famous for her role as Brenda Walsh on the original 1990s teen drama *Beverly Hills 90210*. She is similarly well known for her inability to get along with anyone she works with. This talent is exemplified first in her feuds on the set of *90210*. Costar Tori Spelling is frank about Doherty's actions in her autobiography *sTORItelling*. She claims that the set was much more relaxed after Doherty left the show. Another costar, Jennie Garth, finally admitted that though she and Doherty got along at times, they did physically fight once. Doherty denies this. In keeping with tradition, reports also surfaced that Doherty's guest spot on the new *90210* series didn't earn her many friends either. According to www.popcrunch.com, the new star, Shenae Grimes, told friends that Doherty was hard to get along with and an "effin bitch" on set.

Shortly after leaving the original *90210*, Doherty landed a role on *Charmed* costarring Alyssa Milano. The two starlets apparently had a good relationship during the first two seasons, but by the third season they were at each other's throats. Some claim Doherty grew jealous of Milano's popularity and endorsement deals, but Milano insists that their personalities simply clashed. Whatever the reason, Doherty was dismissed from the show at the end of the third season.

In 2003 Doherty fought (some claim physically) with Paris Hilton, who had a relationship—and made her infamous sex tape—with Doherty's then-husband Rick Salomon. Though the time line is questionable, it seems likely that their relationships with him overlapped. There is still bad blood between these two.

3. LINDSAY LOHAN

Lindsay Lohan's clash with Paris Hilton wasn't her first, and won't be her last. Lohan's first brush with controversy began in 2002 with fellow teen star Hilary Duff. Teen heartthrob and singer Aaron Carter, who reportedly dated both girls simultaneously, eventually dropped Lohan for Duff, which sparked the controversy. This guy must be quite the catch, because Carter reportedly reconciled briefly with Lohan after his split with Duff. This war continued with music battles, guest list exclusions, and media jabs until the girls reconciled in 2007.

In 2005 reports surfaced that Lohan had clashed with Ashlee and Jessica Simpson, barring them from her MTV

Movie Awards party. Lohan was upset by the rumor that Ashlee had hooked up with Lohan's ex-boyfriend Wilmer Valderrama. When Lohan arrived at Jimmy Fallon's MTV party later that same evening, the girls had to be kept apart. All three girls deny any bad blood, and Lohan's rep commented that their names must have been unintentionally omitted from Lohan's party list.

More recently Lohan has been at odds with Scarlett Johansson, allegedly writing nasty things about her on a bathroom stall. However, Johansson claims she doesn't know Lohan, which could very well be true. Lohan's infamous dispute of 2009 is with the family of her ex-girlfriend Samantha Ronson. While they were dating, Samantha's sister, Charlotte, banned Lohan from her party; it is alleged that the Ronson family was instrumental in breaking up the couple. With her career on hiatus, and personal life in ruins, it seems that Lohan could really use a friend, rather than more enemies, right now.

4. ROSIE O'DONNELL

Actress and television personality Rosie O'Donnell was known as the "queen of nice" but that all changed in when National Rifle Association (NRA) supporter Tom Selleck appeared on *The Rosie O'Donnell Show* in 1999. He thought he was there to promote his upcoming film *The Love Letter*, but O'Donnell had other ideas. She quickly turned the interview towards Selleck's involvement in the NRA and views on gun control. The typically lighthearted show grew very uncomfortable as tempers flared. Selleck tried to handle the situation diplomatically, and when asked about the incident in an interview with *Access Hollywood* in August 2007, almost ten years later, he merely said that Rosie should "stop thinking everyone who disagrees with her is evil."

Apparently Rosie enjoyed speaking her mind, for during her short stint on *The View* (2006–2007) she was part of some intense feuds. During one episode she offended Donald Trump when she shared her views on his decision to keep Tara Conner as Miss USA after pictures surfaced of her out drinking underage and doing drugs. O'Donnell went on to impersonate Trump and call him a snake oil salesman. The Donald did not take her insults lying down but reciprocated with insults of his own, threatening to sue her and calling her a loser. The duo traded insults, but no lawsuit ensued. Though their feud eventually died down, O'Donnell won't be on *The Celebrity Apprentice* anytime soon.

O'Donnell's departure from *The View* was facilitated by a feud with fellow cohost Elisabeth Hasselbeck in 2007. The liberal O'Donnell and conservative Hasselbeck often clashed onscreen, but one day it got out of control. O'Donnell accused Hasselbeck of not defending her against right-wing criticism, and the arguing grew so intense that the two women were shot on a split screen. Furious over the split-screen effect and hurt by Hasselbeck's words, O'Donnell left *The View* three weeks before her contract expired.

5. TOM CRUISE

While many celebrities refuse to discuss controversial issues or their personal beliefs publicly, Tom Cruise is not one of them. Cruise, a devout Scientologist, has argued with numerous people as a result of his staunch religious beliefs. One of his most famous feuds occurred in 2005 when he criticized Brooke Shields for using anti-depressants and seeking therapy while struggling with postpartum depression following the birth of her first child. On a subsequent episode of the *Today* show, news anchor Matt Lauer questioned Cruise about his comments. Lauer and Cruise got into a heated debate during which Cruise told Lauer that Lauer's problem was that he did not know the history of psychiatry—as Cruise supposedly did. Cruise ultimately called him "glib," and dismissed Lauer's comments. Both outbursts garnered numerous media coverage, but Cruise has since patched up relations with both Shields and Lauer.

Cruise showed that he didn't consider his religion or his sexuality a joking matter in 2006 when *South Park* aired an episode that made fun of both. Though Cruise denies this, reports surfaced that after the episode aired Cruise was upset and made threats to Viacom (the company that owns both Comedy Central and Paramount) stating that he would not promote his upcoming Paramount film *MI:3* if they re-aired the episode. The rerun was pulled leading fans to cry censorship. Shortly thereafter however, Paramount did not to renew Cruise's contract with the company. Cruise's representatives of course claimed he had already planned to leave. The Paramount–Cruise rift has apparently been mended, and in 2009 Cruise signed on to star in the fourth installment of the *Mission Impossible* franchise.

6. KANYE WEST

Kanye West isn't afraid to disagree with someone, and seems to enjoy the media attention his feuds bring. This makes it difficult to tell when he is truly upset, and when he is simply yearning for attention. He and rapper 50 Cent were embroiled in a fake feud in 2007 when they both announced the release of an album September 11, 2007. Probably for publicity, they engaged in a duel of words. At one point 50 Cent said he would never put out another solo album if West sold more copies than he did. He later retracted that statement, which was fortuitous because West's album *Celebration* far outsold 50 Cent's album *Curtis*.

West also fake-feuded with comedian Stephen Colbert after Colbert revealed Operation Humble Kanye asking fans to buy *A Colbert Christmas* from iTunes to knock West's album from the number one spot. West responded through Twitter with: "Who the f*** is Stephen Colbert." The two were later seen hugging it out, and yes, Colbert won the iTunes battle. But West doesn't seem any humbler.

Though the previous two feuds were primarily for media attention, West seemed genuinely at odds with President George W. Bush in 2005. During the live NBC Concert for Hurricane Relief following Hurricane Katrina, West, one of the speakers, deviated from the prepared script, and instead made his own speech that included the statement, "George Bush doesn't care about black people."

His most recent feud with singer Pink is less drastic, but West managed to enrage Pink during a 2009 Stella McCartney fashion show when, she alleges, he continually commented that there should be more fur in the show. Pink, a vegetarian and PETA advocate was severely offended and later commented about West in the July 2009 issue of *FHM* saying, "There are so many people who I think are a waste of skin and he's up there. I should wear him."

7. STAR JONES

Most well-known as one of the cohosts on *The View*, Star Jones's bad blood with Rosie O'Donnell occurred before O'Donnell even joined the show. While on *The View* Jones underwent a massive physical transformation, dropping about 160 lbs. Questions abounded as to how Jones lost such a massive amount of weight, and she insisted it was through diet, exercise, and a mysterious medical intervention. O'Donnell criticized Jones for not being honest about having gastric bypass surgery. In 2007 Jones finally admitted to having undergone the procedure in 2003. Why did she keep mum? She was afraid of what people would think of her. In 2009 O'Donnell and Jones allegedly put their feud behind them.

One war that has no end in sight, however, is Jones's feud with her former boss from *The View*, Barbara Walters. In 2006 producers for *The View* decided not to renew Jones's contract. Walters claimed it was because of Jones's lack of popularity with viewers. Incidents such as Jones's mysterious weight loss and shameless wedding promotion had turned people off the cohost. Instead of letting the network handle her departure, Jones took matters into her own hands surprising everyone on June 27, 2006 by announcing that she would be leaving *The View* at the end of that season. Walters was blindsided by the announcement, and dismissed Jones from the show that day. This feud has become a "she said, she said" as both have appeared in numerous media outlets telling her side of the story and chiding the other.

8. JANICE DICKINSON

Anyone familiar with Janice Dickinson, the self-proclaimed first supermodel, isn't surprised to see her on this list. Dickinson's lack of a filter for her mouth seems to land her in hot water with almost everyone. But she doesn't care. She speaks her mind. One of her most legendary feuds is with fellow model Jerry Hall. The bad blood between the women resulted from dating the same man: Mick Jagger. Dickinson and Jagger dated for about eight months during the late 1970s, after which she claims she dumped him because she didn't want to move to England. After their falling-out Jagger immediately moved in with Jerry Hall in England. Whether Jagger chose Hall over Dickinson or chose her after Dickinson dumped him is where the discrepancy lies. In one interview Dickinson claimed that Hall threatened to shoot her, and the bad blood remains almost thirty years later.

Dickinson is also embroiled in an ongoing feud with model Tyra Banks, which began after Dickinson was fired from her position as a judge on the hit reality show *America's Next Top Model* after the fourth season. Producers made it seem like Dickinson walked away to pursue other opportunities, but she was quite vocal about what really happened. Dickinson said she was fired for being honest with the contestants, which at times was harsh—but then so is the modeling industry. She claimed she made the show a success and was irreplaceable. Though having now completed thirteen seasons, the show has somehow managed to survive without Dickinson. She continues to make jabs at Banks and *ANTM* in the media. It seems that Dickinson never forgives and forgets.

After *ANTM* Dickinson appeared in the fifth season of the Vh1 Reality TV show *The Surreal Life*. There, she found another sparring partner—Omarosa Manigault of *The Apprentice* fame. These outspoken women were obviously set up to clash, and clash they did. The season consisted of numerous shouting matches, lots of name-calling, and Janice even waving a knife. Needless to say, Dickinson and Manigault have not kissed and made up.

9. VICTORIA BECKHAM (AKA POSH SPICE)
Victoria Beckham's seemingly chilly exterior and haughty attitude has not earned many friends in England or in the U.S. She has quite a list of enemies, which led to the compilation of a list of people who were banned from attending any Spice Girls reunion concert. The list includes singer Lilly Allen, singer/model Sophie Ellis Bextor, soccer couple Peter and Jordan Andre, actress Denise Van Outen, and comedian Graham Norton, among others. While Beckham's dislike of many of these stars is unknown to Americans, her feud with Lilly Allen began when Allen sang about Beckham in her song "Smile." Allen reinforced her dislike of Beckham in a November 2007 interview with Britain's *You* magazine (a section of the *Daily Mail*) when she called Beckham a monster who was famous for no reason and whose only goal in life is to be famous. Harsh.

Naomi Campbell might have been another person on Beckham's "persona non grata" list, since when she and Beckham met at party Campbell cattily asked Beckham why she is called "Posh." Beckham then called Campbell "a complete cow" on TV, and Campbell responded by saying Beckham was "a talent-less cow." Such brilliant wordplay.

10. LAUREN CONRAD

Ok, so Conrad's feuds might be staged for television, because they all take place on the Reality shows *Laguna Beach* or *The Hills*, but it's still amazing that one girl has enraged so many people. She's always at war with someone. Though she made many enemies, some of Conrad's feuds have received more media coverage than others.

Conrad's initial feud was with 2004–2005 costar on *Laguna Hills*, Kristin Cavallari. Conrad and Cavallari fought over a boy, Stephen Coletti. Coletti was good friends with Conrad (though she wanted more) and with at times, with Cavallari's boyfriend.

In 2006 Conrad received her own spin-off show, *The Hills*. Controversy quickly followed. Conrad's friend and roommate, Heidi Montag, began dating Spencer Pratt, to whom Conrad took an instant—and not unfounded—dislike. The general opinion about Pratt is now in agreement with Conrad, so Conrad's initial instinct seems to have been correct. However, Montag was smitten and didn't appreciate Conrad's vocal disapproval of Pratt, and a rift was created between the girls. When Montag decided to move in with Pratt, and Conrad accused the two of them of starting rumors of a Conrad sex tape, the girls officially became enemies.

Most recently Conrad has added former friend Audrina Patridge to her enemy list. As with Montag, Conrad repeatedly lets her dislike of Patridge's on-again-off-again boyfriend, Justin Bobby, be known. Though Conrad's blatant dislike of Bobby had caused some tension, a full-blown feud didn't erupt until rumors began swirling that Conrad hooked up with Bobby in October 2008. Conrad insists that she never even talked to Bobby when Patridge wasn't present, but Patridge claims she was upset because Conrad didn't talk to her face-to-face about the rumors, and chose instead to go through the media. Producers probably cooked up the rumors for publicity, but these girls have been playing right along.

Celebrity Spotlight

Teen Idols

Every few years a new teen becomes famous and sets other teenage hearts aflutter. Madness ensues, but the question in the back of everyone's mind is how long his or her fame will last. Though most teen sensations fade shortly after their fifteen minutes never to be thought of again, the idols of this list stand apart from the mass of famous teens as the most famous idols of the 1980s, 1990s, and today.

1. THE BRAT PACK

This group of teen idols is number one because they transcend the generations. In the 1980s, the members of the Brat Pack and their films were the embodiment of cool and they are still watched and admired by teens today. What girl doesn't want to be Molly Ringwald in *Sixteen Candles* or *Pretty in Pink*. Who wouldn't want to spend their Saturday in *Breakfast Club*–like detention?

David Blum coined the term "Brat Pack" (playing off the 1950s "Rat Pack") in a cover story he wrote about the group of actors for *New York Magazine* in 1985. Just who belong to this mythic this group? There are, in fact, numerous websites dedicated to answering just this question. Most people tend to agree that the following actors are members of the Pack: Molly Ringwald, Ally Sheedy, Emilio Estevez, Anthony Michael Hall, Rob Lowe, Andrew McCarthy, Demi Moore, and Judd Nelson. Arguable members are Robert Downey Jr., John Cusack, Tom Cruise, Charlie Sheen, Matthew Broderick, and Matt Dillon. Some of the most well known Brat Pack films are *The Breakfast Club* (1985), *St. Elmo's Fire* (1985), *Less Than Zero* (1987), *Pretty in Pink* (1986), *Sixteen Candles* (1984), and *Class* (1983). Though the Brat Pack has long since disbanded, the films resonate with teens today and continue to build its fan base.

2. BRITNEY SPEARS

Little did Britney Spears know how famous she would become when the Jive record label released her debut single ". . . Baby One More Time." The single catapulted the sixteen-year-old to instant world fame, remaining atop the charts for three weeks, and the midriff-baring, Catholic-schoolgirl uniform video landed her in her first controversy. In early 1999 her debut album was released and topped the charts for six weeks, selling over ten million albums within the year.

Little did anyone know what a success this 1992 *Star Search* winner and girl from a town of less than one thousand people would become. Shortly after her debut album's release, Britney-mania gained speed, for she was wildly popular with teen girls and boys alike. Britney is often labeled the "Pop Princess" and the first female pop star of her generation, coming onto the scene before Christina Aguilera, Jessica Simpson, or Mandy Moore.

Britney's success continued with her second album, churning out numerous hits, yet her innocent teenage girl image didn't last long. From 1998–2002 she dated the "Pop Prince" of the time, *NSYNC front man Justin Timberlake, and though she proclaimed that she would remain a virgin until marriage her videos and performances—namely at the MTV Music Awards—suggested otherwise.

Britney Spears doing what she does best on the 1999
. . . Baby One More Time tour.

I have to admit that it would be difficult coming of age as
Britney had to—maturing in the media spotlight—with fans
wanting the same young girl image and music that made her
famous. Even her songs, such as "I'm A Slave 4 U," "I'm Not
A Girl, Not Yet A Woman," and "Overprotected," reflected her
struggles with life in the limelight. In 2002 her relationship
with Timberlake ended and Spears announced she was taking a break from her career. Nonetheless, *Forbes* sill named
her "The World's Most Powerful Celebrity."

When Britney returned to work she did not reclaim her previous success. Personal matters soon overshadowed her career, and the whole world watched as Britney spiraled out of control. In 2008 she reemerged under her father's conservatorship. She appears to be on the road to recovery, at least professionally, and is managing to rein in her personal life. Britney's comeback is detailed in the chapter "Celebrity Comebacks."

3. BOY BANDS

From the dawn of music there have been boy bands and they have always enjoyed legions of fans. The last three decades are no exception producing such groups as New Kids on the Block, Backstreet Boys, and *NSYNC. These teen boys drove girls wild, for there was always a boy in each band to appeal to any girl's taste. Girls who liked clean-cut boys could drool over Nick Carter (Backstreet) or Justin Timberlake (*NSYNC). Prefer a rebel? Try AJ of Backstreet or Donny Wahlberg of New Kids.

Album sales and merchandising tells the story. New Kids sold 80 million albums worldwide. Not only have the Backstreet Boys sold over 120 million albums, they also ranked first in concert and album sales from 1997–2005. *NSYNC sold 9.9 million albums in 2000, which is a record for albums sold in a single year. From t-shirts to pillowcases—even action figures—you name it; they found a way to put their name or picture on it.

However, even idolatry gets old after awhile. One New Kid said, "Sometimes . . . it got real scary. . . . The crowd could get out of control." Others said they reached a point where they just wanted to be regular guys. Eventually, each of these groups parted ways. Apparently being a regular guy isn't all it's cracked up to be, for both New Kids on the Block and the Backstreet Boys have attempted to reunite, but the now thirty-somethings have failed to reclaim their idol status or achieve their previous musical success so far.

4. THE COREYS

Corey Feldman and Corey Haim burst onto the scene when they costarred in *The Lost Boys* in 1987. Feldman was known for his roles in *The Goonies* (1985), *Stand By Me* (1986), and *The 'Burbs* (1989). Haim was best known for his role in the popular film *Lucas* (1986), in which he starred alongside Charlie Sheen and Winona Ryder. As a duo, however, they were more popular than either had been (or has been since) on his own. It was the beginning of "Corey Mania" where they graced the cover of teen magazines and were reportedly the highest paid teen actors of the 1980s.

After eight films together, the Coreys split up, thinking each could make it on his own. Unfortunately, it was their combined power that was the key to their success. Both Coreys battled drugs in the 1990s and acted in unmemorable films. Feldman starred in the short-lived TV series *Dweebs*, released multiple albums with his band Corey Feldman's Truth Movement (yes, really), and recorded a solo album. Feldman's most well known venture since the break up of the Coreys was his stint on the first season of Vh1's *The Surreal Life.*

Haim filed for bankruptcy in 1997 and, with rehab behind him, tried to restart his acting career with roles in *Without Malice* (2000) and *Universal Groove* (2007) and *Lost Boys: The Tribe* (2008) (the sequel to *The Lost Boys*). In 2007 Feldman and Haim reunited on the A&E Reality TV show, *The Two Coreys*. To date, two seasons have aired with moderate success. Ultimately A&E canceled *The Two Coreys*, but it would have been difficult to continue anyway since Feldman posted on his personal blog that he would not have contact with Haim until he overcame his drug addiction.

5. RIVER PHOENIX

Successful, misunderstood, tragic; all these words describe River Phoenix's short life. He grew up in an atypical family.

In the late 1960s his parents joined the Children of God cult and moved the family to South America. When Phoenix was seven, the family returned to the United States, put down roots in Los Angeles, and changed their surname from Bottom to Phoenix. This was in honor of their new beginning in California.

His film debut came in the forgettable 1985 film *Explorers*. However, he quickly found success with roles in *Stand By Me* (1986), *The Mosquito Coast* (1986), *Indiana Jones and the Last Crusade* (1989), and *Running on Empty* (1988), for which he received an Academy Award nomination as Best Supporting Actor.

While Phoenix was adored by young women and was featured in numerous teen magazines, he never became comfortable with his fame. Shy by nature, he once stated, "If I see my face on the cover of a magazine . . . I shut myself out and freak." After a while—perhaps as a result of his fame or because he became disillusioned with the film industry—others began to notice a change in Phoenix. A dedicated environmentalist, a strict vegetarian, and animal-rights advocate and member of PETA, Phoenix had been staunchly anti-drugs. River left acting to take a break from the spotlight and started a band, Aleka's Attic, with his sister, Rain. However, he returned to Hollywood in 1993 to film *Dark Blood* and was set to costar in *Interview With A Vampire* alongside Tom Cruise. Tragically, early on October 31, River died of an overdose outside The Viper Room (a club owned by his close friend Johnny Depp) as a result of multiple drugs he had ingested.

There are songs that were written in Phoenix's memory, and many web sites dedicated to him. His future as an actor was bright and one can only wonder if perhaps his story is the result of teen idol status gone wrong. Phoenix's own words were foretelling: "I would rather quit while I was ahead. There's no need in overstaying your welcome."

6. LUKE PERRY AND JASON PRIESTLEY

Whether you preferred the good boys or bad ones, the teen drama *Beverly Hills. 90210* had both: boy-next-door Brandon Walsh, played by Jason Priestley, and rebel Dylan McKay, played by Luke Perry. *Beverly Hill, 90210* debuted in 1990 and the cast members became teen sensations overnight—though few of them were actually teenagers at the time. Priestly described the hype surrounding them as "madness." Perry allegedly received more than 3,000 fan letters each week.

Like many teen heartthrobs, Priestley and Perry struggled to avoid being pigeonholed. Perry left the cast from 1995-1998 to pursue other projects, but returned having found little success outside the famous zip code. Priestley left the cast in 1998 but continued to be involved with the series as an executive producer.

Since the end of the series Perry has appeared in numerous TV guest spots on series such as *Will and Grace*, *Law and Order SVU*, *Family Guy*, and *Oz*. He has also performed onstage on Broadway and London's West End. Both Perry and Priestley tried their luck in other television series, but neither with any lasting success. Perry appeared in *Jeremiah* and Priestley in both *Tru Calling* and *Love Monkey*. Priestley has had moderate success as a director, even directing a few episodes of the reincarnated *90210*. Though their teen idol days may be well behind them, Perry and Priestley still work steadily and make occasional appearances at industry events, and still cause the hearts of former *Beverly Hills, 90210* fans to beat a just a little bit faster.

7. ZAC EFRON

Zac Efron is the most recent teen idol whose level of worship rivals those of boy band stars Nick Carter and Justin Timberlake. Before Efron, Disney had pumped out numerous female teen idols such as Hilary Duff, Lindsay Lohan, and most recently, Miley Cyrus. But his starring role in the made-for-TV *High School Musical* movies brought Efron teen stardom previously unachieved by his female counterparts. The first film drew 255 million viewers and led to sold out stage shows, concerts, theme park attractions, and record-setting DVD sales. And Zac has proved that though *HSM* made him an idol, his popularity is not directly tied to *HSM*, by also starring in *Hairspray*, *17 Again*, and *Me and Orson Welles*. While none of these roles are a major departure from Efron's golden boy role as *HSM*'s Troy, he says that right now he's just having fun.

8. THE OLSEN TWINS

Their acting careers began when they were just a few months old and their mother took them to audition for a sitcom. When producers held them and they didn't cry, they got the part. I guess that's all you can ask of babies. As a result, the girls shared the role of Michelle Tanner on *Full House* for the next eight years.

Michelle Tanner merchandise was so popular that the twins' parents decided to create Dualstar Entertainment to handle their merchandising endeavors. This began a slew of straight-to-video films, some of which were produced by the twins making them the youngest producers in history. In total, their entertainment company has released forty videos, which have sold over thirty million copies; six albums, selling over one and a half million copies; and a young adult book series, totaling over twenty-nine million copies sold. Upon entering their teenage years, the girls started a clothing and lifestyle line sold exclusively through Wal-Mart. At age eighteen, the girls became copresidents of Dualstar and are worth an estimated one hundred million dollars. They've been on the *Forbes* "Celebrity 100 List" since 2002 and in 2007 *Forbes* collectively ranked them as the eleventh on their list of the richest women in entertainment.

Since their eighteenth birthday Mary-Kate and Ashley have pursued different career paths. Mary-Kate is trying to find acting success outside the tween realm and has had little success, landing a recurring guest role on the third season of *Weeds* and a role in the 2008 Indie film *The Wackness*. Ashley is more devoted to the every-day workings of Dualstar, especially in trying to create more fashion lines. Though the twins have met with mediocre success since their teen idol heyday, they seem happiest out of the public eye.

9. LEONARDO DICAPRIO

DiCaprio didn't land his breakthrough Hollywood role until his teenage years were almost over, but his youthful appearance made him popular among teen girls. His first critically recognized role was in *This Boy's Life* (1993), and his first nominations for Golden Globe and Academy Awards appeared in the same year for his role as Arnie in *What's Eating Gilbert Grape* (1993). His performances in *The Basketball Diaries* (1995) and as Romeo in the updated Shakespeare classic *Romeo and Juliet* (1996) first catapulted him into teen-idol status. But it was not until the box–office smash *Titanic* (1997), in which he played the romantic hero, Jack Dawson, that he arguably became the most adored movie star of the time.

It would be impossible for any film to top the success of *Titanic* (at the time it was the highest grossing movie of all time and tied *Ben Hur* for most Academy Awards) but DiCaprio's next two films, *The Man in the Iron Mask* and *The Beach*, actually flopped at the box office. These would turn out to be minor setbacks for DiCaprio, who rebounded with numerous critically acclaimed roles, successfully shedding his teen image and growing into a respected leading man.

10. DEBORAH "DEBBIE" GIBSON

Before Britney, Christina, and Rihanna, there was Debbie,

who some might call the *original* "pop princess." With her crinoline skirts, sneakers, oversized jackets, and perky blond hair, she burst onto the music scene in the mid 1980s at age sixteen. While she is often confused with 1980s mall pop star Tiffany, Debbie is remembered as the one with talent. She still holds the Guinness world record she set at age seventeen for being the youngest person to write, produce, and perform a number one single, her song "Foolish Beat." Her first single, "Only in My Dreams" topped charts worldwide, her debut album *Out of the Blue* sold five million copies, and her sophomore album went triple platinum. She even shared the 1989 ASCAP (American Society of Composers, Authors, and Publishers) Songwriter of the Year Award with Bruce Springsteen. Aside from her successful music career, Debbie was a teen icon appearing in, and on the covers of all the teenybopper magazines. Her fashion, like her music, was in demand, and she created a perfume with Revlon and teamed up with Natural World Cosmetics to create a line of cosmetics for teen girls.

Debbie went on to record three more studio albums, as well as an independent record, but none achieved the success of her earlier releases. While Debbie faded from the public eye in the 1990s, she found success on the stage, appearing in numerous musicals both on Broadway and in London, including *Les Miserables, Grease,* and *Beauty and the Beast*; she continues to perform onstage today. Some of her other credits include posing for *Playboy* in 2005, judging the contestants on the short-lived *American Juniors*, and competing on *Skating with Celebrities*.

Comeback Kids

Children who become celebrities are not destined to have the highest success rate in life. On the contrary, it is not uncommon for people who find fame and fortune at a very young age to have difficulty handling such success and consequently end up running their career—and often their life in general—into the ground. However, the children on this list were not only famous during youth, but have managed to find success as adults in the entertainment industry.

1. RON HOWARD

Ron Howard played some of the most famous characters on television in the 1960s and 1970s. His most famous role was as Andy Griffith's son Opie on *The Andy Griffith Show* from 1960–1968. He continued his success on television when he played golden boy Richie Cunningham on the sitcom *Happy Days* from 1974–1980. Rather than fall victim to the pressures of fame, as some young celebrities do, Howard has thrived.

He used his weight as an actor to learn his true passion, how to work behind the camera. He struck a deal with Roger Corman that he would act in Corman's film *Eat My Dust* (1976) if Corman would help Howard direct his first film, *Grand Theft Auto* (1977) in return. Howard enjoyed working behind the camera so much that he founded Major H Productions, producing and directing the hit film *Splash* (1984), which established him as a bankable director. In 1986 Howard cofounded Imagine Films Entertainment with his friend Brian Grazer, which has produced—and through which Howard has directed—numerous films including *Backdraft* (1991), *Apollo 13* (1995), *A Beautiful Mind* (2002), and *The Da Vinci Code* (2006). The production company has also generated numerous TV shows, such as *Felicity*, *24*, and *Arrested Development*. Married to his high school sweetheart, the father of four children, and an award-winning director and producer, Howard really does seem to live up to the "golden boy" characters he played in his youth.

2. DREW BARRYMORE

Drew Barrymore made many headlines before even reaching the age of ten: from her memorable performance as Gertie in *E.T. The Extra Terrestrial* (1982), to becoming the youngest *Saturday Night Live* host at age seven, receiving a Golden Globe nomination for her role in *Irreconcilable Differences* (1984), to making John Willis's list of Promising New Actors of 1984. But not long after the flurry of positive headlines, Barrymore seemed to spiral downward, which was young even by Hollywood standards. She was a regular at Studio 54 at age nine, entered rehab for drug and alcohol abuse at age thirteen, and attempted suicide at age fourteen, which led to another stint in rehab.

Though Barrymore was emancipated from her parents at sixteen, and apparently drug-free, her wild ways continued. She seemed destined to go the way of many child actors when she posed for *Playboy* and then flashed David Letterman on his show in 1995. Her godfather, Steven Spielberg, even sent her a note telling her to cover up.

So, with her friends support, Barrymore decided to change her life's direction. She took a small role in the horror flick *Scream* (1996), and then chose roles in such films as *The Wedding Singer* (1998), *Ever After* (1998), and *Never Been Kissed* (1999), which quickly made her one of America's Sweethearts. Since the mid–1990s, Barrymore's career has continued on an upswing, leading to the establishment of her own production company, Flower Films, directing, and a spot on the Hollywood A-list.

3. SARAH JESSICA PARKER

Sarah Jessica Parker gained recognition on the Broadway stage as the lead in *Annie*, which led to a role in the television show *Square Pegs*. This role transformed her into the nerdy teen for which she is remembered. Though the show was canceled after only one season, Parker was noticed, and subsequently cast in such teen films as *Footloose* (1984) and *Girls Just Want to Have Fun* (1985).

When she re-emerged into the spotlight in the 1990s, she was cast in more glamorous, adult roles, in films such as *Honeymoon in Vegas* (1992) and *First Wives Club* (1996). Of course, she became a fashion icon and A-list actress when she landed the role of Carrie Bradshaw in the HBO series *Sex and the City* from 1998-2004, and then reprised the role for the big screen.

4. JODIE FOSTER

Entering the acting business at age three by landing work in commercials, Jodie Foster became Disney's darling of the 1970s, starring in such Disney films as *Freaky Friday* (1976), *Bugsy Malone* (1976), and *Candleshoe* (1977). But Foster's acting wasn't all kid stuff. She received a nomination for the Best Supporting Actress Oscar for her role as a child prostitute in *Taxi Driver* (1976).

Foster did not fall into the typical trap, like many younger Hollywood stars. Instead, she went to college, attending Yale University and embraced a more traditional youth. Her college years were not unaffected by her fame, though and Foster was troubled by multiple stalkers.

Upon graduation from Yale she returned to acting and over time established herself as a legitimate adult actress. Her critically acclaimed performances in *The Accused* (1989) and *Silence of the Lambs* (1991), each of which earned her a Golden Globe and an Academy Award. Now Foster can pick and choose her roles, and still take time to raise her children. Even though she's not a staple on the Hollywood red carpet, she is still profitable at the box office, as seen in such films as *Maverick* (1994), *Contact* (1997), *Anna and the King* (1999), and *Inside Man* (2006).

5. CHRISTINA APPLEGATE

Christina Applegate spent her awkward teenage years in front of millions of viewers playing Kelly Bundy on the popular television sitcom *Married . . . with Children*. Though her career began when she was just a baby on the soap opera *Days of Our Lives*, ten seasons (1987–1997) on *Married . . .* made her one of the most well-known teen celebrities of the time. And while some former teen stars are a dime a dozen, Applegate has made a solid name for herself as an actress.

Immediately following *Married . . .*, Applegate was cast in her own sitcom, *Jesse*, but it was canceled after two seasons. She went on to accept acting roles, for both the big and small screens, and earned two Emmy Award nominations (2003 and 2004) and one Emmy win (in 2004) in the category of Outstanding Guest Actress in a Comedy Series for her recurring guest spot on *Friends*. Applegate tried her hand once more at sitcom with ABC's *Samantha Who?*, but it seemed the third time was not the charm, and after two seasons the series was canceled in 2009, despite critical praise.

As a result of Applegate's 2008 battle with breast cancer, she has been in the spotlight honestly speaking publicly about her fight, treatment, and recovery. She topped *People* magazine's Most Beautiful People list in 2009, becoming not only a successful actress but an inspiration as well.

6. CHRISTIAN BALE

Christian Bale began his career with much critical acclaim for his performance in the film *Empire of the Sun* (1987) at age thirteen. This initial success led to a role in *Treasure Island* (1990) opposite Charlton Heston. After gaining recognition for roles in films geared toward an adult audience, he starred in more age-appropriate films like *Newsies* (1992), *Swing Kids* (1993), and *Little Women* (1994), all three of which gained him legions of teenage fans. Allegedly, Bale auditioned for, and almost won, the role of Jack Dawson in *Titanic* and he was also considered for the role of Will Turner in *Pirates of the Caribbean*.

Bale had no trouble transitioning into the film industry as an adult. Accustomed to serious roles, Bale returned to severe characters in the independent films *American Psycho* (1999) and *The Machinist* (2004). His performances earned him enormous admiration as an actor, for the roles required massive strain on his physique and intense psychological preparation. Over the past several years, Bale has increased his mainstream popularity by taking on the role of Batman in *Batman Begins* (2005), and *The Dark Knight* (2008), and by replacing Arnold Schwarzenegger as John Connor in the fourth installment of the Terminator series *Terminator Salvation* (2009).

Bale will likely continue to vacillate between challenging roles in independent projects and more mainstream roles that increase his visibility box-office profits, and will, no doubt, continue to be a prominent Hollywood actor for years to come.

7. CHRISTINA RICCI

Christina Ricci became a recognizable child star when she played Wednesday Addams in *The Addams Family* (1991). She reprised the role in *The Addams Family Values* (1993) and her success led to teenage roles in such films as *Casper* (1995) and the coming-of-age film *Now and Then* (1995). She credits her mother for making acting a positive experience for her as a child, and not behaving as a "stage mom." It was Christina and her siblings who begged their mom to let her act, not the mother pushing expectations on the child.

Though her popularity ebbed as she matured, she has continued to work. Her most popular projects include *The Opposite of Sex* (1998) (for which she was nominated for a Golden Globe), *Sleepy Hollow* (1999), *Monster* (2003), and *Penelope* (2008). Ricci has found her niche in the independent film industry, which she personally finds more interesting, and she has been rewarded with much critical praise for her work in these lesser-known roles.

8. NEIL PATRICK HARRIS

The television show *Doogie Houser, MD* made teenager Neil Patrick Harris's face known throughout America and Harris became synonymous with his character long after the show ended in 1993 after four seasons. Though Harris continued to act—primarily on the stage with some guest star roles on TV—he failed to break out of the shadow of Doogie Houser. When he played himself in the film *Harold & Kumar Go to White Castle* (2004), Harris surged back into the Hollywood spotlight and landed a starring role on the sitcom *How I Met Your Mother*, which has become successful and for which he has been nominated for multiple Emmy and Golden Globe Awards. Harris's career definitely seems to have been given a second life and the actor is taking it all in stride. This time around, the character he plays on TV does not outshine the actor himself, and it is likely Harris's career will continue long after *How I Met Your Mother* ends.

9. KIRK CAMERON

Kirk Cameron was a teen heartthrob from 1985–1992, when he played trouble-making teen Mike Seaver on *Growing Pains*. Once the show ended, Cameron had a difficult time finding work. He married his on-screen girlfriend Chelsea Noble and left blockbuster movies behind in favor of working on film projects that reflected his Christian religious beliefs. A surprising choice, coming from a life in Hollywood, true, but Cameron has found his niche and turned it into a lucrative career.

In 2002 Cameron founded The Way of the Master ministry, which produces a TV show—cohosted by Cameron—and a radio program, publishes books, and offers religious education courses. His work in film continues as well; he produces and performs in Christian-themed films, such as the film series adapted from the wildly popular book series, *Left Behind*. The first two films in the series made over $100 million combined, and allegedly cost only $17 million each to make. According to CNN.com, his independent film *Fireproof*, which was released in theaters, grossed over $33 million, making it the highest grossing independent film of 2008.

Obviously Cameron is proof positive that mainstream entertainment is not the only way to succeed in the industry.

10. ANTHONY MICHAEL HALL

Anthony Michael Hall is best known for playing the role of the geek in numerous John Hughes films. After Hughes noticed his performance as Rusty Griswold in *National Lampoon's Vacation* (1983) he first cast Hall as geeky "Farmer Ted" (he is actually credited as "The Geek") in the Brat Pack classic *Sixteen Candles* (1984). He reappeared as the geeky Brian in *The Breakfast Club* (1985), and finally the geeky Gary in *Weird Science* (1986). While this type of role gained Hall notoriety in Hollywood, he did not enjoy being typecast and decided to turn down the role of Duckie in *Pretty in Pink* (1986) and the title role in *Ferris Bueller's Day Off* (1986), both of which Hughes created with Hall in mind.

As often happens when one strays from his or her niche, Hall experienced numerous film flops, finding only minor success in *Edward Scissorhands* (1990) and little else thereafter. Throughout the 1990s Hall continued to find work playing minor roles, but did not reemerge in Hollywood until he landed the lead role in the TV drama *Dead Zone*, which aired for six seasons, from 2002 to 2007. This role allowed Hall to break free from the stigma of his youth and clear the way for more diverse roles.

Try, Try Again

Everybody loves a good comeback story, but few celebrities have successfully pulled it off. The celebrities on this list managed to run a successful career into the ground and then rise again to A-list status.

1. MICKEY ROURKE

In 2008 Mickey Rourke captured the hearts of audiences all over the world and the attention of Hollywood with his return to the spotlight in the film *The Wrestler*. Rourke's performance was seen as a critical success, winning him a Golden Globe award, and was bringing him *this close* to winning the Best Actor Oscar for his portrayal of wrestler Randy Robinson. Robinson's story seemed to mirror Rourke's own: after achieving acting fame in Hollywood in the 1980s, Rourke left his career behind to pursue boxing in the 1990s. When he returned he was a mere shell of the man Hollywood once knew.

Rourke achieved success as an actor in the 1980s primarily in action and thriller films, including *Body Heat*, *Angel Heart, Rumble Fish*, *The Outsiders*, and *91/2 Weeks*. However, his success went to his head and he developed a reputation for being "difficult." He turned down numerous major roles in such films as *Silence of the Lambs, Beverly*

Hills Cop, *Rain Man*, and *Tombstone*. Poor film choices and a bad attitude led to a decline in his career. In 1991 Rourke announced his retirement from acting to pursue boxing, which had been his passion as a teenager. He is later reported as saying that he had to go back to boxing because he felt he was self-destructing and had no respect for himself as an actor. Rourke was actually a successful boxer, never losing a match during his three years as a professional. However, numerous boxing injuries, which required reconstructive surgery, greatly altered his appearance. Rourke admitted to the *Daily Mail* that he went to "the wrong guy" for his surgeries, and acknowledged that his facial features were a mess.

In 1994 Rourke returned to acting, and after performing in several minor film roles (some of which were straight-to-video releases) he landed the lead role in *Sin City*, and a supporting role in the film *Domino* in 2005. But it was Rourke's award-winning performance in *The Wrestler* that has officially put him back on the map, inviting more mainstream film offers, including a role in the much-anticipated *Iron Man 2*. Even people who haven't watched *The Wrestler* have fallen in love with Rourke's honest comments and affection for his dogs, namely his Chihuahua, Loki, who died a week before the Oscars (she was scheduled to accompany Rourke to the event). Replacing the "difficult" label with one that reads "humble" seems to have provided Rourke with a second round in Hollywood.

2. ROBERT DOWNEY JR.

Robert Downey Jr. enjoyed minor acting roles throughout the 1980s until his breakthrough in the Brat Pack film *Less Than Zero* (1987). His career seemed to be on an upswing when he played Charlie Chaplin in the 1992 biopic *Chaplin*, for which he received an Oscar nomination, but soon after his drug addiction overshadowed his acting ability. He was in and out of jail for violating drug probation, which also led to stints in rehab facilities in 1996 and 1998. But old habits die hard and after each stint in jail or in rehab Downey found himself battling the same problems. In 2001 Downey Jr. was arrested again and instead of further jail time the exasperated judge ordered him to rehab. The third time was indeed the charm for Downey. He told Oprah in 2004, "I finally said, 'You know what? I don't think I can continue doing this.'"

In 2002 Downey was cast in the film *The Singing Detective* (2003) thanks to his friend Mel Gibson, and this film paved the way for others, like the 2003 thriller *Gothika*. Because of his history, producers withheld 40 percent of Downey's salary until the film wrapped, and similar clauses are now allegedly standard in his contracts. Downey's star has continued to rise with roles in *Good Night and Good Luck* (2005) and *A Scanner Darkly* (2006), and exploded after his 2008 hit *Iron Man* (for which two more sequels are planned), and the comedy *Tropic Thunder*, which earned him another Oscar nomination. Hollywood has always acknowledged Downey's talent, but for the first time he is being considered a truly bankable actor. Staying on the straight and narrow seems to be both Downey's and Hollywood's best interests.

3. **MARIAH CAREY**

Nicknamed Mirage in high school because she rarely showed up to class, Mariah Carey has had a long, bumpy career. Mariah Carey's self titled debut album hit record stores in 1990, and her career took off quickly. Her first album produced four straight number one singles and success continued throughout the decade, being the only artist with a number one song each year of the 1990s. With eighteen number one singles, she is second only to The Beatles.

As the 1990s closed, Carey seemed to be unstoppable, and this feeling was reinforced in early 2001 when she signed an eighty-million-dollar-contract with Virgin Records for her next four albums. Later that year, both her personal and her professional lives took a downturn and in July and again in September, Carey was hospitalized for a physical and emotional breakdown. There was extensive speculation and rumors regarding what actually plagued Carey, but she insisted that she was merely rundown and needed a few days to rest. The ensuing failure of her movie *Glitter* and the accompanying soundtrack further damaged her image, which prompted Virgin to buy out her contract for twenty-eight million dollars in 2002. Carey's artistic stock was plummeting and the label opted to lose some money rather than risk losing even more by producing four more unsuccessful albums with her.

Island Records picked Carey up for twenty-two million dollars, and led her back to greatness. In 2005 Carey released her tenth album, *The Emancipation of Mimi*, to much praise from critics and fans alike. It was the best-selling album of 2005, and won her three Grammy Awards. Since then Carey has remained in the public eye, partially for her music, which has found new life, as well as for her marriage to actor Nick Cannon.

4. CHARLIE SHEEN

Charlie Sheen first came to prominence as a member of the Brat Pack and is famous for his roles in numerous box office hits, such as *Platoon* (1986), *Wall Street* (1987), *Young Guns* (1988) and *Major League* (1989). In the mid–1990s, however, Sheen developed a reputation for being a partying womanizer, and the incidents that reinforced this image negatively affected his career. In 1995 he testified during the Heidi Fleiss trial, admitting to spending $50,000 on $2,500-a-night prostitutes. In 1996 ex-girlfriend Britney Ashland charged Sheen with physical abuse, to which he pleaded no contest. In 1998 he hit rock bottom, almost dying from a drug overdose. He was hospitalized and then entered rehab, which he left after one day. However, he has since remained sober.

Sheen's career took an upward swing upon entering the twenty-first century. He was chosen to replace Michael J. Fox on the sitcom *Spin City* from 2000-2002. The following year he landed the lead in the sitcom *Two-and-a-Half Men*, which is now in its seventh season. Sheen is currently the highest paid actor on television, receiving a reported $825,000 per episode. He has endured many ups and downs in his personal life, including a bitter divorce from and custody battle with Denise Richards, but currently seems to be right on track with his career and enjoying life as a new father to twin boys, even if his marriage to third wife Brooke Mueller is on the rocks.

5. BRITNEY SPEARS

Britney Spears appeared on the pop scene in late 1998 and was quickly dubbed the Pop Princess. She was the first artist to have her first four albums debut at number one on the Billboard charts. Spears's image took a hit as pictures of her drinking and smoking began to surface. Further damage was done by her fifty-five hour marriage to childhood friend Jason Alexander in Las Vegas in January 2004, and then by her quickie wedding (in September of the same year) and tumultuous 2-year marriage to backup dancer Kevin Federline. Spears's relationship with Federline seemed to bring out the worst in her, and she didn't seem concerned about her public image or her career. The couple had two children together before Spears filed for divorce in November 2006.

Upon hearing that Spears had filed for divorce her fans seemed to think, "Finally, Britney's come to her senses. She can return to her position as the Pop Princess we all know and love." Not quite. Spears started off her single life with a lot of hard partying, which led to various visits to rehab throughout February and March of 2007. It also led to a shaved head and a good deal of irrational behavior. By the time her divorce was finalized she had lost custody of her sons, had to undergo random drug testing, and had to meet with a parenting coach twice a week. Who would have thought Federline would be the more responsible parent?

In January 2008 Spears was hospitalized for a psychological evaluation and *People* magazine reported that she was diagnosed as bipolar, though neither she nor any of her representatives has ever confirmed this diagnosis. In February 2008 her father, Jamie Spears, gained legal control over her assets. Since then her career has been on a steady rise. She appeared as a guest star on the sitcom *How I Met Your Mother*, won three MTV Video Music Awards, her new album, *Circus*, debuted at number one, her *Circus* tour is a success, and she is now the new spokesmodel for Candie's. Though she is definitely not the Britney Spears of the 1990s, and it's hard not to feel that her every movement is controlled by her puppeteer father, we can only hope that she can gradually take control over her own life and destiny.

6. THE WOMEN OF *DESPERATE HOUSEWIVES*

Ok, so not *all* of the women of on the hit ABC dark comedy *Desperate Housewives* fit into this category—the show kicked off Eva Longoria's career and Felicity Huffman was not as widely recognized before *Housewives*—but the show did infuse some much-needed life into the careers of its three other leading ladies: Teri Hatcher, Marcia Cross, and Nicolette Sheridan. At an age when most actresses stray from the A-list, these ladies are enjoying more fame now than earlier in their careers.

Teri Hatcher even admitted, "I couldn't have been a bigger has-been." She shot into the spotlight while costarring with Dean Cain in the hit television show *Lois and Clark* from 1993–1997, but after the show wrapped she had a difficult time finding work. Her career was sustained by some made-for-TV movies and commercials.

Marcia Cross costarred on the 1990s hit television show *Melrose Place* where she played the evil Dr. Kimberly Shaw from 1992–1997. After that, Cross put her acting career on the backseat while she got her Master's degree in psychology, acted in little-known films and making occasional guest appearances on TV. The role of Brie Van De Kamp placed her into the limelight like never before.

Nicolette Sheridan appeared on *Knots Landing* from 1986–1993, afterwards appearing in forgettable roles after losing out to Debra Messing for the role of Grace Adler on *Will & Grace*. In 2004 she was cast as the naughty sexpot neighbor on *Housewives*, reminding audiences everywhere just how sexy women in their forties can be. Sheridan left *Housewives* in 2009, and all of Hollywood will be watching to see if she can propel her visibility into further success.

7. ROB LOWE

Rob Lowe was a central member of the Brat Pack in the 1980s, starring in the films *The Outsiders* (1983) and *St. Elmo's Fire* (1985). However, his playboy image caught up to him during the 1988 Democratic National Convention, when of a sex tape of Lowe with two girls, (one was only 16) surfaced. Lowe settled out-of-court with the girl and received a mere twenty hours of community service. The judged believed Lowe when he said he didn't know the girl was underage, since they met at Club Rio, which she was too young to enter legally. Though he was cleared of charges, his image and his career both suffered.

It wasn't until 1999 when he was cast as Sam Seaborn on the TV drama *The West Wing* that Rob Lowe reemerged as a Hollywood player. He left *The West Wing* in 2003 amid salary and screen time disputes. He went on to try his luck with other TV series, but met with cancellations. He found some success in the miniseries genre with *The Stand* (2004) and *'Salem's Lot* (2004) and on the big screen with his performance in the film *Thank You For Smoking* (2006). After missing out on a huge career opportunity by taking himself out of the running for the starring role of Dr. Derek Shepherd on the hit ABC medical drama *Grey's Anatomy*, Lowe gained some visibility by joining the cast of *Brothers and Sisters* from 2006–2010. He initially appeared as a guest star, but the episode on which Lowe appeared received the highest ratings since the show's premiere, and Lowe immediately became a show regular. Hopefully the notoriety from this show will provide Lowe with more acting opportunities pen to keep him in the Hollywood spotlight.

8. JOHN TRAVOLTA

John Travolta's career has had numerous ups and downs throughout his near forty years as an actor. In the 1970s, Travolta first found recognition on the small screen in the TV sitcom *Welcome Back Kotter*. His film roles in *Saturday Night Fever* (1977) and *Grease* (1978) quickly created legions of female fans who swooned over his smooth dance moves. However, after *Urban Cowboy* (1980) Travolta didn't have another box office success until 1989 with *Look Who's Talking*. Travolta's long-term career resurgence came in 1994 with his Oscar-nominated performance as Vincent Vega in *Pulp Fiction*. Travolta was once again a bankable actor and film offers began pouring in. Travolta had a streak of hit films including *Get Shorty* (1995), *Face Off* (1997), and *Primary Colors* (1998), but the glory of the 1990s soon wore off. *Battlefield Earth* (2000) and *Swordfish* (2001) didn't fare as well at the box office, signaling another downturn in Travolta's career. As the current decade draws to a close he is back on track with box office successes such as the surprise hit *Wild Hogs* (2007). Travolta's subsequent roles in *Hairspray* (2008) and *Bolt* (2009) further cemented his return. Hollywood loves a comeback story, and Travolta keeps creating them.

9. ELLEN DEGENERES

Ellen Degeneres entered the entertainment industry as a stand-up comic in New Orleans. She found success in Los Angeles when she received her own TV sitcom simply titled *Ellen* (1994–1998). The self-titled show was reasonably popular, lasting four seasons before its cancellation. The show might have lasted longer, but Degeneres announced she was gay on *Oprah*, and subsequently her character on the show admitted she was gay as well. Apparently *Ellen*'s core audience was not interested in a show that explored homosexual issues; ratings plummeted after the "coming-out" episode.

After the swift demise of her show, Ellen returned to stand-up comedy, and eventually attempted another sitcom, *The Ellen Show* (2001–2002). Unfortunately, her second sitcom found no success. Though the odds were against her, Ellen put together another television show, but instead of a sitcom she tried her luck in the daytime talk show arena. Now, many other celebrities have made similar attempts (think Megan Mullaley, Ricki Lake, and Roseanne Barr), but Ellen is one of the few successful crossovers. *The Ellen Degeneres Show* premiered in 2003 and its audience has continually grown. Her energy and humor make audience members and guests feel at ease. After its first season the show received eleven Daytime Emmy nominations, winning four, including Best Talk Show. Ellen's talk show has made her career more successful than ever. She has hosted the Academy Awards and the Primetime Emmy Awards shows. She is a spokesperson for American Express, and is a spokesmodel for Cover Girl cosmetics. Even her 2008 marriage to actress Portia de Rossi did not derail her popularity. It seems that this time around not even Ellen's personal choices will minimize her appeal. In September 2009 she was tapped to replace Paula Abdul as a judge on *American Idol*, a plum primetime gig that shows just how in-demand she is and that the sky is the limit.

10. PATRICK DEMPSEY

Patrick Dempsey first became famous for his film roles in the late 1980s and early 1990s where he was cast as the awkward yet lovable guy who managed to attract women both young and old. His film debut came in 1985 with *Heaven Help Us* and he quickly landed parts in other teen films, becoming most famous for his roles in *Can't Buy Me Love* (1987) and *Loverboy* (1989). However, his personal life—Dempsey married his forty-eight-year-old manager when he was only twenty-one—and less than stellar career choices caused a decline in his popularity.

After fading from the spotlight in the 1990s, Dempsey reappeared in a recurring guest roles on both *The Practice* (1997) and *Will and Grace* (1998) that showed him in a sexier and more mature light and putting him back in the Hollywood loop. He landed a supporting role in the romantic comedy *Sweet Home Alabama* (2002), which increased his visibility even further. In 2004 he unsuccessfully auditioned for the role of Dr. Gregory House on *House, M.D.*, but the following year he won the part of another TV doctor. Dempsey still holds the role Dr. Derek "McDreamy" Shepherd in *Grey's Anatomy*, which quickly became a hit ABC drama. His popularity on TV has led to leading film roles in such box office hits as *Enchanted* (2007) and *Made of Honor* (2008). Though Dempsey's career has been choppy in the past, it currently looks like smooth sailing ahead.

Just Add Water

People struggle for years, or an entire lifetime, searching for the "big break" that will turn them into celebrities—or at least into A-list actors earning millions of dollars. For most, instant fame is merely a dream, but the celebrities on this list went from nobodies to paparazzi magnets almost overnight.

1. DANIEL RADCLIFFE

Plucked out of relative obscurity to play Harry Potter, the most famous modern literary character, Daniel Radcliffe went from an ordinary British boy to one of the most recognizable celebrities in the world virtually overnight. Prior to landing the role of Harry Potter in the film adaptations of J. K. Rowling's famous series, Radcliffe had appeared in one made-for-TV movie, *David Copperfield* (1999) and one film, *The Tailor of Panama* (2001), neither of which made him a recognizable actor. When Radcliffe accepted the role of Harry at age eleven he knew the book series was popular, but did not realize that all the fame and popularity of the character would be focused directly on him. When the seventh and final book in the series was published it sold 8.3 million copies in the first twenty-four hours in the United States alone. That is a lot of very dedicated fans.

Since the release of the first Harry Potter film in 2001, Radcliffe has been famous worldwide, making normal life a virtual impossibility. In 2007 Radcliffe ranked thirty-third on Britian's Richest Youths list, and at sixteen became the youngest non-royal to have an individual portrait on display in Britain's National Portrait Gallery. Aside from his role as Harry, Radcliffe has built his resume, appearing in a few stage productions and films. However, it will be difficult for the public to accept him as anyone other than Harry Potter, having given this beloved character a face and brought him to life onscreen. It may be a blessing for Radcliffe that his future interests lie in working behind the camera as a director and producer. It could certainly allow him to carve out a place for himself in the entertainment world—apart from Harry Potter.

2. ROBERT PATTINSON

Prior to his role as Edward Cullen in the film version of the popular vampire book series *Twilight*, Pattinson had only tasted fame as a character in two of the Harry Potter films and it was rumored that he was considering quitting acting to pursue a music career. As Cedric Diggory, a student at Hogwarts, Pattinson was on the edge of Potter-mania, but costarring in *Twilight* quickly made him the center of his own fan frenzy to the extent that only Daniel Radcliffe could understand. However, Radcliffe had an advantage over Pattinson, for he knew how famous the Harry Potter series was before undertaking the role. Pattinson had never read or heard of the *Twilight* series before reading the film role; he was completely unprepared for the hordes of fans that now follow him. Fellow cast members confirmed this, commenting that Pattinson is paranoid about paparazzi and is somewhat "freaked out" about his newfound idol status. And he's not just a "teen" idol, with fans ranging from young girls to grown women.

In an interview with the Spanish magazine *Panetalla Nacional* Pattinson says that he doesn't think fame has changed him, but it has changed how people see him. He tries to live an ordinary life, but it is impossible—he is instantly recognized and his every step is watched. Pattinson is trying to build his acting resume while completing the remaining films in the *Twilight* series, but to his female fans he may always be the romantic vampire, Edward Cullen.

3. ZAC EFRON

Who knew that a Disney channel made-for-TV movie would bring instant superstar status to its cast? *High School Musical* premiered in January 2006 to 7.7 million viewers, and the DVD sold even more copies. The second installment of the franchise debuted on the Disney Channel in 2007 to 17 million viewers. The big screen release of *High School Musical 3* raked in $42 million its opening weekend and *HSM* merchandise, such as dolls, backpacks, and clothing are wildly popular as well.

HSM heartthrob Zac Efron definitely had no clue what he was in for when he auditioned for the role, and claims he really isn't special. In an interview with *Details* magazine he said, "There's really only one audition for a Disney Channel movie that separates me from 2,000 other brown-haired blue-eyed guys in L.A." Maybe any good-looking teen guy who won the role of Troy Bolton would have garnered legions of young fans, but Efron's cool demeanor doesn't hurt. Efron has been called "the biggest teen star in America" and "a poster boy for teeny-boppers" and was on the *Forbes* Celebrity 100 list in 2008.

Efron admits that he misses being a "normal guy" who can walk outside without being hounded by paparazzi or asked for his autograph, but he knows he's lucky to have achieved such a high level of success in such a short period of time. He wants to ensure he's not just a passing fad in the entertainment industry, and so he is working to diversify his resume, but it has yet to be seen if he can hold his own with an adult audience.

4. MEGAN FOX

Megan Fox shot to fame as the "hot girl" in the 2007 block-buster *Transformers*. Prior to her role in *Transformers* she had appeared in guest spots on a few television shows, including *What I Like About You*, *Two and A Half Men*, and *Hope and Faith*. She also played supporting roles in the Mary-Kate and Ashley Olsen movie *Holiday in the Sun* and *Confessions of A Teenage Drama Queen*, starring Lindsay Lohan. Apparently, it took running for her life from robots in tiny shorts and tight tops to really catch Hollywood's eye. She continues to receive more attention for her body than for her body of work, but she does not seem too bothered by that. In 2008 Fox received the title of Sexiest Woman Alive by *FHM* magazine. When asked in an interview with the UK *Sunday Times* if being typecast as "just pretty" ever upsets her, Fox responded that she doesn't think it's bad to be thought of as pretty, and acknowledged, "If I weren't attractive I wouldn't be working at all. . . . People don't expect anything from me, so even mediocre blows people away."

Fox has been quick to say she does not want to overstep her abilities as an actress, so don't expect her to appear alongside Scarlett Johansen or Keira Knightly anytime soon. She is perfectly content with her bombshell status, and it seems like she will have a lucrative acting career until the next hot chick comes along.

5. JENNIFER ANISTON

Ok, so *Friends* turned all six of the show's costars into household names, but Jennifer Aniston, most famously known as Rachel Green, became the most famous of them all, seemingly overnight, ensuring she never has to return to telemarketing or waiting tables—both jobs she worked prior to finding fame.

Perhaps it was her hairstyle (which became known as "The Rachel") or the fact that she dated, and married, established actors (think Tate Donovan and Brad Pitt). Furthermore, while each of the costars attempted film careers, Aniston's has been the most successful. She has found success in such films as *Office Space* (1999), *The Goodbye Girl* (2002), *Bruce Almighty* (2003), and *Marley & Me* (2008), maintained a large fan base, and continues to intrigue the masses, though sometimes more for the drama surrounding her personal life than for her work. So long as she is in Hollywood, Aniston will continue to draw attention.

6. MONICA LEWINSKY

Monica Lewinsky went from being a no-name, twenty-two-year-old White House intern to being known worldwide literally overnight. When news broke in 1997 alleging that she and then–U.S. president Bill Clinton had engaged in a sexual relationship, Lewinsky's face was plastered all over the news and she was placed under a microscope. Not only was her behavior criticized, so was her appearance. Everyone wanted to answer the question, "Why her?"

Lewinsky was at the center of one of the most infamous investigations in the U.S., and it will forever have a place in history, leading to an impeachment vote for Clinton. After the scandal, Lewinsky cashed in on her fame, appearing on various TV shows, becoming a spokeswoman for Jenny Craig, designing her own line of handbags, and publishing an autobiography in 2004 titled *My Life*. Retiring from the public eye, Lewinsky has earned a Master's degree from the London School of Economics, but when ABC News caught up with her ten years after the scandal, she admitted it's been difficult to return to normal life and find a job because the Clintons are connected to the top employers in her field, which makes them reluctant to hire her. This is particularly unfortunate since the other players in this incident—Bill Clinton, Linda Tripp, Paula Jones—have been able to move on with their lives, but Lewinsky, if only by the mere fact that the scandal is named after her, is synonymous with it.

7. TIFFANY

Known as the "shopping mall sensation," Tiffany bounded onto the music scene in 1987 with her debut album *Tiffany* and proceeded to tour shopping malls across the U.S. Her debut album sold over four million copies and she became the youngest person to have a debut album top the charts. It was amazing that singing in shopping malls gained her such a large fan base. Screaming teenagers flooded malls to hear her, and she graced the covers of numerous teen magazines. Unfortunately for Tiffany, the craze was short-lived. Legal issues among her manager, her parents, and herself stalled her career and by the time they were sorted out music tastes had shifted.

8. ORLANDO BLOOM

It's difficult to believe that British actor Orlando Bloom was an unknown actor before landing the role of Legolas in the *The Lord of the Rings* trilogy (*LOTR*). Bloom had acted in a few small roles on British television and in the film *Wilde* (1997), but it was his performance in a school production at the Guildhall School of Music and Drama in 1999 that led to his big break. As fate would have it, *LOTR* director Peter Jackson was in the audience one night, and was so impressed by Bloom that he asked him to audition for his upcoming movie, *The Fellowship of the Ring,* the first of the *LOTR* movies. Bloom initially auditioned for the role of Faramir, but was cast as Legolas. That stroke of luck propelled

Bloom to worldwide fame, gained him a legion of female fans, and won him the 2002 MTV Movie Award for Breakthrough Male Performance. Soon he was consistently ranked among Hollywood's most attractive men, including a spot on *Teen People* magazine's 25 Hottest Stars Under 25 in 2002 and *Elle* magazine's 15 Sexiest Men in 2007. Since the *LOTR* trilogy, Bloom has increased his popularity with roles in such films as *The Pirates of the Caribbean* trilogy, *Troy* (2004), and *Kingdom of Heaven* (2005).

q. RENÉE ZELLWEGER

Ok, so she's not famous for being a bombshell or a teen idol, and she doesn't have fans screaming at her wherever she goes, but a single film brought Zellweger to the top of the A-list where she remains.

Uncertain about making the leap to Hollywood, Zellweger began her acting career in her home state of Texas. She met Matthew McConaughey while filming *The Return of the Texas Chainsaw Massacre* (1994) and also acted alongside him in *Love and A .45* (1994). The latter movie earned her enough critical praise that she decided to take the chance, and give Hollywood a shot. She quickly won a role in *The Whole Wide World* (1996). Her performance in that film grabbed Cameron Crowe's attention, and he asked her to audition for his upcoming film *Jerry Maguire* starring Tom Cruise. Zellweger beat out such Hollywood stars as Cameron Diaz, Marissa Tomei, Winona Ryder, Bridget Fonda, and Mira Sorvino, managing to hold her own opposite one of the world's most famous actors, and even receiving a Screen Actor's Guild award nomination for her performance. This role turned the no-name newcomer into a hot Hollywood commodity. By carefully choosing her roles, Zellweger has cemented her A-list status, receiving three Oscar nominations (one win) and six Golden Globe nominations (three wins). She is also currently one of the highest paid actresses in Hollywood, consistently appealing to both the critics and the box office.

10. HANSON

You might have blocked them—or at least their smash hit single "Mmmbop"—from your memory, but their chart-topper seemed to have a stranglehold on radio stations in 1997. The song, which didn't consist of many real words, and the brother band alike were fixations to the young girls who propelled the unknown group to stardom overnight. The interest in this brother band led to numerous documentaries and biographies. In 1998 they hit the road in a successful summer tour, and were actually nominated for three Grammy awards. Hanson's success was short-lived owing to creative disputes with their label, Island Def Jam in 2000. They went on to record under their own label, 3CG Records, though they have never regained the success they attained in the late 1990s. Older and hopefully wiser, Hanson has a new album set to hit stores in Spring 2010 for a whole new generation of fans.

The Real Deal

Reality TV shows have become extremely popular in the twenty-first century. Though these shows differ greatly in subject matter, they all have one thing in common: the possibility of fame and fortune. Being on TV will change the life of each contestant; for some the change will be life-altering. While most fade back into oblivion, the few on this list have parlayed their appearance on Reality TV into achieving celebrity status and spawning a successful career.

1. RYAN SEACREST

Ryan Seacrest was one of the many young people who move to L.A. in search of fame. Unlike most, he has achieved great success in the entertainment industry. Seacrest landed his first DJ job at a local radio station in Atlanta, Georgia while still in high school and had then been recruited by ESPN to host the game show *Radical Outdoor Challenge* as a college freshman. While Seacrest would probably have climbed his way to a great career in Atlanta, he had bigger dreams. He dropped out of college, left his hosting gig with ESPN, and moved to L.A.

In L.A. he found some obscure TV hosting jobs for kids programming but had more trouble breaking into the competitive radio industry. His break came with a local radio station that gave him a show called "Ryan Seacrest for the Ride Home," which Seacrest turned into L.A.'s leading daily afternoon radio show.

As everyone knows, however, Seacrest's big break came in 2002 when he landed a cohosting spot on what would become the hit FOX reality show *American Idol*. His cohost left after the first season and since then Seacrest has hosted the show alone. He is the mediator among the judges as well as a comforter to the contestants. He's the man stuck in the middle, but he's so effortlessly smooth that the show moves seamlessly. Seacrest's *Idol* success has helped him land other positions; he took over Casey Kasem's radio program *American Top 40* in 2004, and he landed a nationally syndicated morning radio program, *On Air with Ryan Seacrest*, in 2005 (replacing Rick Dees). That same year he also cohosted *Dick Clark's Rockin' New Year's Eve* and is now the sole host and a producer of the show. Seacrest also launched his own clothing line The R Line, and received a star on the Hollywood Walk of Fame. In 2006 he signed a three year $21 million contract with the E! Network to develop, produce, and host various programs. Forbes estimated he earned $14 million in 2007 alone. *American Idol* renewed his contract for three years in July for $45 million, tripling his previous salary. Seacrest has certainly made the most of big break and diversified his projects into lucrative businesses that will sustain him long after *Idol* ends.

2. ELISABETH HASSELBECK

Few reality stars parlay their fame into legitimate television gigs, but Elisabeth Hasselbeck has done just that. After appearing on *Survivor: The Australian Outback* in 2001 Hasselbeck landed a cohosting role on the popular daytime talk show *The View*. Before her reality show debut, Hasselbeck attended Boston College and then worked as a shoe designer for Puma. Her first on-screen hosting gig was for the show *Stylemakers* on the Style Network. Immediately after appearing on *Survivor* she hosted the Style Network show, *The Look for Less,* until she won a seat on *The View* in 2003 after Lisa Ling's departure.

Since then she has single-handedly held down the conservative end of the table and has feuded with numerous cohosts. Her outspoken right-wing stance has been the only credential she's needed to be invited to the White House and to introduce Sarah Palin at a rally during the 2008 election campaign. Despite numerous rumors that she was leaving the program, Hasselbeck has stayed put, maintaining the visibility she surely hopes to make another career leap.

3. **AMERICAN IDOLS**

Ryan Seacrest isn't the only person *American Idol* has launched into fame. More contestants off *Idol* have become famous than any other reality program. While not all of the winners have achieved success, many winners have become fixtures in the music industry, and some of the losers have become idolized as well.

Season one–winner Kelly Clarkson went from waiting tables in Burleson, Texas, to releasing a hit single. She has released four CDs, won two Grammy awards, and according to Sony Music has sold over twenty million albums worldwide. She won *Idol* in 2002 and in 2009 she is still topping the charts; the first single, "My Life Would Suck Without You," from her fourth album, flew to number one on the Billboard chart.

Jennifer Hudson came in fourth place when she appeared on *Idol's* third season, yet she went on to beat out season three–winner Fantasia Barrino, for the part in the award-winning film *Dream Girls.* That role won her a Golden Globe award, an Academy award, a BAFTA, and a Screen Actor's Guild award for Best Supporting Actress. Since then she has appeared in the films *The Secret Life of Bees* and the *Sex and the City* movie. She has been so busy that she just released her first album in 2008, which debuted at number two on the Billboard charts, and for which she received a Grammy. Not winning *Idol* may have been the best thing to happen to her.

Carrie Underwood is arguably the most successful *Idol* winner to date. She grew up in a small town in Oklahoma and was a college student before her friends convinced her to try out for *Idol*. Since winning, she has become a well-respected country music singer, surpassing some of the most seasoned and well known female country singers, such as Faith Hill and Martina McBride, to take home various Best Female Vocalist awards. She has won numerous Academy of Country Music awards, Country Music Association awards, and Country Music Television awards. She is also the first country singer to debut at number one on the Billboard Hot 100 chart. It looks like Underwood has a long musical career ahead of her.

Other notable *Idol* contestants are Chris Daughtry whose band Daughtry has attained success in the rock genre, Kellie Pickler who has also found a home in country music, and Clay Aiken who had a loyal following of "Claymates" and appeared on Broadway, until he returned to his home of North Carolina where his primary role is as a dad to his twin boys.

4. TIM GUNN

While the design reality show *Project Runway* is stocked with famous judges, such as supermodel Heidi Klum, renowned American fashion designer Michael Kors, and then fashion director of *Marie Claire* magazine Nina Garcia, it is the soft-spoken, understanding-yet-firm mentor, Tim Gunn who stands out as a fan favorite. His innate sense of style and infamous usage of the phrase "Make it work" has helped him find success in both the entertainment and the fashion industry.

Before landing his role on *Project Runway* in 2004, Gunn held the position of Dean of the Fashion Design Department at the prestigious Parsons School of Design, in New York City, where he had worked for over two decades. In 2007 Gunn joined Liz Claiborne, Inc. as Chief Creative Officer, a position he holds in addition to his television gigs. Aside from *Project Runway*, Gunn has been a guest star on numerous programs, and cohosted the 2009 ABC red carpet arrivals for the Academy Awards. His book, *Tim Gunn: A Guide to Quality, Taste, and Style* (2007), has since expanded into his own TV show on the Style Network, *Tim Gunn's Guide to Style*, making Gunn among the most turned-to of fashion gurus.

5. PARIS HILTON

Paris Hilton may have first been noticed when infamous her sex tape, with then-boyfriend Rick Salomon was released in 2004, but her reality show *The Simple Life* put her in the mainstream spotlight, a place where she's stayed ever since. Hilton was just one of many heiresses on the party circuit before her video and reality show set her apart. *The Simple Life* debuted on FOX to thirteen million viewers. There were five seasons of the show, the final two of which aired on the E! Network. The show played to the "spoiled rich girl" stereotype, setting Hilton and sidekick and fellow heiress and BFF Nicole Richie in the homes of "real" people and highlighting just how difficult it was for them to function without money and without privilege. Though it was cringeworthy at times, it was also addicting to watch. The show not only propelled Hilton into the paparazzi spotlight, but also led to numerous other projects. She has tried her hand at acting, guest-starring on the teen drama *The O.C.*, and having more prominent roles in the box office flops *The House of Wax* (2005), *The*

Hottie and the Nottie (2008), and the straight-to-DVD movie *Pledge This* (2006).

With the aid of ghostwriters, Hilton has also authored books including *Confessions of an Heiress: A Tongue-in-Chic Peek Behind the Pose* (2004).

She tried her luck as a singer, producing 2006 album under her own label, Heiress Records. Though her self-titled album, *Paris*, sold 77,000 copies its first week, which isn't terrible, and two tracks actually hit the radio, it was not well reviewed and there has not been a follow-up album.

She has had her hand in video game development, night club ownership, has appeared in advertisement campaigns, created her own fragrances, and gets paid hundreds of thousands of dollars to appear at clubs. It's hard to believe Hilton has only been on the radar since 2004, what was the celebrity scene even like before she came along?

6. JILLIAN MICHAELS

Jillian Michaels has become one of the most well-known fitness trainers in America, but unlike most trainers who become famous for the celebrities they've trained, Michaels's fame has come from training average people. She gained popularity as the tough-talking trainer on the hit NBC Reality show *The Biggest Loser*. She doesn't tolerate whining from her contestants and the viewers love her for it. She gets results: more often than not, the show's winner comes from her team.

Michaels is also a trainer on the Australian version of the show, and still finds time for her own projects as well. She operates Empowered Media, LLC, which puts out a line of her workout videos; has created a fitness game for the Nintendo Wii, *Jillian Michaels Ultimatum 2009*; she's written numerous diet and fitness books; has teamed up with eDiets to create her own meal delivery system; has her own website with two million subscribers; hosts a weekly radio show and has gotten her own spin-off show on NBC called *Losing It With Jillian Michaels* premiering in 2010. She has used her visibility and success on a Reality show to create an incredibly successful fitness empire.

7. CARSON KRESSLEY

"Five gay men. Out to make over the world. One straight guy at a time." That tagline sums up the premise for the wildly popular reality show *Queer Eye for the Straight Guy*, which ran from 2003 to 2007. During each episode, the five gay hosts help out one straight guy in need of a life makeover. The show was instantly popular and though there were five hosts, Carson Kressley stood out, quickly becoming a household name and a recognized fashion expert. In 2003 Barbara Walters featured Kressley on her *Ten Most Fascinating People of 2003* special. Since the end of *Queer Eye*, Kressley has hosted *Entertainment Tonight*, the 2007 Oscar red carpet, and the Lifetime Network show *How to Look Good Naked*. He was also a judge on *Crowned: The Mother of all Pageants*, and is a frequent guest on the *Today* show and *Good Morning America*. Though none of his appearances may garner the same sort of attention that *Queer Eye* did, he has become a respected member of the fashion industry and appears to be in Hollywood to stay.

8. OMAROSA MANIGAULT

There's Oprah, Tyra, Madonna, and now Omarosa. Well, ok, so all Omarosa has in common with these other women is that she's known by a single name, but her goal is to be another Oprah, so being known by a single name is a first step. In 2004 Omarosa Manigault appeared in the first season of Donald Trump's Reality TV show *The Apprentice*. Omarosa quickly stood out from the other contestants and was labeled "The Most Hated Woman in America." She may not have won, but most people don't remember who did, and "Omarosa" is a household name. Omarosa used her fame to open other doors in the entertainment industry. She appeared on major talk shows such as the *Oprah Winfrey* show, the *Today* show, the *Tonight Show*, and *Larry King Live*. She landed her own talk show deal, but the idea died in development. She also wrote the book *The Bitch Switch: Knowing How to Turn It On and Off* and she extended her fifteen minutes of fame by appearing on other Reality TV shows including *The Surreal Life*, *Fear Factor*, and *The Celebrity Apprentice*.

According to her website, she is currently a business and political contributor on MSNBC, CNBC, CNN, and FOX. She has also served as a special entertainment correspondent for the TV Guide channel, the Style Network, and *Extra*.

9. JULIANNE HOUGH

Julianne Hough easily danced into the role of America's Sweetheart when she landed a job as one of the professional dancers on *Dancing with the Stars* season four less than a year after graduating high school. Her bubbly personality and bright smile made her stand out from the other dancers and she became an instant hit with viewers. She won both seasons four and five.

However, she wasn't content just being a dancer, and had always dreamed of a career as a country music singer. In 2008 she released her self-titled debut album, which sold more than 67,000 copies the first week, which *People* reports is the best selling country debut since Kellie Pickler in 2006. Summer 2008 she toured with Brad Paisley, one of the most popular country singers today, and announced that she would not return to *Dancing with the Stars*. Producers made her an offer she couldn't refuse: partnering with then-boyfriend and fellow country singer, Chuck Wicks.

In March 2009, the Academy of Country Music (ACM) announced that Hough won the award for Top New Female Vocalist and in April she won the ACM award for Top New

Artist. Apparently Hough can do it all and people just can't get enough of this multi-talented sweetheart.

10. LAUREN CONRAD

Lauren Conrad, known as "LC," appeared on the celebrity scene in 2004, when she was only eighteen, when MTV chose to document Conrad and some of her classmates at Laguna Beach High School during their senior year in the new MTV series *Laguna Beach: The Real O.C.* Conrad claims that she initially thought it was merely going to be a documentary and had no idea it would become a hit television show. Throughout the two seasons she appeared on the show, Conrad was at odds with the main female star, Kristin Cavallari, who appeared to have the brighter future in the entertainment industry. However, it was Conrad who was offered her own spin-off show, *The Hills*, which premiered in 2006. The show followed Conrad when she moved from Laguna Beach to Los Angeles to pursue her dream of becoming a fashion designer, attending design school and interning at *Teen Vogue*.

In 2006, 2007, and 2008, Conrad won the Teen Choice Award for Favorite Female Reality Star, beating out *Laguna Beach* rival Kristin Cavallari in 2006. Conrad's appeal to American teens is further cemented by the fact she has appeared on the covers of numerous teen magazines such as *Teen Vogue*, *CosmoGirl*, and *Seventeen*. She is also the face of mark., Avon's line of cosmetics geared toward teens and young women. She debuted the Lauren Conrad Collection clothing line at L.A. Fashion Week in 2008, after the third season of *The Hills* became MTV's highest rated show of 2007. Conrad officially left *The Hills* after its fourth season and seems to be doing well with her *New York Times*–bestselling novel *L.A. Candy* (2009) and its sequel *Sweet Little Lies: An L.A. Candy Novel* (2010). But will Hollywood still remember her when the cameras are turned off?

Don't Give Up Your Day Job

Some celebrities aren't content with being famous for one reason, and seem to think that success in one area will carry over into any other venture they attempt. Though a select few succeed in multiple fields, most do not. The celebrities below are some of the most notable crossover failures.

1. HEIDI MONTAG

Some people would argue that Heidi Montag has to actually *have* a career in order to unsuccessfully stray from one. Whether or not "Reality TV show personality" is really a career is debatable, but she and her husband, Spencer Pratt, are sure trying to make it one. The duo managed to earn millions of dollars from their gig on *The Hills*, and even more money from promotional appearances and endorsement deals. The fact that this fame-hungry pair keeps money rolling in is both amazing and a bit sad—just when you think they're gone from the spotlight, they force their way back into the news. In a way, it's a gift.

It is, however a gift that does not extend to singing. Apparently no one has mentioned this to Montag or Pratt (her manager), or perhaps they've just refused to listen. People gave Paris Hilton grief about her attempt at a musical career, but Hilton's singing is ten times better than Montag's music. Montag has released numerous songs on iTunes and on Ryan Seacrest's radio show, but not one has made it into the radio play rotations. She actually made a music video for one song with Pratt as videographer with a handheld camera. Enough said.

Unfortunately Montag has also shown the world that she is also *not* a talented fashion designer. She signed a one-year contract with Anchor Blue to produce "Heidiwood," a clothing line she designed. The dismal review *New York Magazine* online published on April 16, 2008, explains the problems with the clothing and probably why Anchor Blue did not renew its contract with Montag. The clothes were relatively inexpensive for a celebrity clothing line, but not inexpensive enough to justify the cheap materials used and the poor construction. Montag should probably stick to what she does best—being a "Reality TV show personality". . . whatever that means.

2. CHARLIE SHEEN

Charlie Sheen is a talented TV and film star, with numerous awards and a large bank account to prove it. But when he tried his hand at a more introspective art form the results were not as successful. In 1990 Sheen self-published a book of poetry titled *A Peace of My Mind*. For his sake, I hope there's more going on in his mind than the fruits of his poetic attempt. Though the book is rated with five stars on Amazon.com, at least some of the seven reviewers are his friends. Poetry critics were less enthusiastic about the book and it's rhyming poetry. *The Huffington Post* went so far as to comically suggest that perhaps Denise Richards's discovery of the book had led to their divorce. Since Sheen has not yet published a further volume of his work, we can assume he is keeping his musings to himself and sticking to what he does best—reading other people's words.

3. MARIAH CAREY

Mariah Carey's attempted crossover into the acting world is one of the most infamous and most disastrous cases to date. *Glitter* (2001) is the original *Gigli* (2003), showing that celebrity does not guarantee carte blanche success. Worse than the failure of the movie itself, this career move negatively impacted Carey's very lucrative music career, and led her to take a break from work. Today she once again reigns at the top of the music charts, and is trying her luck at acting again, though in smaller, more inconspicuous roles. There is a rumor that she is writing a children's poetry book, but no word yet from Carey on that project.

4. GARTH BROOKS

Garth Brooks is a country music legend, adored by millions of fans and respected by his fellow country artists. However, Brooks felt there was a part of himself that could not be expressed through the country music genre. And so, Garth Brooks created an alter ego: Chris Gaines. Brooks was supposed to assume this other personality for a film project for which he was recording the soundtrack, but the film was never produced, leaving just a rock album *Garth Brooks in . . . The Life of Chris Gaines* (1999) and Brooks looking like he had a split personality. Brooks's fans were confused and mainstream audiences didn't know what to make of this country music star turned fake rock star. Predictably, album sales were lower than expected and, because the album was released before the film, the film's production company halted production indefinitely (i.e., forever). Since then Brooks has stuck to his country roots, though he has largely stayed away from the music industry entirely since announcing his retirement in 2001.

5. GEORGE FOREMAN

George Foreman had a very accomplished career as a boxer, with two World Heavyweight Champion titles to his credit. He went on to make his fame work for him and established himself as a successful product endorser—who hasn't heard of the George Foreman Grill? Acting, however, cannot be counted among his talents.

For some reason ABC green-lighted the sitcom *George* in 1993, starring George Foreman as retired boxer who works with troubled kids. The show was short-lived, but the real surprise was that it made it to prime time to begin with. These days TV executives know that the way to capitalize on a celebrity is to give them a reality show. With ten kids, the *Foreman Show* would have been pretty entertaining Reality TV.

6. CINDY CRAWFORD

An American icon and supermodel during the early 1990s, Cindy Crawford has found success even after ending her career as a model. Crawford has produced a series of work-out videos, a skincare line, and even a home goods line. Between 1989 and 1995 she was the host of MTV's *House of Style*; but speaking well on camera does not an actor make. Film executives and audiences discovered this quickly with the release of the film *Fair Game* (1995) in which Crawford costarred alongside William Baldwin. Though the film's $11.5 million take at the box office was not terrible, it did not live up to the expectations it had as a major action picture. Crawford earned three Razzie Award nominations, and learned her lesson. She's stayed away from major acting roles ever since.

7. SHAQUILLE O'NEAL

At 7' 1" Shaquille O'Neal made a big splash in the NBA as 1992's first draft pick. He's won numerous awards and has been a player on four NBA championship teams. O'Neal has not restricted his career to the basketball court, but none of his endeavors have been huge successes. In 1993 O'Neal released his first of five rap albums. Reviewers were critical of the albums, but even so, O'Neal's first album has been certified platinum. With song titles such as "What's Up Doc" and "I'm Outstanding" though, it's hard to take his rapping career seriously. O'Neal has also acted in such films as *Kazaam* (1996) and *Steel* (1997) but none were box office successes. O'Neal is undeterred by the less than favorable reviews of his extracurricular pursuits; who knows what can be expected of him next?

8. MICHAEL JORDAN

Michael Jordan is one of the most famous and success-ful athletes of all time. His achievements in basketball are legendary, and he has inked some of the most lucrative endorsement deals ever. In 1993, after three consecutive NBA championship titles, Jordan announced his basketball retirement and subsequent plans to pursue baseball. Unlike Dion Sanders, who successfully pursued dual careers play-ing professional baseball and football, Jordan did not fare as well. In 1994 he played for the Birmingham Barons, a minor league team, but was never called up to the major league. Jordan quickly decided to come out of basketball retirement and led the Bulls to three more championships. When asked about why he decided to pursue baseball, Jordan said he did it for his dad who loved the sport and was tragically murdered in July 1993.

9. WILLIAM SHATNER

Most famously known for his role as Captain Kirk in *Star Trek* the television series films, William Shatner also pursues a career in music. To say that Shatner sings is a bit of a stretch: essentially he just speaks with musical accompani-ment. His albums were widely mocked and criticized, for his combination of contemporary music with Shakespeare. He would "sing" a rendition of a popular songs, such as "Mr. Tambourine Man" or "Lucy in the Sky with Diamonds," and intersperse dramatic readings from Shakespeare throughout.

Wisely, Shatner took some time away from his music, focusing on acting, but in 2005 he emerged with another album titled *Has Been*, which varied greatly from his earlier work. The album was produced, arranged, and cowritten by Ben Folds, a respected musician, and the album actually received some positive reviews, despite the lack of Shakespeare. Shatner's music career isn't a total bust, but it is his prominent acting career that has kept him in the public eye and allowed him to dabble in the music industry.

10. CELEBRITY AUTHORS

It's not uncommon for celebrities to write memoirs or tell-alls, but celebrity fiction is a relatively new phenomenon, and usually, it's better left unread. Classified as fiction, these books usually recount a story that is suspiciously similar to events in the star's actual life, with just enough alteration to names and events to keep them from libel suits. It's pretty brilliant because typically it is a star's fans that read this book, and fans can usually identify which real person a fictional character represents. Some stars that have written novels include Pamela Anderson (*Star: A Novel*, 2004) and Nicole Richie (*The Truth About Diamonds*, 2005). Paris Hilton's book *Confessions of an Heiress* (2004) is usually classified as a biography, but her dog Tinkerbell's book, *The Tinkerbell Hilton Diaries* (2004) is certainly an attempt to cash in on the celebrity fiction train.

Why Are They Famous?

*C*elebutante. Originally coined in 1939 by society colum-nist Walter Winchell, the word is a combination of the words "celebrity" and "debutante," and is used to describe young socialites whose fame stems from using their wealth, not their accomplishments, to gain media attention to the extent that they are regarded as celebrities. Unlike some so-cialites who have made a name for themselves with careers of their own, or by helping run the family business (such as Ivanka Trump, Holly Branson, Aerin Lauder, and Georgiana Bloomberg), celebutantes are primarily famous for their name alone.

1. PARIS HILTON

Paris Hilton may not be the first celebutante but she certainly began the wave of the most recent celebutantes, and she has set the gold standard for a celebutante. Hilton originally broke onto the scene because of her status as a Hilton heir-ess, but she has made a name for herself, primarily through the paparazzi. Hilton keeps people interested in her by changing up her act, thus the media continues to swarm her wherever she goes. From her infamous sex tape, to her real-ity show, relationships, jail time, acting roles, books, albums, and product lines, Hilton (or someone on her payroll) is a media genius. While many of the ladies on this list attempt the same feats, they do not have the certain *je ne sais quois* that the public can't seem to get enough of. Hilton actually makes a few million dollars from her endeavors. She commanded around $300,000 for a private appearance as of 2007 as per Forbes.com, but now probably because of the economic down turn and Hilton's overexposed image, the price is rumored to be closer to $100,000. Still, not a bad chunk of change. Though Hilton may be known as an "heir head" heiress, she has to be smarter than she looks to be such a success.

2. KATIA VERBER

Known as the "Paris Hilton of Russia," Katia Verber currently embodies the definition of a celebutante perhaps even better than Paris Hilton, for Verber does not make her own money. Well, Verber probably does receive a salary, for she is technically a buyer for Mercury, the company that owns such brands as Gucci, Dolce & Gabbana, and Prada, and for which her father, Alla Verber, is vice president. Verber's job description however, seems to primarily include posing for photo shoots and attending parties.

While unknown to most Americans, Verber attracts much media attention in Russia, and is the "It" girl on Moscow's social scene. *Marie Claire* magazine brought the Russian heiress to America's attention when it conducted an in-depth interview with the Verber, shadowing a day in her life. The day consisted of being chauffeured in a $250,000 gold Bentley, talking on her $7,000 cell phone, eating sushi, shopping (for clothes for herself), and clubbing. Sounds just like a day in the life of an American celebutante. Apparently some things permeate cultural divisions.

3. NICOLE RICHIE

Nicole Richie, whose birth name was Nicole Camille Esco-vedo, is the adopted daughter of singer Lionel Richie. She initially became famous as Paris Hilton's sidekick in the reality show *The Simple Life*, but Richie has since become a celebutante in her own right. Richie first made headlines with a change in style from funky to glamorous, while simul-taneously shedding major pounds. She garnered numerous headlines for feuding with Paris Hilton, having a suspected eating disorder, and a DUI arrest for which she was sentenced to four days in jail (of which she served eighty-two minutes), rehab, and three years probation.

Richie now lives a quieter life since going to rehab and prison and having two children with boyfriend, Joel Madden (of the band Good Charlotte), but she still maintains a place in the public eye. Instead of attracting negative attention, Richie makes news these days as a full-time mother, jewelry designer, and philanthropist who uses her fame to promote charitable causes, such as the Richie Madden Children's Foundation and organic gardening. While still not famous for doing much, she seems to lead a healthier and happier life.

4. CHARLOTTE CASIRAGHI

Charlotte Casiraghi is famous for being Grace Kelly's grand-daughter and fourth in line to the throne of Monaco, which is currently ruled by her uncle, Prince Albert II. She has lived a privileged life, even receiving a small island off the coast of Sardinia from her paternal grandparents for her fifth birthday. Not holding a royal title, however, keeps her free from royal duties. Of course, she and her siblings are present for major royal events, but they have no day-to-day royal responsibili-ties, leaving her time to focus on cultivating hobbies of her own. Charlotte was raised in France away from the media spotlight, but it has made her all the more intriguing to the media, making any appearance cause for media frenzy.

London's *Sunday Mirror* reported on May 12, 2002 that at age sixteen Charlotte ranked tenth on the list of the World's Most Eligible Women, and in 2006 *Vanity Fair* magazine placed her on their International Best Dressed List. Her love life is a source of constant media attention, as are her appearances at fashion shows, art exhibits, and other high profile events. Her popularity has spawned numerous fan websites that document her pictures throughout the years. Charlotte's personal accomplishments are few as of now, but her family's history and her fashionable good looks have catapulted her into fame of her own. More demure than most American celebutantes, Charlotte is an example of a celebutante with class.

5. PEACHES HONEYBLOSSOM GELDOF

Peaches Honeyblossom Michelle Charlotte Angel Vanessa Geldof certainly has a celebutante's name, and she lives up to the title. Her father is musician and political activist Sir Bob Geldof and her mother was British TV personality Paula Yates. Though Peaches has three sisters, she garners—or more accurately demands—the majority of the media spotlight.

Peaches seems to relish media attention much like the American celebutantes on this list. She is a favorite of the British paparazzi because she can be counted on to perform newsworthy antics and does not censor her comments. She is a regular on Twitter, where she posted a picture of herself holding a gun to a friend's head, and on the London club scene, where is regularly seen partying with such people Pete Doherty (Kate Moss's ex) and Lindsay Lohan.

Like any good celebutante she has starred in her own Reality TV shows, such as *Peaches Geldof: Teenage Mind* (2005), *Peaches Geldof: Teen America* (2006), and *Peaches: Disappear Here* (2008). She has worked as a celebrity reporter, dabbled in modeling (making her debut during London

Fashion Week in 2007), and is a Scientologist. Her popularity has led her to procure celebrity endorsement deals with Australian fashion line Dotti and the Miss Ultimo collection.

Peaches has also secured her spot as a top celebutante by eloping with Max Drummy, a member of the American music band Chester French. They even married at the Little White Chapel in Las Vegas, Nevada (the site of Britney Spears's quickie wedding to Jason Alexander) in August 2008. Though the duo had their names tattooed on each other, they divorced in February 2009. In March 2009 she announced on Twitter that she had married her female DJ friend, perhaps taking a page from Lindsay Lohan's headline-making relationship with Samantha Ronson. Whatever Peaches pursues in the future, she probably won't do it quietly.

6. BRITTNY GASTINEAU

Aside from Paris and Nicole, Brittny Gastineau is probably the most "successful" American celebutante. Gastineau's social status comes courtesy of her father, the legendary New York Jets defensive end Mark Gastineau, and she brought herself into the public eye through the E! Network Reality TV show *Gastineau Girls*. The show followed Brittny and her mother Lisa's daily life from 2005 to 2006. Aside from her TV career, Gastineau has also modeled, though with limited success. She was also a part of the short-lived 2005 Reality TV series *Filthy Rich: Cattle Drive*, which kept her in the public eye. With her mother Gastineau has also started a line of accessories and jewelry. It remains to be seen if Gastineau can sustain the public's interest and continue to profit from her endeavors.

7. KIMBERLY STEWART

The daughter of music legend Rod Stewart, Kimberly Stewart, is a celebutante by association. On her own, she does

Celebutante Brittny Gastineau making the
rounds in 2007. *lukeford.net*

not garner much media attention, but in the company of
others, such as childhood friend Paris Hilton, she becomes
tabloid fodder. Stewart has tried her hand at acting, modeling, and singing, but none have proven lucrative careers, or
even steps towards fame in her own right. Stewart garnered
the most media attention during 2005 when she was slated
to replace Nicole Richie in the fourth season of *The Simple
Life*. Stewart and Hilton were seen all over L.A. together and
Stewart even created some buzz of her own when she became engaged to Talan Torriero (from the Reality TV show
Laguna Beach). However, the engagement ended at about
the same time as Stewart's hopes for TV fame. Fox can-

celed *The Simple Life*, and when the E! Network picked up the fourth season they wanted Richie not Stewart. Stewart is still photographed out in Hollywood occasionally, but her celebrity status has taken a downturn since her glory days as Hilton's sidekick.

8. COURTENAY SEMEL

Courtenay Semel's father is former Yahoo! CEO Terry Semel. Semel, however, has chosen not to follow in her father's footsteps, preferring instead to help her father spend all that money. Her one attempt at a "career" of her own was her appearance on the ill-fated Reality TV show *Filthy Rich: Cattle Drive* (2005). She later decided to stick with what she did best: shopping and partying. Some media attention was drawn her way when rumors surfaced about a possible relationship between Semel and Lindsay Lohan. Lohan's reps denied this, saying the girls were merely good friends. Semel moved on to Internet and Reality TV star, Tila Tequila with whom she had an on-and-off-again relationship through October 2008. In January 2009 Semel hit an all-time low when she allegedly beat up ex-girlfriend and fellow heiress Casey Johnson (of the Johnson & Johnson fortune), in an attack that included burning Johnson's hair.

Terry Semel cut his daughter off from her trust fund shortly thereafter, which led Semel to turn to her last resort: rehab. The general speculation was that Semel's behavior and subsequent admittance to rehab was a result of substance abuse, but she has denied these rumors. Semel insisted that she checked into rehab for exhaustion, and (according to *The Insider*) from a desire to restore her relationship with her family.

9. BIJOU PHILLIPS

While East Coast celebutantes are known for staying *out* of the tabloids, Bijou Phillips defies the standard, for in her teenage years she was known as New York's Wild Child. The daughter of The Mamas and the Papas singer and songwriter John Phillips, Bijou grew up in anything but a traditional household. Both her mother and father suffered from drug addictions, which resulted in a lack of parental supervision. Phillips began modeling at thirteen, became emancipated at fourteen, and then quit school and moved to New York City. She was the youngest model to appear on the cover of Italian *Vogue*, and had a successful career as a model. Her personal life, on the other hand, was a disaster. She began drinking and doing drugs, which led to many volatile public episodes that were documented in the media. She had a tumultuous affair with Cher's son Elijah Blue, tried to French kiss a female interviewer, and was linked with Sean Lennon, Leonardo DiCaprio, and Elijah Wood. By the time she was seventeen her father sent her to rehab to dry out.

Despite her unconventional teenage years, Phillips has reemerged a semi-successful model, recording artist, and actress. Though most of her acting roles have been in lesser-known films, critics have praised her performances. Phillips is now engaged to Danny Masterson of *That '70s Show* fame, and seems to be content living a quieter life. Phillips still makes regular appearances at clubs and Hollywood events with her fiancée, but now she leaves much less drama in her wake.

10. AMANDA HEARST AND LYDIA HEARST-SHAW

Amanda and Lydia Hearst are the great-granddaughters of newspaper tycoon William Randolph Hearst. They represent the traditional East Coast socialites who attract media attention, though they try to avoid it. The Hearst girls do not dance on tables, stumble out of clubs, release sex tapes, or end up in rehab. They have have been nothing short of elegant so far.

Amanda Hearst was once quoted in *Harper's Bazaar* magazine as claiming to spend $136,360 per year in self-maintenance, but she claims her words were taken out of context. Amanda graduated from Fordham University with a degree in Art History, but seems to be more interested in philanthropy than in art. As she told *Vanity Fair*, "Doing philanthropy just seems natural." She technically has a job as the global ambassador for Tommy Hilfiger, which she described in an interview with *The Telegraph* as "like being a spokesperson I guess, but more active?" Apparently, since she phrased it as a question, she's not exactly sure of her job description either. The interviewer reported that Hearst knew nothing about Hilfiger's upcoming line, so perhaps the job is more about socializing and less about the fashion business. Whatever the case, the well-mannered socialite is a pretty, all-American face for the brand.

While a staple on the New York social scene, Lydia Hearst is one celebutante whose modeling career isn't a joke—Lydia actually *is* a successful high fashion model. Her work for such well-known brands as Prada, Clinique, MAC, and Heatherette, and appearances in numerous fashion magazines has earned her the 2007 Michael Award for Model of the Year, and the title of Best International Supermodel in 2008. While still actively modeling, she is trying to cultivate an acting career, making a guest appearance on the teen show *Gossip Girl* and a supporting role in the indie flick *The Last International Playboy* (2009). She hopes to follow in Milla Jovovich's footsteps, which would be a success great enough earn her own celebrity and lose her "celebutante" status.

More Than a Pretty Face

Perhaps second only to Olympic gymnasts, models have one of the shortest career spans of any profession. The prime age for a model's discovery is about seventeen and if she's lucky she'll work in the industry until age twenty-five. Some of today's most famous models outlive this standard—Heidi Klum still models at the ancient age of thirty-seven—but are now preparing for their twilight years by using their celebrity to pursue other endeavors to keep them in designer clothes and the spotlight for years to come. The models on this list walked beyond the runway to maintain their celebrity status.

1. TYRA BANKS

Tyra Banks began modeling at age fifteen and at seventeen went to Paris. After being there a mere two weeks she booked an astounding twenty-five fashion shows thereafter. Aside from making a name for herself in the modeling world, Banks is now expanding her resume. She lands at number one on this list because she has extended into areas uncharted by other models. While many models begin clothing or makeup lines, Banks is building an entertainment empire. She is creator, producer, host, and a judge on the hit Reality TV show

America's Next Top Model and creator, producer, and star of *The Tyra Banks Show. Forbes* says that Banks is "making a credible run at becoming the next Oprah Winfrey for the younger set." Banks is further following in Winfrey's footsteps by announcing she is ending her talk show to pursue other projects. She also has numerous television shows in production via her company, Bankable Productions.

Banks has also taken a stab at acting. Her credits so far include the movies *Higher Learning* (1995), *Coyote Ugly* (2000), and *Life-Size* (2000). She tried singing, cutting the single "Shake Ya Body," but even she sees it as a mistake, admitting, "I don't know what I was thinking." She wasn't alone.

In addition to her entrepreneurial endeavors, Banks has created a leadership and life skills development program she dubbed TZONE for underprivileged girls in the L.A. area. So far, more than 250 girls have participated. Not only does Banks know how to make money, but she knows how to give back to her community too.

2. HEIDI KLUM

Heidi Klum entered the modeling world in 1992 upon winning a national model contest in Germany called "Model 92". She didn't find instant success though, because American agencies considered her too large to model. It wasn't until she began modeling for Victoria's Secret in 1997 that Klum's career really took off, and it shows no signs of slowing down.

Following Banks's lead, Klum entered the entertainment industry as a producer and host of the Emmy-nominated Reality TV show *Project Runway*. The show scored high ratings and its original station, Bravo, saw *Project Runway's* audience grow 468 percent between its debut and second season finale—making it the most-watched telecast in the network's history. This explains why the network put up such a fight to keep the show, which ended up moving to the Lifetime network in 2009. In 2005 Klum also began hosting *Germany's Next Top Model*, the hit German version of Banks's show.

Klum is involved in areas outside entertainment as well. She created her own clothing lines that were featured in the German mail-order catalog *Otto*, as well as a line called "Heidi Klum" for Jordache. She has designed shoes for Birkenstock and jewelry for Mouawad, created perfumes ("Heidi" and "Me"), and designed swimsuits, which were featured in the *Sports Illustrated* 2002 Swimsuit Issue. Her Mouawad jewelry collection debuted on the QVC shopping network and fourteen of the sixteen styles sold out in only thirty-five minutes. Everything she touches turns to gold.

3. JANICE DICKINSON

The self-proclaimed "World's First Supermodel," Janice Dickinson, began modeling in the early 1970s. She broke the popular model mold of the time—looks like all-American Cheryl Tiegs were then in vogue. Dickinson's dark hair and full lips, were considered too Mediterranean-looking to make it in the modeling industry. Allegedly, she made her own big break when she showed up on a photo shoot and announced that she was the model expected, even though she wasn't. The photos taken during that session finally landed her a contract with Wilhelmina, one of the top modeling agencies in New York City.

Aside from modeling, in which she still dabbles even in her fifties, Dickinson participated as a judge in four cycles of *America's Next Top Model* and was a participant on the first season of the celebrity Reality show *The Surreal Life*. She left *Top Model* to host her own model Reality show, *The Janice Dickinson Modeling Agency*, which follows her as she builds her own modeling agency.

Dickinson also has designed her own jewelry line, which sells on HSN and has authored two memoirs: *No Lifeguard on Duty: The Accidental Life of the World's First Supermodel*

(2002) and *Everything About Me Is Fake—And I'm Perfect* (2004). Allegedly, six months before the publication of the latter book Dickinson underwent sixty thousand dollars worth of plastic surgery. At least she's honest.

4. KIMORA LEE

Part Asian and part black, Kimora Lee's mixed heritage gives her a unique look that helped make her a highly sought-after model. Lee began modeling at age fourteen when she signed an exclusive contract with Chanel. At age twenty-four she married Def Jam Records owner and mogul Russell Simmons. She helped him run his business, Phat Fashions, which representst the clothing line Phat Farm and Baby Phat. Baby Phat is one of the most popular lines of urban clothing and beyond women's wear also includes infant, junior, and plus size clothing as well as lingerie, accessories, shoes, and cosmetics. (She and Simmons split in 2006, but they continue to work together professionally.)

Lee has also branched out from her clothing line. She authored the book *Fabulosity: What It Is & How to Get It* (2006), stars in the Style Network's Reality show *Kimora: Life in the Fab Lane*, and created her own Barbie doll.

5. CINDY CRAWFORD

Cindy Crawford is probably one of the most recognizable faces in America. Her signature mole helped her stand out from the crowd and propelled her to supermodel status in the early 1990s. The Pepsi campaign featuring Crawford further helped make her a household name nationwide. Now in her mid-forties, Crawford still looks camera-ready, but has turned her sights away from modeling and toward other interests. From 1989 to 1995 she was the host of MTV's show *House of Style* and then put herself in front of the camera starring in her own best-selling workout videos. In 1995 Crawford tried her hand at acting, starring in the movie *Fair Game*, but neither the film, nor her performance could be considered a success.

Outside of the entertainment industry, Crawford created the skincare line Meaningful Beauty with Parisian doctor Jean Louis Seabagh, and she has her own furniture line, Cindy Crawford Home, which is sold exclusively through Rooms To Go.

6. KATHY IRELAND

Kathy Ireland may not be a household name today, but she was internationally renowned as one of the world's most famous models after appearing on the cover of the 25th Annual Swimsuit Issue of *Sports Illustrated* in 1989.

Ireland has appeared in a handful of films including *Side Out* (1990), *Loaded Weapon I* (1993), and *Backfire* (1995), as well as a guest star on TV's *Melrose Place*, *Suddenly Susan*, and *Touched By An Angel*. She also lent her voice to the animated series *Fantastic Four*, *Duckman*, and *The Incredible Hulk*. While many models have written their memoirs, Ireland has written children's books including *What Do Mommies Do?* and *An Angel Called Hope* (2005), and a self-help book, *Powerful Inspirations—8 Lessons That Will Change Your Life* (2004).

A certified fitness instructor, Ireland has also released her own best-selling workout videos, and served as a consultant for the ESPN-2 series *Body Shaping*. In addition to her writing and entertainment endeavors, Ireland is the founder, CEO, and chief stylist of Kathy Ireland Worldwide Product Empire. Her company, which grosses over $1.5 billion annually, inspired *Forbes* magazine to dub her "Super-Model-Turned-Super-Mogul."

7. CLAUDIA SCHIFFER

This blond-haired, blue-eyed German import came to fame during the 1990s after a national Guess campaign plastered her image on billboards across the U.S. Initially, she aspired to become a lawyer in her father's law firm, but dropped that ambition when she was spotted in a discotheque at age seventeen and was signed to the Metropolitan Model Agency.

Aside from modeling, Schiffer, like many models before her, also created a line of workout videos, *Claudia Schiffer's Perfectly Fit*, which reached the best-seller list. She has appeared in numerous popular films, such as *Richie Rich* (1994), *Zoolander* (2001), and *Love Actually* (2003) and has guest-starred on the sitcoms *Dharma and Greg* and *Arrested Development*. She was also a joint-owner of the short-lived restaurant Fashion Café in New York.

8. PAMELA ANDERSON

During the summer of 1989 Pamela Anderson attended a Canadian Football League (CFL) game; little did she know that her decision to wear a Labatt's beer t-shirt would drastically change her life. During the game, a camera focused in on Anderson; when it put her on the jumbo-tron screen, the crowd went wild! Labatt's representative noticed the response, and the fact that she was wearing a Labatt's shirt cemented the deal. Anderson began modeling for the Canadian brewery, which posted her face across Canada.

Soon after, Ken Honey, a freelance photographer, took a few pictures of Anderson and submitted them to Playboy on her behalf. Playboy liked what it saw and Anderson posed for the cover of the October 1989 issue. With her career taking off, Anderson moved to Los Angeles where in addition to modeling she also began acting. Anderson landed a small part on the sitcom *Home Improvement* as the Tool Time Girl and then her most famous role as C. J. Parker on *Baywatch*. She also starred in a short-lived sitcom *Stacked* (2005–2006). She is the most successful Playboy model in history, gracing the cover a record five times.

Anderson is the author of the novel *Star* and its sequel

Star Struck. She still attracts attention for whatever she does, makes appearances on the entertainment scene, and still has one of the most coveted bodies in Hollywood.

9. ELLE MACPHERSON

In 1982, Macpherson skyrocketed to fame when she starred in a TV commercial for TAB cola. TAB has since gone the way of the Dodo but Macpherson is still going strong. In 1986, *Time* magazine gave her the name "The Big Elle" and ran a cover story about her career, which included numerous magazine covers like a record five *Sports Illustrated* Swim-suit Issue covers. She also had a relatively successful acting career, appearing in ten movies in two years, including *Jane Eyre* (1996), *The Mirror Has Two Faces* (1996), and *Batman & Robin* (1997), and on the small screen in five episodes of *Friends*. In 2010 she was announced as the host of and an executive producer on *Britain's Next Top Model.*

In 1990 Elle Macpherson Initmates was launched in Australia and New Zealand. In 2000 it took off in the UK and more recently in the Gulf States, Canada, and United States. Today, Macpherson Intimates is one of the most recognized lingerie brands in the world. However, Macpherson didn't stop at that. In 2005 she launched Elle Macpherson, The Body, a bath and body collection in the UK. She also serves on the board of directors at Hot Tuna International, an Australian surf-fashion label, overseeing design, management, and strategy. Recently, MacPherson added a cosmetics collection to her bath and body line. Among the various awards that Macpherson has won for her many and varied achievements, her business savvy also earned her the 2005 Fig Leaves Entrepreneur of the Year Award.

10. GISELE BÜNDCHEN

Gisele Bündchen is still at the peak of her modeling career, but is rapidly expanding her business ventures. She was discovered in her native Brazil at age thirteen and the following year entered the national Elite Look of the Year contest. She took second place and then placed fourth in the world competition in Ibiza, Spain.

However, she is probably more successful than the girls who placed ahead of her in both competitions, earning an estimated $35 million in 2008, and ranking her as the world's highest-paid supermodel according to *Forbes*. While she may still be a supermodel, she isn't wasting any time diversifying her career. She has acted, costarring in the film *Taxi* (2004) alongside Queen Latifah and Jimmy Fallon, and created her own line of sandals produced by Brazilian sandal-maker Grendene. The line has sold over one hundred million pairs since 2001 and contributes about $8 million of her income. Other ventures include a licensing deal with Luxottica's Vogue Eyewear and partial ownership of Brazil's fashionable Palladium Executive Hotel. If Bündchen has done so much while still being at the top of the modeling world, who knows what she will accomplish when she actually retires from modeling.

Product Pushers

Endorsements have become an incredibly lucrative venture for the celebrity, often bringing more revenue than the career for which they have become famous. Unattractive behavior has made some of the celebrities below fall from the grace of endorsers only to find themselves on higher ground than before. Other celebrity endorsers on this list were merely ironic choices by the respective companies, who ultimately negatively affected the company's image.

1. KATE MOSS

Kate Moss is largely responsible for the rise of the "heroin chic" look in the modeling industry in the 1990s. However, a 2005 tabloid picture of the model snorting cocaine led to the loss some lucrative endorsement contracts. Apparently, Moss's employers merely wanted her to look like a drug addict not actually *be* one. Fashion houses Chanel, Burberry, and H&M reportedly dropped the model from their ad campaigns. However, after completing rehab Moss's endorsement offers were even more lucrative. She signed contracts with numerous companies including Calvin Klein, Bulgari, Stella McCartney, and Virgin Mobile. Britain's *The Independent on Sunday* reported that Moss's endorsements post-rehab are worth about $17 million, compared to the mere $10 million she had before.

2. MICHAEL PHELPS

Though the golden boy (literally, he has won fourteen Olympic gold medals) in the pool, Michael Phelps has shown that his perfection does not extend to his day-to-day life. After a nearly perfect showing at the Athens Summer Olympics in 2004 Phelps was arrested for driving under the influence of alcohol (DUI) and given eighteen months probation. However, he apologized profusely and the public seemingly forgave him. But when Phelps was photographed using a bong in February 2009 there was a bit more outrage. He was using an illegal substance! Granted, not a performance-enhancing drug—marijuana rarely makes anyone do anything faster—it is an illegal substance. Plus, he is a role model for children. Heck, he turned down the opportunity to be on the cover of a Wheaties cereal box in favor of Frosted Flakes. And everyone knows that impressionable young children prefer the sugarcoated flakes.

At the risk of being sued ten years down the road by parents whose children's drug habits inevitably began after following in the footsteps of arguably the most amazing, yet pot smoking, Olympic athlete, Kelloggs let Phelps's contract expire, citing that the photo of Phelps smoking a bong "is not consistent with the image of Kellogg." However, Phelps's other endorsers, such as Subway, Speedo, and Omega, stood by him. Phelps even gained an endorsement contract with H_2O Audio in June 2009. Ironically, Kellogg's stock has fallen since parting ways with Phelps.

3. KOBE BRYANT

Basketball star Kobe Bryant was an instant success on the court, moving straight from high school basketball to the NBA, so it's no surprise that endorsement deals soon fol-

Michael Phelps—in one of his finer moments—winning gold medal number 8 in 2008. *Bryan Allison*

lowed. Bryant was the face of popular ad campaigns with corporate giants McDonald's, Coca Cola, and Nike. However, a 2004 encounter with a nineteen-year-old hotel employee, who charged that Bryant sexually assaulted her, put all that on hold. McDonald's eventually dropped Bryant, as did Nutella. Coke and Nike put their campaigns with Bryant on hold. Once the charges were dropped and the civil case was settled out of court endorsers welcomed Bryant back and new endorsement offers followed.

4. CYBILL SHEPHERD

In 1987 the Beef Industry Council hired model turned actress Cybill Shepherd for their "Real Food for Real People" meat campaign. However, there was one little problem—Cybill Shepherd wasn't much of a meat-eater. She admitted in a *Family Circle* magazine interview, "I've cut down on fatty foods and am trying to stay away from red meat." Shepherd was promptly dropped from the campaign, prompting many people to wonder why she agreed to endorse the product in the first place.

5. MARY-KATE OLSEN AND ASHLEY OLSEN

Mary-Kate and Ashley Olsen were tween queens with hordes of adoring young fans. So, who better to endorse milk to make it seem cool and edgy? Well, maybe someone who actually drinks milk, or at least looks like they drink milk. The Olsens' "Got Milk?" campaign began in 2004, plastering them all over magazines. The twins claimed, "We love the campaign and we want to help make sure our fans are healthy like us." However, the campaign hit a sour note when Mary-Kate checked herself into a rehab clinic to get help for an eating disorder. The Olsens' milk campaign was halted immediately, allegedly out of sensitivity to the Olsens' current situation.

6. O. J. SIMPSON

There was a time when O. J. Simpson was known for playing football, first for the Buffalo Bills and then for the San Francisco '49ers. His notoriety led to numerous endorsement contracts, including a long-running relationship with Hertz beginning in the 1970s and lasting until he came under suspicion for the murder of his wife Nicole Brown Simpson and her friend Ronald Goldman. Though they immediately disassociated themselves from Simpson, many people will always associate the two.

7. MAGIC JOHNSON

Magic Johnson was a star basketball player for the L.A. Lakers during the late 1970s and 1980s, and in 1996 he was named one of the 50 Greatest Players in NBA History. He stunned the world when retired in November 1991 after announcing that he was HIV positive. He also disclosed that he had become infected as a result of extramarital affairs. At the time of his announcement Johnson had endorsement deals with such companies as Converse and Pepsi that were estimated to be worth $12 million. However, Johnson reportedly lost all of his endorsement deals within six months of making his announcements. Though Johnson remained in the public eye, returning to basketball for two short stints, he did not receive any new endorsement contracts until July 2003 when he signed a deal with Lincoln Mercury.

8. MICHAEL JACKSON

Michael Jackson's Pepsi campaign was one of the most successful in history. The relationship between Pepsi and Jackson seemed on solid ground throughout the 1980s and into the 1990s, until Jackson was accused of child molestation. Though the case was settled out of court—for a reported $20 million—Jackson's image was irreparably damaged. Obviously Pepsi wants to be a child-friendly product, but association with Jackson would have been insensitive and inappropriate.

9. ERIC CLAPTON

In 1988 Michelob turned to rock legend Eric Clapton for the theme song for its new ad campaign. A version of Clapton's song "After Midnight" was selected as the background song for a new Michelob television commercial. Apparently Anheuser-Busch executives (who own Michelob) didn't realize that Clapton and alcohol don't mix; prior to the campaign Clapton underwent treatment for various addictions, and

Clapton admitted to *Rolling Stone* magazine that when the campaign debuted he was battling alcoholism in a detox facility.

10. **MADONNA**

Pepsi added Madonna to its stable of celebrity endorsers when it signed her to a one-year, five-million-dollar contract. Not only did the contract require Madonna to appear in the typical commercials, but it required Pepsi to sponsor her upcoming tour. Pepsi's first collaborative commercial with Madonna was set to feature her new single "Like a Prayer." The video/commercial was a hit, but Madonna's music video for the song, which debuted on MTV shortly thereafter, was highly controversial, featuring burning crosses and inter-racial sex.

In response to the video, numerous right-wing and religious groups threatened to boycott Pepsi until it disassociated itself with Madonna. The last straw came when the Pope banned Madonna from appearing in Italy. Pepsi succumbed to the pressure and cut all ties with Madonna, even letting her keep the five-million-dollar advance so as to make a clean break. For all of the controversy, Madonna's *Like a Prayer* album and song skyrocketed to the top of the charts in thirty countries, making Madonna a household name worldwide.

Last-Chance Celebrities

F ame is fleeting, and celebrities are constantly reinventing themselves to remain in the spotlight. Reality TV has brought the careers of many celebrities back from the grave. Almost always, celebrities who appear on Reality TV shows are trying to reclaim their celebrity status. For many celebrities this route had indeed led to renewed success and fame, bringing many a career back from the grave and none more so than the reinvented celebrities on this list.

1. PAULA ABDUL

Paula Abdul got her start in the early 1980s when she became a Laker Girl, a cheerleader for the L.A. Lakers basketball team. She also landed the spot of head choreographer, which opened the way for numerous other jobs as choreographer for such performers as Janet Jackson and Mick Jagger, as well as for movies such as *Coming to America* (1988). In 1989 Abdul released her third single, "Straight Up," which became an instant hit. She had three more number one hits off her debut album that sold over ten million copies worldwide. Her sophomore album was also a success, with two number one singles.

The 1990s brought trouble for Abdul, first with a stint in rehab for bulimia, and then with her divorce from actor Emilio Estevez. By the time she released her third album, musical tastes had changed and none of the songs on the album broke into the top twenty. Though her music career faltered and Abdul fell out of the public eye, she kept busy choreographing and appearing in small television roles.

Everything changed in 2002 when Abdul was chosen as one of the three judges for *American Idol*, which brought her celebrity status again. Her success on *Idol* has opened numerous doors, including a spot as a guest host on *Entertainment Tonight*, a short-lived Reality series of her own called *Hey Paula* (2007), and the chance to record a new album. *Idol* has put Abdul back on the map, for better or for worse. In August 2009 Abdul announced via Twitter that she would not return to *Idol* leaving many to wonder if her success will continue.

2. TYRA BANKS

Tyra Banks was a supermodel throughout the 1990s. She stood out as one of the few successful black models in America, becoming only the third African-American woman to contract with a large cosmetics company when she signed with Cover Girl. In 1996 she became the first black model to be featured on the covers of the *Sports Illustrated* Swimsuit Issue, *GQ*, and the Victoria's Secret catalog. However, her most visible job was as a Victoria's Secret model, which garnered her legions of fans.

A model's career is relatively short, and even though Banks's career lasted longer than most, she announced her retirement from modeling in 2005. Though Banks faded from the spotlight as a model, she had a new career path. As a co-owner of Bankable Productions, she started the UPN Reality TV show *America's Next Top Model*, which she has hosted and produced since its inception in 2003. The show put her in the role of mentor, which she developed further when she began her own talk show *The Tyra Banks Show*, which has become a hit with teen girls everywhere. Banks even won a Daytime Emmy for Outstanding Informative Talk Show. Though her days as a model may be over, she is building an empire that will outlast even the longest modeling career.

3. HULK HOGAN

"Hulkamania" surrounded the 1980s when Hulk Hogan burst onto the wrestling scene and became the most famous professional wrestler of the era. He defeated Andre the Giant in his debut fight in 1980, was cast in the 1982 film *Rocky III*, and won the WWF championship belt in 1984—a title he held for three more years. Hogan's popularity led to mass marketing of his image, and Hogan even starred in a few films including the wrestling movie *No Holds Barred* (1989), *Mr. Nanny* (1993), and *Santa with Muscles* (1996).

But Hogan was forced to leave the sport and abandon his film career when he admitted to drug abuse while testifying against his former WWF boss. Though he returned to wrestling fame in 1996, joining Ted Turner's World Championship Wrestling as part of the New World Order, he revived his popularity when he allowed cameras inside his home to film the reality series *Hogan Knows Best* (2005–2007). Viewers saw a softer side of Hogan as he dealt with his teenage children preparing to leave the nest and with everyday life. The show placed the entire Hogan family in the public eye and made Hogan an American icon again. Though the fame that has accompanied his revival has not always been welcome—his son was tried and jailed and Hogan and his wife went through a nasty divorce—he is back in the fame game. Since then, Hogan cohosted the Reality show *American Gladiators* and is the host and executive producer of *Hulk Hogan's Celebrity Championship Wrestling*. He also appears on his daughter's spin-off Reality TV show *Brooke Knows Best*.

4. DONALD TRUMP

During the 1970s and 1980s Donald Trump became famous for his wheeling and dealing as a very successful New York real estate developer. He and his wife, former model Ivana Trump climbed to the top of New York society; at one point the Trump empire was valued at $1.7 billion. In 1990 Trump took a major hit when the value of his empire plummeted to a mere $500 million, forcing him to take on massive loans and declare corporate bankruptcy, allegedly with debts equaling $3.5 billion. He was almost forced into personal bankruptcy as well—his personal debt at the time was reported as $900 million.

Trump and his businesses reemerged in the 1990s and Trump received some publicity for his second marriage to and then second divorce from Marla Maples. But Trump's celebrity did not reach the general public until he hosted the Reality show *The Apprentice*, of which he is also co-executive producer. Trump's star rose by leaps and bounds as the show took off. He now earns a reported $3 million per episode, which is testament to the show's success and his popularity. He has become synonymous with the phrase "You're fired," (which he has attempted to trademark). He has appeared on numerous talk shows, including *Larry King Live* and took on Rosie O'Donnell in a much-publicized war of words. He has undertaken numerous other ventures, including an online university, a line of menswear, a fragrance, and a brand of vodka. He also hosts the reality show *The Celebrity Apprentice*. Trump remains in the spotlight, even though the nation's financial crisis is affecting his business ventures as well. According to the *Huffington Post*, Trump Entertainment Resorts filed for Chapter 11 Bankruptcy in February 2009. If the past is any indication though, Trump will rise again.

5. JANICE DICKINSON

Janice Dickinson began modeling in the mid 1970s at age

fourteen. She soon became a recognizable face for her exotic, dark features, and graced the cover of *Vogue* magazine (the American and European versions) thirty-seven times and modeled for such fashion greats as Armani, Versace, and Calvin Klein.

However, as she aged, she took up work behind the camera, working as a photographer. Dickinson returned to the spotlight in 2003 when she was cast as a judge for Tyra Banks's Reality TV show *America's Next Top Model*, a position she held until 2005. Was Dickinson fired or did she leave? It's a battle of "she said, she said," but Dickinson's visibility as the tough judge who wasn't afraid to speak her mind, gave her the opportunity to appear on *The Surreal Life* in 2005. The Oxygen Network picked up on Dickinson's popularity and offered her a Reality show of her own, *The Janice Dickinson Modeling Agency*, where Dickinson becomes agent and mentor to aspiring models. Though she is now in her fifties, her popularity has led to an advertising contract with Orbit Gum. The loud-mouthed beauty has found her way back to the spotlight and it appears she doesn't plan on leaving it anytime soon.

6. MARIO LOPEZ

Playing the school jock in the hit teen sitcom *Saved by the Bell* from 1989 to 1993, Mario Lopez soared to fame. The big debate among teen girls at the time was "Zack or Slater?" referring to Mark-Paul Gosselaar and Mario Lopez's characters on the show. Luckily, there were plenty of female fans to go around. *Saved by the Bell* was so popular that it spawned two spin-off shows (though much less successful than the original), two movies, and a comic book series. Since the end of *Saved by the Bell*, Lopez worked on a few forgettable television series and talk shows, but did not come back into the celebrity spotlight until appearing on the third season of *Dancing with the Stars*. He garnered attention for his dancing skills (he was the runner-up) and for his two-year romance with his dance partner, Karina Smirnoff.

Though the romance burned out, Lopez's career has been shining brightly. He joined the cast of the sexy TV drama *Nip/Tuck* from 2006 to 2009; hosted the Miss America and the Miss Universe pageants in 2007; and also landed hosting gigs for the Reality shows *America's Best Dance Crew* and *Top Pop Group*. In addition to acting in a few made-for-TV movies he also made his Broadway debut in 2008 in a revival of the classic musical *A Chorus Line*.

7. GENE SIMMONS

Since the late 1970s, Gene Simmons has been known by millions of KISS fans for the demon makeup he wore and his seven-inch tongue. KISS sold more than eighty million albums and played more than two thousand concerts in their time; but as the years went on, band members came and went (as did the makeup) and they fell out of the spotlight. They announced their reunion tour in 1996 and tickets sold out in forty-six minutes.

Simmons was introduced to a whole new generation—and reintroduced to his legion of loyal fans—in a different light when he and his family appeared in the A&E Reality show *Gene Simmons Family Jewels*. The show has run for four seasons and has been successful, documenting Simmons's life with his partner of over twenty years, Sharon Tweed, and their two surprisingly normal children, Nick and Sophie. The show exhibits a softer side of Simmons as the family man as opposed to Simmons the rock legend.

Since the premier of the family Reality show, Simmons has expanded the KISS brand and brought it into the forefront of a new audience. New merchandising products include the KISS Coffeehouse in Myrtle Beach, South Carolina, and KISS Him/KISS Her beauty, shampoo, and fragrances. Simmons appeared on the first season of *The Celebrity Apprentice* and continues to use his entrepreneurial skills to further his KISS merchandising opportunities.

8. OZZY OSBOURNE

People may have assumed that Ozzy Osbourne was lying in a gutter somewhere, brain dead from all the drugs and alcohol he ingested during his career with the band Black Sabbath and then as a solo act. However, Osbourne is very much alive (though maybe a little less sharp than he once was) as revealed on his family's reality show *The Osbournes*. The show was created after MTV Cribs filmed an episode in the Osbourne house and it was extremely successful. The Emmy Award winning show aired from 2002 to 2005 and was the highest-rated program in MTV history. The show gave the public a chance to see Osbourne away from his stage persona and in a family atmosphere. Though the Osbournes are an unusual family, the show highlights their strong bond, which has been reinforced by the hardships they have endured on- and off-camera, such as their children's weight issues, drug abuse, and Sharon's battle with colon cancer. Public interest in the family has continued even beyond the end of the series.

Aside from numerous gigs for his family members, Osbourne released his first solo album in six years in 2007 and followed it up with another album in 2009.

9. FLAVOR FLAV

In the late1980s Flavor Flav was part of a founding member of the rap group Public Enemy, which became quite popular during the decade. However, by the 1990s the group and Flav had fallen out of the spotlight. After numerous trips to rehab and multiple stints in prison, Flav resurfaced on the third season of Vh1's Reality show *The Surreal Life* (2004), standing out from the other housemates for his unique style and his in-house relationship with Brigitte Nielsen. Viewers were so intrigued by this odd couple that Flav and Nielsen were offered a spin-off show in 2005, *Strange Love*. When *Strange Love* ended with Nielsen returning to her husband, Mattia Dessi, Vh1 offered Flav his own Reality show to find love. *The Flavor of Love* aired for three seasons (2006–2008), but he failed to find love with any of the women. He actually met a girl after the show ended, proposed on-air during a *Flavor of Love* special, and now they have a son together (Flav's seventh child). Even after finding love, Flav kept his place in the spotlight starring in the short-lived sitcom *Under One Roof*. Eccentric Flav seems to have staying power in the continually entertaining his viewers.

10. BOBBY BROWN

Bobby Brown became famous in the 1980s first as part of the boy band New Edition and then as a solo artist. However, after the early 1990s, Brown's popularity diminished and his third solo album, released in 1998, was a commercial disappointment.

Brown rebounded in 2005 when a Reality show premiered starring him and his famous wife Whitney Houston. Though it was Brown's show, it is rumored that the Bravo network only agreed to the project after Houston agreed to regular appearances. Though *Being Bobby Brown* received high ratings, it only lasted one season after Houston refused to participate further and then filed for divorce from Brown in October 2006. However, the single season breathed some life into Brown's career, and in 2008 he became a contestant on the reality show *Gone Country,* costarred in the CMT spin-off *Outsider's Inn*, and the seventh season of Vh1's *Celebrity Fit Club*. Though Brown isn't as famous as he once was, his short-lived Reality show increased his visibility and gave him at least C-list celebrity status while he tries to revive his singing career.

Only the Good Die Young

The death of any celebrity is newsworthy and mourned by the entertainment community, but celebrities who die with seemingly untapped potential receive even more attention. "What if's" abound that can never be answered. Below are ten of the most unfortunate untimely deaths from illness, accident, or outside influence from the 1980s, 1990s, and 2000s.

1. HEATHER MICHELLE O'ROURKE— DECEMBER 27, 1975–FEBRUARY 1, 1988

Heather O'Rourke isn't a household name today, but at six years old she spoke the memorable line "They're here…" as Carol Anne Freeling in the 1982 film *Poltergeist*. Her fame from *Poltergeist* led to roles on the TV shows *Fantasy Island*, *Webster*, *Chips*, and *Happy Days* as well as in the movie's 1986 sequel, *Poltergeist II*.

Just before she began filming on *Poltergeist III* Heather developed flu-like symptoms that caused her hands and feet to swell. She was initially diagnosed with influenza, but the illness persisted and she was later diagnosed with Crohn's disease, an autoimmune disorder which manifests in the gastrointestinal track. She was put on medication to contain the symptoms, and managed to finish filming. Her illness persisted and ultimately resulted in her death from cardiac arrest in February 1988. Some reports allege that O'Rourke's cardiac arrest was caused by septic shock and infection that was brought on by congenital intestinal stenosis (blockage) and that she was misdiagnosed with Crohn's disease, which could have been managed with medication and treatment.

2. DIANA, PRINCESS OF WALES— JULY 1, 1961–AUGUST 31, 1997

August 31, 1997, Americans awoke to the shocking news that the beloved Princess Diana was dead at age thirty-six. The world was particularly saddened because not only was this famous royal not only loved by all, but also because she seemed to be on the verge of a rebirth, having recently divorced Prince Charles. She was deeply involved in charity work and was exploring a new relationship with Dodi Fayed, son of Egyptian billionaire Mohamed Al-Fayed, when her life was cut short. Diana died from injuries sustained in a catastrophic car accident in Paris, France. Paparazzi were pursuing Diana and Fayed when the couple's car—traveling at almost twice the speed limit—crashed into a pillar in the tunnel under the Pont de l'Alma. Diana was alive upon arrival at the hospital, but was pronounced dead at 3:57am.

The paparazzi received much blame immediately following the incident, however Diana and Fayed's driver's blood alcohol level was above the legal limit. Many conspiracy theories have surfaced surrounding this event. Was the royal family behind her death to prevent her from having Fayed's child? Was she killed by British intelligence to preserve the monarchy? Was the crash aimed at killing Fayed over bad business dealings? These are only a few of the many rumors, and though there is no solid evidence to support any of them suspicion remains. The film *The Queen* (2006) addressed some of the issues the royal family faced after Diana's death and numerous books have surfaced pertaining to the incident, but the public will never know for sure what happened that fateful night.

3. JOHN LENNON—OCTOBER 9, 1940–DECEMBER 8, 1980

According to the BBC, December 8, 1980, was an ordinary day for Lennon and his wife Yoko Ono. Lennon spent most of the day recording music at Record Plant Studio in New York City. Numerous news outlets reported the events of Lennon's death as follows: at approximately 11:00 pm he and Ono arrived at The Dakota, their apartment building on the Upper West Side. Upon entering the building Mark Chapman pulled out a gun and shot Lennon four times in the back. He was rushed to the hospital, and was pronounced dead on arrival. The official cause of death was hypovolemic shock, which is caused by the severe loss of blood and fluid volume.

There was no funeral for Lennon, but Ono asked that people pause for ten minutes of silence. On December 14, millions of people around the world participated in the ten minutes of silence. Thousands around the world gathered to honor the legendary Lennon; approximately thirty thousand in the musician's hometown of Liverpool, England, and over one hundred thousand mourned together in New York's Central Park.

Chapman confessed to the shooting, saying that voices in his head told him to kill Lennon. He was found guilty of second-degree murder and sentenced to twenty years to life in jail. He has come up for parole numerous times, but each time parole has been denied.

4. JOHN F. KENNEDY, JR.—
NOVEMBER 25, 1960–JULY 16, 1999

John F. Kennedy, Jr. was remembered as the "American Son" and a member of the American family most closely resembling royalty. Having lived through the assassinations of both his father, president John F. Kennedy and uncle Robert Kennedy, John, Jr.'s untimely death is sometimes thought to be part of a "Kennedy curse."

He was a lawyer, a journalist, and a socialite, whose photos and news often appeared in the celebrity magazines. Kennedy dated actresses Darryl Hannah and Sarah Jessica Parker, and was even named *People* magazine's Sexiest Man Alive in 1988, an honor usually reserved for Hollywood actors.

In July 1999, while flying a plane from New York City to Cape Cod, in the company of his wife, Carolyn Bessette Kennedy and her sister Lauren Bessette, Kennedy's plane went down off the shore of Martha's Vineyard. There was no problem detected with the plane, it seemed it just plunged into the water. The National Transportation Safety Board determined that crash was due to pilot error: Kennedy failed to maintain control of the airplane during descent over the water at night, which led to spatial disorientation. A licensed pilot for only one year, Kennedy was relatively inexperienced and visibility was limited that night. An extensive search was conducted, but it was four days before the remains of the airplane were discovered, 150 feet under water.

All three victims were buried at sea, which led some to speculation that not all the bodies were found. The Bessette's filed a wrongful death lawsuit, which was settled out of court. Thus, the Prince of Camelot and future of the Kennedy line was buried, leaving his sister Caroline as the only living member of JFK's immediate family.

5. BRUCE LEE—NOVEMBER 27, 1940–JULY 20, 1973
BRANDON LEE—FEBRUARY 1, 1965–MARCH 31, 1993

Though Bruce Lee's death occurred in 1973, the fact that both father and son experienced untimely deaths—even twenty years apart—is unusual. Bruce Lee was a Chinese icon, well-known for his chiseled body and roles in martial arts films. Lee died after going into a coma while taking a nap. Much speculation has surrounded the thirty-two-year-old's death, and the coroner's report was inconclusive. Doctors agreed that his death was caused by cerebral edema (swelling of the brain caused by congestion of fluid), but there was debate about what caused the cerebral edema. Two substances were found in his stomach: trace amounts of cannabis and Equagesiac, which is a combination of aspirin and a muscle relaxant. There are numerous theories as to why Bruce Lee died, including substance abuse and various conspiracy theories. The explanation most agreed upon by numerous doctors is that that Bruce's system was hypersensitive to the tablet he ingested, since, aside from brain swelling, his body showed not other symptoms or ailments. There wasn't enough cannabis in his system to have had any affect.

Brandon Lee followed in his father's acting footsteps and was making his name in Hollywood when his career was cut short by a fatal accident that occurred while filming *The Crow* (1994). Blanks were used during gun scenes, but due to poor gun safety and maintenance procedures, a leftover cartridge was lodged in the barrel and when the gun was fired with blanks, this cartridge was forced out of the barrel and struck Brandon Lee. Cast and crew did not realize what had happened until Brandon failed to get up after the director yelled, "cut." He was rushed to the hospital, but died after surgery.

With only eight days of filming left, Brandon's mother agreed to allow the studio to complete the film using a stunt double and special effects to put Brandon's face on the stunt double's body. It was the final homage to the twenty-eight-year-old's tragically short life and career.

6. RIVER PHOENIX—AUGUST 23, 1970–OCTOBER 31, 1993

River Phoenix was a famous teen heartthrob in the early 1990s with Hollywood at his fingertips, and his pick of high profile film roles. Shy by nature, Phoenix struggled with his fame, and turned to drugs as a coping mechanism.

According to findadeath.com, the story begins on October 30, 1993, when Phoenix and a group of friends were at the L.A. club The Viper Room. Allegedly, River was in the bathroom doing drugs when someone offered him some "high-grade Persian Brown"—a combination of meth amphetamines and opiates. Upon snorting it he began vomiting and trembling. He briefly passed out in the club and asked to go outside; Joaquin, his brother, and Phoenix's date, actress Samantha Mathis, obliged. Once outside he collapsed and began seizing violently. When paramedics arrived he was in cardiac arrest. Even with the valiant efforts of the ER physicians who tried to revive him, Phoenix was pronounced dead at 1:51am, October 31. The official cause of death was "acute multiple drug intoxication."

7. HEATH LEDGER—APRIL 4, 1979–JANUARY 22, 2008

The world was stunned when news broke that twenty-eight-year-old actor Heath Ledger had died. Ledger had become a respected A-list actor after receiving an Oscar nomination for his role in the controversial film *Brokeback Mountain* in 2005. He was a regular on the tabloid scene for his relationship with actress Michelle Williams with whom he had a daughter, Matilda. Ledger had just completed filming the much-anticipated Batman sequel *The Dark Knight* (2008), and had recently wrapped filming on the Bob Dylan biopic *I'm Not There* (2007). At the time of his death Ledger was filming *The Imaginarium of Dr. Parnassus*.

The details surrounding Ledger's death are still not entirely clear. The time line is believed to be as follows: at approximately 12:30 pm Ledger's housekeeper arrived, saw him lying on his bed and heard him snoring; at 2:45 pm his masseuse arrived, saw him sleeping on the bed, and set up her massage table, but when she tried to wake him up he was unresponsive. The masseuse called Mary-Kate Olsen and told her that Ledger was unconscious. Olsen called her private security team in New York and sent them over to

Ledger's apartment. The masseuse then called 911 and said he was not breathing. When paramedics arrived, Ledger was pronounced dead at the scene. Many people have wondered why Olsen was the first person called. Whether they were in a relationship or if she had some connection to the drugs Ledger ingested is unknown. Olsen has never publicly commented on the incident. She was questioned by police, who were satisfied that she was unconnected to Ledger's death.

CNN reported that multiple types of drugs were found in Ledger's system, including painkillers, sleeping pills, and anti-anxiety medication. The New York City medical examiner determined that the cause of death was not suicide, but an accidental overdose resulting from abuse of prescription medications. Doctors told *People* magazine that the drug combination in Ledger's system likely caused "polydrug intoxication," which led to respiratory arrest that slowed his breathing until it stopped entirely. Ledger had been vocal about his difficulty sleeping, telling the *New York Times* in a November 2008 interview that he probably slept an average of two hours a night and was probably "stressed out a little too much" over his role as Bob Dylan. His use of sleep aids is therefore not terribly surprising, though the number of drugs he used—six were found in his system—is.

In 2009 Ledger posthumously won the Oscar for Best Supporting Actor for his role as the Joker. At twenty-eight years old, Ledger was a respected, prosperous actor and a loving father, who undoubtedly had a bright future ahead of him, before his life was, tragically, cut short.

8. BERNIE MAC—OCTOBER 5, 1957–AUGUST 9, 2008

The death of comedian and actor Bernie Mac on August 9, 2008, came as a surprise to the public. The media had reported that Mac, star of *The Bernie Mac Show*, and known for his roles in the *Ocean's Eleven* (2001) trilogy, and *Guess Who* (2005) was admitted to the hospital on August 1 with pneumonia, but was expected to recover fully. However, eight days after he was admitted Mac died from complications from pneumonia. *People* magazine reported that medication to combat an infection resulting from sarcoidosis had weakened his immune system. This made Mac more susceptible to illnesses like pneumonia and complicated his subsequent recovery. His wife of thirty years, and his daughter were with him when he died.

q. JOHN BELUSHI—JANUARY 24, 1949–MARCH 5, 1982

Comedian and actor John Belushi came to national attention as a *Saturday Night Live* cast member from 1975 to 1979 and is infamous for his role in the cult film *Animal House* (1978). As Belushi's film career took off, so did his drug use, and his already fast lifestyle got even faster. Belushi had been in and out of rehab, with no permanent results, and his substantial drug use finally took its toll. March 5, 1982, was an ordinary evening for thirty-three-year-old Belushi. According to numerous media outlets he partied at celebrity hot spot On the Rox in L.A., and then returned to his hotel room at the Chateau Marmont with some friends, including Robin Williams and Robert DiNiro. The party continued and alcohol and drugs circulated, but eventually everyone left except for a groupie, Cathy Evelyn Smith. Allegedly, Belushi asked Smith to shoot him up with a speedball (heroine and cocaine) and she obliged. He passed out and Smith left the room for a while. While she was gone, Belushi's physical therapist arrived and discovered Belushi's body.

Belushi's death was ruled an accidental overdose and Smith was released after questioning. However, a few years later in an interview with the *National Enquirer* she admitted to shooting Belushi up. She was arrested and sentenced to three years in prison for supplying the drugs. Belushi was buried in Abel's Hill Cemetery on Martha's Vineyard. His widow moved his grave, after discovering that fans were desecrating it, and it is now unmarked.

The legendary, not to mention highly exclusive, Chateau Marmont.
Gary Minnaert

10. MICHAEL JACKSON—AUGUST 29, 1958–JUNE 25, 2009

Prior to the King of Pop's death, celebrity media outlets speculated that Jackson was not in good health, but the fact that he was spending hours each day preparing to make a comeback weakened these reports.

The exact cause of the cardiac arrest, which led to Jackson's death, is unknown. Jackson was surrounded by his own team of private doctors and was on numerous medications. After much speculation and several autopsies, the L.A. county coroner released a statement on August 28, 2009 concluding that Jackson's manner of death was homicide, caused by acute Propofol intoxication.

The loss of the King of Pop is especially tragic since it seemed like Jackson was getting himself together, and working on his upcoming concert tour. The world will never know if Jackson could have recaptured his former glory, but the immense outpouring of grief is indicative of the love and respect that Jackson still received from his fans.

Celebrity Looks

Skinny Minnies

Celebrity figures are constantly under the microscope, so it's not unusual that most celebrities are slim and fit. This being said, it takes a *very* skinny person to stand out from the crowd of stars who are already much smaller than the average American. This list is comprised of the celebrities who have received extensive media coverage for their extraordinarily thin, at times almost emaciated-looking, forms.

1. VICTORIA BECKHAM

This British import reigns supreme over all svelte celebrities in Hollywood. She doesn't hide under baggy clothes to deflect gossip, as do many suddenly-skinny starlets. Instead, she flaunts her pin thin legs in mini dresses, tight jeans, and high heels. One would almost think she relishes the attention.

However, Beckham insists that she does not have an eating disorder. She admits that while she was part of the Spice Girls she was obsessive about her weight—constantly dieting and even bingeing. These days, though she is tinier than she ever was as a Spice Girl; the *Daily Mail* reported that she has a 23-inch waist, requiring her to commission some of her clothes, since many designers don't carry sizes smaller than

24 inches. Beckham credits very controlled eating habits with crafting her slender frame. According to *People* magazine, she claims to subsist primarily on fish, veggies, and fruit (and probably not much of that!). In a September 2008 issue of *The Sun* Beckham says that being in L.A. has made her a happier and healthier person. The success of her fashion line certainly must have brought her happiness; and as for the healthy part, she says she no longer goes hungry (she even eats carbs!) and she runs four miles every single day. Well, even with all that eating she's doing, she still manages to be one of the skinniest girls in L.A., which is quite a feat.

2. NICOLE RICHIE

Nicole Richie came to fame as the chubby (relatively speaking) sidekick to Paris Hilton in the hit reality series *The Simple Life*. When the third season of the show premiered in 2003, Richie was noticeably slimmer. She was praised by fashion and media outlets for her new style and body transformation, which she gladly said came with working with a personal trainer, eating more healthfully, and hiring a stylist. However, by 2005 comments started flying that Richie looked too thin. Pictures of her on the beach looked like pictures of a starving child in a third world country and garnered serious media attention.

Richie spoke in her own defense, adamantly denying that she had an eating disorder and insisted she had hired a nutritionist and therapist to help her deal with her stress-related weight loss. Richie entered rehab in May 2007, reportedly to deal with both drug abuse and an eating disorder. Richie continued to deny all rumors of an eating disorder.

While Richie continues to be thin, these days she doesn't look quite so sickly. Becoming a mother seems to have altered Richie's life for the better. In an interview for the June 2008 issue of *Harper's Bazaar* Richie confessed she wants to have five children. So far she's two down, three to go!

3. **MARY-KATE OLSEN**

This half of the mighty Olsen twin empire is one of the most famous skinny celebrities. In 2004 Mary-Kate and her sister Ashley received a star on the Hollywood Walk of Fame and onlookers were shocked at Mary-Kate's skeletal frame. In June 2004 the tiny star entered treatment for an eating disorder and drug abuse following reports that her weight had slipped to below 90 pounds. *Us Weekly* reported that she was treated for anorexia, though Mary-Kate has never commented on her eating disorder and reports that she had a drug problem were vehemently denied by her spokesperson.

Today it is difficult to tell exactly what size Mary-Kate is because her clothing is oversized—affectionately labeled "homeless chic." In December 2008 some pictures were taken of Mary-Kate that looked like she had gained a little weight, estimated to be about 102 lbs, and rumors that she was pregnant began to circulate. Those rumors were soon found to be false. Geez, this girl just can't win. Maybe she's just getting healthy!

4. **LARA FLYNN BOYLE**

Lara Flynn Boyle starred in the television dramas *Twin Peaks*, *The Practice*, and *Law and Order* and also became well known as Jack Nicholson's girlfriend from 1999 to 2001. She has always been quite thin, but she appeared noticeably thinner around the turn of the century and tongues began to wag that she was battling an eating disorder. For years, Boyle has repeatedly denied these rumors.

When asked about whether she was a good role model for young girls during an interview with the *Sunday Mirror* in 2001, Boyle argued that surgically enhanced stars set a worse example for impressionable young girls than anorexic-looking actresses. She criticized stars that undergo breast implants, face-lifts, and other surgical procedures, which didn't go very far to making her friends in Hollywood. It can certainly be argued that eating disorders and elective surgical procedures two sides of the same coin—both idealizing an unrealistic body type and both often indicative of self-image problems. Ironically, Boyle acknowledged that one of her role models was Calista Flockhart, an actress who was widely thought to have battled with an eating disorder while starring in *Ally McBeal* (1997–2002). Maybe not the best choice while simultaneously denying your own food issues.

5. THE GIRLS OF *90210*

In 2008 the CW network debuted a spin-off of the hit 1990s teen show *Beverly Hills 90210* and brought skinny to a whole new level. All of the girls on the show are thin, but Jessica Stroup and Shenae Grimes have garnered the most attention for their twig-like frames. *Us Weekly* estimated Stroup's weight to be 100–105 lbs, which is incredibly low for someone who is 5ft. 8in. Grimes's weight was estimated to be about 90 lbs. and she is 5ft. 3in. The article reported that the girls were thin when cast, but had lost a lot of weight since then due to the Hollywood pressure to look perfect.

Us Weekly also reported that the CW had sent notice to their representatives to address weight issues with the girls, ordering them to gain weight. Because the CW reportedly beats other networks in the 12–34-year-old demographic for *90210*'s time slot, it is incredibly important that healthy weights are represented.

6. STEVEN TYLER

Aerosmith's front man Steven Tyler is refreshingly honest when it comes to his eating habits. Posted on Hollywood-backwash.com, Tyler admits that he might be "manorexic." He constantly diets because he fears being unable to fit into his pants from his previous tour. He is obsessive about staying at 145 pounds, and not looking like a washed-up rock star on stage. He claims that he works out a lot and does not

Steven Tyler posing for fans aboard the USS Nimitz in 2007. *U.S. Navy*

usually eat during the day, usually only eating wild salmon and broccoli for dinner. With a mantra like "nothing tastes as good as being thin feels," no wonder he can maintain his slim physique.

7. LINDSAY LOHAN

Lindsay Lohan became famous as a precocious Disney actress, starring in the 1998 remake of *The Parent Trap*, and developed into a stunningly beautiful, curvaceous teenager, starring in such hit films as *Freaky Friday* (2003) and *Mean Girls* (2004). Fans loved her because she looked real and seemed like a normal teenager.

However, as tends to happen in Hollywood, Lohan began running with the young Hollywood crowd, befriending super-skinny socialite Nicole Richie and stylist Rachel Zoe, frequenting clubs, and becoming noticeably thinner. Her once curvy figure became rail-like and she dyed her beautiful red hair blond. By 2005 she was almost unrecognizable to her fans. Initially Lohan claimed that she did feel pressure to be thin in Hollywood, but that the transformation came as a result of a personal trainer and healthy eating. In a 2006 *Vanity Fair* interview Lohan admitted that when she saw herself hosting *Saturday Night Live* she realized she was too thin. "My arms were disgusting . . . I was sick," Lohan explained. Though she denied she had an eating disorder, claiming the magazine had used her quotes out of context.

Lohan appeared to be back on track to health (at least weight-wise) for a while, but in late 2008 pictures surfaced of Lohan looking dangerously skinny again. Her spokesperson denied the rumors, stating that Lohan had merely been under a lot of stress, which resulted in her weight loss. This may actually be true, for her relationship with Samantha Ronson had been on the rocks for months, and with the dissolution of their relationship it's possible that Lohan's weight might plummet further.

8. KATE BOSWORTH

When Kate Bosworth burst onto the Hollywood scene with a starring role in *Blue Crush* (2002) she looked like a healthy, strong, sexy surfer girl. Bosworth dated Orlando Bloom from 2002 to 2006 and coincidentally by late 2006 she looked unusually thin. *Us Weekly* estimated her weight to have dropped to 105 lbs, which is considered unhealthy for someone that is 5 ft. 7 in. tall.

In the February 2008 issue of *Vanity Fair* Bosworth explained that it was a very troubling, dark time in her life that caused her to lose weight. She even said that her mother and grandmother both lose weight when they are upset. Pictures of Bosworth in her 2008 *Vanity Fair* photo shoot made it seem like she had returned to a healthy weight and has maintained a healthy appearance, though don't misunderstand, she is still *very* thin.

9. TERI HATCHER

Teri Hatcher's reemergence on the Hollywood scene as part of the ensemble cast of the TV drama *Desperate Housewives* brought her obviously thinner figure into the spotlight. When she starred in *Lois and Clark* from 1993 to 1997 she was a bit curvier and her face was much fuller. Age could have thinned her face, but fewer people are naturally thinner in their forties than they were in their thirties.

As *Desperate Housewives* has continued, Hatcher has seemed to lose even more weight. A 2005 picture of Hatcher jogging on stick-thin legs put the rumor mill in full gear. In an interview with *Closer* magazine, Hatcher said, "The only thing I'm guilty of is being too athletic and refusing to eat garbage." Apparently, Hatcher has not heard about "exercise bulimia," which is defined as excessive exercising, usually attached to feelings of guilt about eating. I'm not saying she does, in fact, have an eating disorder, but there is such a thing as too much exercise.

10. ELLEN POMPEO

Ellen Pompeo was made famous by her role as Meredith Grey in the hit television drama *Grey's Anatomy* that debuted in 2005. She came on the scene when Lindsay Lohan and Nicole Richie were garnering much media attention for their unnaturally thin frames. At 5 ft 7in. and approximately 100 lbs, Pompeo says she has always been skinny (her nickname is

Straciatella, meaning "little rags" or "strings") and was very self-conscious of her thin figure throughout her childhood. She wants to stay healthy, so she does not chow down on junk food, but she wishes that she could gain weight, explaining that she has hired a trainer and started weight training to gain a size. Apparently her super quick metabolism requires that she eat 3,000 calories per day. Is that even legal in Hollywood? Unless we are actually on the *Grey's Anatomy* set we will probably never be able to confirm her eating habits. But maybe we can give her the benefit of the doubt and just envy her a little more for that (isn't it enough that she already gets to kiss Patrick Dempsey every week?).

Hot Mamas

The saying about baby weight, "Nine months on, nine months off" does not seem to apply to most celebrities. There are exceptions to the rule—like Salma Hayek and Debra Messing who claim to have taken their time losing their pregnancy weight—but most celebrities see post-pregnancy weight loss as a sprint, exercising as much as possible and eating as little as possible to become camera-ready ASAP. While these celebrities look like supermoms, and make us mere mortals who are lucky to find time to take a shower a week after having a baby look bad, remember you'd snap back into your pre-pregnancy clothes too if your multimillion dollar job depended on it and you had a couple of nannies, a chef, and a personal trainer on staff.

1. HEIDI KLUM

Heidi Klum is known for her unearthly body, even after four pregnancies, but getting her body runway-ready eight weeks after giving birth to her second child in 2005 was amazing even for her. Sure there are tricks for looking like you've lost baby weight, but when strutting down the catwalk mostly naked in the Victoria's Secret televised (and remember the camera adds ten pounds!) Christmas special, there is no-where to hide extra curves.

So how did she do it? The website FitSugar.com breaks it down for us. Klum reportedly followed David Kirsch's Ultimate New York Diet and exercised a lot. She ate five small meals a day, eating every three hours between 7am and 7pm. For the first two weeks, Klum avoided "starchy" carbs, such as dairy and fruit, which Kirsch says cause bloating. Then he allowed her to incorporate healthy carbs like lentils and quinoa, yet focusing on eating high protein, low carb meals. Off limit foods included bread and alcohol.

What was her workout regimen? Instead of putting Klum on the treadmill, Kirsch opted to train her using the rowing machine, which he says gives you "bigger bang for your buck." It works your legs, butt, arms, back, and core all at once. While you probably won't look like Klum after pregnancy if you didn't look like her before becoming pregnant, following her healthful eating plan and exercising like crazy, you'll likely return to your pre-pregnancy self quickly.

2. KATE HUDSON

Hudson wasn't worried about pregnancy weight gain like many Hollywood moms, but insisted she wanted to have fun during her pregnancy. While pregnant with her son Ryder, she gained approximately sixty pounds! Hudson claims she went a little crazy eating ice cream until her mom literally ripped the spoon out of her hand.

After Hudson gave birth, however, she couldn't waste much time returning to her fabulous form, because she was slated to start filming *The Skeleton Key* (2005) only a few months later. She got down to business: she hired two personal trainers and worked out a reported three hours a day, six days a week while sticking to a strict 1500 calorie a day high protein low carb diet. For her cardio workout she ran both on a treadmill and outdoors, and for muscle toning she followed the Proper Body Exercise routine, which combines Pilates, yoga, and core stability moves. Not surprisingly, the grueling training and dieting paid off and Hudson reclaimed her perfect body in just four months.

3. NICOLE KIDMAN

Much controversy surrounded Nicole Kidman's pregnancy, since she seemed to gain virtually no weight! Ok, in reality she gained about twenty pounds, but because she's extremely thin and five-foot-ten, she looked more like a normal person than a pregnant one. *The Insider* reported that Kidman claimed, "I'm so lucky I'm so tall, so I carried small." I'm sure it didn't hurt that she maintained her grueling exercise routine throughout her pregnancy and as soon as her doctor gave his approval (just a week and a half after giving birth) Kidman started jogging again. Pictures of Kidman two weeks post pregnancy showed no sign of belly bulge. Insiders said it was a result of a strict diet and exercise regimen she began immediately after giving birth, since she was signed on to start filming a movie two months postpartum. Even in Hollywood, Kidman's lightening-quick weight loss is enviable.

4. JESSICA ALBA

Known for her sexy acting roles, it was quite a shock to see Jessica Alba gain twenty-five pounds while pregnant. Alba was the first to admit that she was shocked to see her curvier body, even at only five months pregnant and to have no control over its expansion. However, Alba didn't disappoint, showing off a perfect bikini body four months after daughter Honor Marie arrived.

Unlike other celebrity moms who admit to exercising multiple hours a day, Alba's trainer, Ramona Braganza, said that Alba followed her 3-2-1 Baby Bulge Be Gone plan, which included working out only one hour per day, five or six days a week. Alba's workouts consisted of a mix of cardio, circuit training, and core exercises. Her healthy low-fat, low-carb diet also helped shed pounds.

Alba admitted to wearing a girdle (which apparently has become popular in Hollywood) advocating that it helped strengthen her weakened core muscles and back while reducing the swelling. Alba has been quite vocal about how difficult it was to reclaim her pre-baby body, telling *Elle* magazine: "The workouts were horrible. I cried. And I haven't worked out since." Though we may hate that she has succeeded in returning to perfection, women can appreciate and admire her hard work and dedication. None of that "I lost all my weight through breastfeeding. It just fell off."

5. BROOKE BURKE

Brooke Burke preempted the baby weight struggle by maintaining strength and cardio workouts throughout each of her four pregnancies. Yes, that's right, she's bounced back to her model perfection four times now. After her fourth child, born in March 2008, Burke signed on to participate in the seventh season of *Dancing with the Stars*, which began only five months after giving birth. She went on to win the competition, displaying rock hard abs and a perfectly toned body.

Burke said that she wore a belly wrap during and after pregnancy. Though she acknowledges they aren't comfortable, it works, claiming she wore a wrap night and day for over a month after pregnancy to reduce water retention and strengthen her abs. She said she exercises moderately, jumping on the trampoline and hiking with her family, and is a Pilates enthusiast, all of which she continued during her pregnancy.

As for dieting, she says it's all about moderation. She eats five small meals a day, avoids carbs late in the day and stays away from white flour, sugar, and soda altogether. She drinks lots of water with lemon and hot green or fresh mint tea.

6. JAIME PRESSLY

Jaime Pressly went to extremes to lose forty pounds in less than three months—in time to celebrate her thirtieth birthday in her pre-baby body. According to celebritydietdoctor.com, to lose the first ten pounds, she went on a seven-day detox plan where the first three days she ate only cabbage soup and veggies, adding a potato and grilled chicken by day six. After that she went on a strict protein diet where she ate between four and six mini-meals per day.

In addition to a strict diet regimen, Pressly stuck to a grueling workout schedule. Just ten days after giving birth, she started working out with a trainer for two to three hours per day, five days per week. By doing a mix of cardio and core strengthening work she trimmed four inches off her belly to get back to her 26-inch waist. She said that starting her exercise and workout regimen immediately after giving birth really helped her get on the right path and stay there.

7. MARCIA CROSS

Marcia Cross stands out in this group because not only did she give birth to twins at age forty-five, but she was also confined to bed rest. She had to lose sixty-five pounds in three months, before *Desperate Housewives* was set to resume filming.

Cross lost a lot of strength while confined to her bed, yet she was adamant that she would regain her former body. In an interview on *Good Morning America* she said, "You know, I actually do feel pressure to be back, you know, looking the way I did before I left. But I don't think it's just for TV, because I would feel that way regardless, because I just want to be at my best." She also added in the interview that she maintained a fairly healthy diet during her pregnancy, though she admitted, "I would have loved a few more vanilla milkshakes, but I knew on the other side of it that I wouldn't want to have to spend months and months losing it."

How did she get her body back? Well, she admits she wore Spanx immediately after, however she also exercised a little each day, whether it was thirty minutes on the treadmill, thirty minutes of strength training, or just working out to a BravaBody DVD. Because she breastfed, she had to eat, but she kept it healthy, sticking to protein and veggies.

8. ANGELINA JOLIE

Angelina Jolie has quickly lost baby weight twice. First after giving birth to daughter Shiloh and then after birthing twins, Vivienne and Knox. Both times she lost the weight, twenty-five and fifty pounds respectively. Though Jolie claimed that it was difficult to stop eating the high calorie foods she enjoyed during pregnancy after giving birth, she managed to emerge svelte just a few weeks postpartum. *Us Weekly* magazine reported that she received food shipments from a department store in Berlin to curb her eating habits, while *The Insider* reported that she played the Nintendo DS game *Let's Pilates* for exercise. After Shiloh was born, Jolie said she upped her yoga workouts and drank African ginger root and garlic tea as a natural weight loss aide, in addition to breastfeeding, which she claimed helped her lose weight. After both pregnancies, Jolie appeared even thinner than before, which instigated rumors or an eating disorder, but Jolie vehemently denies these reports.

9. DENISE RICHARDS

Even after having a C-section with both of her pregnancies, Denise Richards managed to look bikini-ready shortly there-after. Five months after giving birth to her eldest daughter, Sam, Richards posed for *Playboy* and two weeks after giving birth to her second daughter, Lola, Richards was seen shopping looking very trim. In an interview with *People* magazine Richards adamantly claimed she did not begin working out until six weeks after giving birth since she had a C-section, but the "stress diet" helped her lose weight quickly. Richards was going through a divorce from Charlie Sheen around the time she gave birth to Lola and was required to be on the set of her TV show, *Sex, Love & Secrets* (which has since been canceled), a mere six weeks after giving birth. Now that's motivation!

Once her doctor gave her the go-ahead, Richards began training with Garrett Warren six times a week for one hour a day. Her workout consisted of a variety of weight training, boxing, kickboxing, and lots of abdominal work. To control her diet, Richards had her meals delivered by Diet Designs.

10. ALESSANDRA AMBROSIA

Just ten weeks after giving birth to her daughter, Alessandra Ambrosia was strutting her stuff on the Victoria's Secret runway. So what's her secret? To work off the extra twenty pounds, Ambrosia focused on regimented eating and exercise habits. Because she had her baby via C-section, she couldn't do core work for a while, so she concentrated on cardio exercise, namely climbing and walking with ankle weights. When her doctor gave approval for her to start working out, she began exercising two hours every day with her trainer Leandro Carvalho using his Brazilian Butt Lift workout, which combines ballet moves, squats, and lunges. You've got to hand it to these Victoria's Secret models, for their dedication to maintaining their bodies.

Coveted Celebrity Facial Features

Most celebrities are beautiful, but which celebrities' pictures do plastic surgeons see most often? The most-requested celebrities are forever changing depending on who's "hot" that year, but there are some staples on the lists. The people listed below are a composite of newcomers and old favorites with envied facial features.

1. LIPS

When you say "lips" Angelina Jolie instantly comes to mind. Ever since her appearance on the Hollywood scene, her sumptuous, full lips have been coveted. Even other celebrities, such as Meg Ryan and Melanie Griffith, have tried to emulate Jolie's full lips, but unfortunately they look more like puffer fish. Interestingly, Jolie's significant other, Brad Pitt, has the most-requested lips among men and Anne Hathaway and James Marsden are new additions to the list of requested lips. So, How much does lip augmentation cost? Expect to pay about $300 for collagen injections, which will last one to three months. Surgical augmentation will last between six months and one year and set you back about $2,000.

2. EYES

If you're female and want to get your eyes "done" there's a good chance you're looking to Halle Berry or Megan Fox as role models. Men look to Daniel Craig and James Franco. The clear blue eyes seem to be in. Blepharoplasty, a procedure that reshapes the upper and/or lower eyelid, costs about $4,000 for both eyes. Lids and eye bags can be augmented, and a face-lift can alter eyes as well to create a more youthful appearance. But be careful, you could easily end up looking more alien than foxy.

3. NOSE

Nicole Kidman's nose has been one of the most coveted celebrity noses for many years. Interestingly, both she and Ashlee Simpson, a newcomer to the list of oft-requested noses, have been the targets of plastic surgery speculation. Kidman looks to have a more defined, smaller nose than she did when she first entered Hollywood. Simpson has all but admitted to undergoing rhinoplasty, since it is obvious that her trademark bump has been removed. Rhinoplasty is one of the most common cosmetic surgery procedures, though most celebrities tend to only admit to having undergone work to repair a deviated septum. Leonardo DiCaprio and Josh Duhamel are among the most requested male noses. There hasn't been any speculation concerning the authenticity of their noses, but men seem to be less scrutinized. Though rhinoplasty will set you back an average of $4,500, the results last forever.

4. CHEEKS

Like rhinoplasty, plastic surgery in the buccal region is probably a process you only have to undergo once. When it comes to cheeks there are only two ways to go: bigger or smaller. Some people desire cheek implants for the appearance of having higher cheekbones, while others want a more chiseled look, opting for buccal fat removal. Costs range from $1,500-$5,000, and some of the most desired celebrity cheeks belong to Cameron Diaz, Heidi Klum, Johnny Depp, and Zac Efron.

5. CHIN
Chin augmentation is not one of the most well known areas for cosmetic surgery, but it can make a huge difference in how a person's face looks and the results are permanent. A chin implant is performed to balance facial features. It can make one's nose look smaller or neck look more regal. George Clooney and Robert Pattinson are two celebrities with popular chins. Depending on the extent of work, cosmetic surgery on the chin region can cost over $5,000.

6. JAWLINE
Cosmetic surgery of the jawline is often paired with chin surgery, with a single jaw implant costing around $3,000. Combining jaw surgery with chin augmentation runs almost $10,000 and would change the look of half your face. That's financial dedication. Jaws can be made longer, more defined, or more square so as to emulate such famous jaw lines as Tyra Banks, Rachel Weisz, Robert Pattinson, and George Clooney.

7. SMILE
One of the first features people notice about another person is their smile; having a million-dollar smile can make or break a face—and not just in Hollywood. You've seen someone who is stunningly good-looking, but the moment they smile you see crooked or yellowed teeth and the whole effect is ruined. No one says, "Oh well, aside from her teeth

he/she's totally hot." If a person's smile is so important to ordinary people, it is absolutely vital for celebrities, who are in constant competition with each other. It is common-place for tweens to get braces, and some celebrities such as Gwen Stefani have gone this traditional route. Katherine Heigl used the less noticeable product Invisalign to fix a few crooked teeth prior to her wedding. However, the popular trend in Hollywood is veneers, which provide a casing for teeth. Tween queens Hilary Duff and Miley Cyrus, as well as *American Idol* contestant Elliott Yamin are among recent stars to gain a perfect smile with veneers. If you're thinking veneers could be the perfect, quick solution keep in mind that they cost approximately $1,000-$2,000 per tooth. You better be smiling a lot!

8. EYEBROWS

Eyebrows are an inexpensive facial feature to alter. One can spend a few dollars and get their eyebrows plucked and waxed at a salon, or it can even be done at home. Though it is a process that has to be repeated every few weeks, it is cheap enough that there's no excuse for anything less than A-list brows, and absolutely no excuse for a unibrow! Some eyebrows are more desirable than others, and a correctly shaped eyebrow can enhance ones face. Model turned actress Brooke Shields is famous for her signature fuller eyebrows, while Jennifer Aniston and Hayden Panettiere have slimmer, more defined eyebrows that are widely coveted.

9. COMPLEXION

A clear complexion cannot be faked. Even in Hollywood where money is no object and skin care products are abundant, some stars stand out for their smooth, flawless skin. Does it come naturally? Probably not. Stars use dermabrasion, skin rejuvenation techniques (such as laser resurfacing), and chemical peels to keep their skin clear and youthful. Cate Blanchett is one actress whose complexion is admired, and she is adamant that she has never had a botox injection. Nicole Kidman however, who also is idolized for her flawless complexion, is reportedly a fan of the procedure that costs between $300 and $1,000 per injection and results last only a few months.

10. **OVERALL FACE**
Though most of us mere mortals would love to look like any celebrity, some stars have more desired faces than others. Among women, Angelina Jolie and Jessica Biel have the most wanted faces; among men, the consensus is for Brad Pitt or David Beckham. It seems fitting then, that Jolie and Pitt have joined forces to procreate; maybe their children will be on the next generation's list.

Shaping Up

A celebrity's body is a key part of their marketability. Most stars don't get their drool-worthy bodies from mere starvation, but exercise intensely to modify or maintain their shape. Not unlike most people, celebrities don't always have the knowledge or the motivation to achieve the jaw-dropping results they need. Enter the personal trainers who force them into shape. Of course, they employ only the best trainers and those on this list are celebrity tested and approved.

1. VALERIE WATERS

Valerie Waters is the "it" trainer of the moment, having trained numerous A-list celebrities including Cindy Crawford, Jessica Biel, and Jennifer Garner. Waters met Garner three weeks before the hit television show *Alias* began filming and Waters had only three weeks to whip Garner into butt-kicking shape. Waters has now trained Garner for eight years, and Garner continues to have one of the most envied bodies in Hollywood.

Waters is a proponent of circuit training, which she believes maximizes calorie burn and quickens the metabolism. Aside from tailoring client workouts to fit their body type and individual goals, Waters designs and builds home gyms, and is the creator of the Muscle Truck, which is an 18-wheel truck that has all the equipment of a high-end gym inside. It has been used by celebrities while filming on sets, such as *A Beautiful Mind* and *The Italian Job*. Waters is the author of *Red Carpet Ready: Achieve the Body of Your Dreams in Just 6 Weeks*, which she says includes the workouts and diets her celebrity clients follow when preparing for Red Carpet season. She emphasizes how hard celebrities work to achieve and maintain their bodies. They workout like mad and maintain strict diets, very rarely splurging. So if you want to have dessert, don't beat yourself up that you're not a size 2. Those are the girls staring longingly from across the room while you enjoy your treat.

2. GUNNAR PETERSON

If you've heard of one celebrity trainer on this list, it's probably Gunnar Peterson. Peterson has become a staple behind the top celebrity bodies in the business. His numerous celebrity clients include Angelina Jolie, Matthew McConaughey, Kim Kardashian, and Jennifer Lopez (he's the one who trained her for her post-pregnancy triathlon and she said he is the best trainer she's ever had).

Peterson knows first-hand what it's like to struggle with weight, having been a Weight Watchers client at age ten. From there his relationship with food and exercise developed and now his work is everywhere; he is featured in numerous magazines such as *Women's Health*, *Men's Health*, *Sports Illustrated*, and *Us Weekly*, as well as on the *Today* show, CNN, *Fox and Friends*, E! Network, and Vh1. In addition to Hollywood celebrities, Peterson has trained athletes in the NBA, NFL, and NHL. He has also created a series of DVDs, authored numerous books, and teamed up with Guthy-Renker to produce the Core Secrets method, which focuses on strengthening the core, primarily through the using of a fitness ball. Peterson's central tip is, "exercising should be a cornerstone of your life, like brushing your teeth. It's not even an option to blow it off."

3. HARLEY PASTERNAK

Who was behind Jessica Simpson's post-John Mayer twenty-pound slim down? Who guided Eva Mendes to her newly sculpted body? Who advised Katherine Heigl on how to achieve her tightened and toned physique? That would be trainer and diet guru Harley Pasternak, whose 5-Factor Diet has become one of the hottest diet and fitness plans in Hollywood. Other major stars he's trained include Miley Cyrus, John Mayer, and Kanye West. He's been featured in the *Washington Post*, *Seventeen*, *Fitness*, and on *Oprah*, and makes regular appearances on the *Today* show.

The diet approach of Pasternak's 5-Factor Diet is discussed later, in the "Fighting Fat" chapter, so what's the basis of the exercise portion of this celebrity favorite? Harley recommends working out at least twenty-five minutes a day, five or six days a week, performing a combination of cardio, strength, and bodyweight exercises in each workout. For more detailed information Pasternak has authored the books *5-Factor Fitness: The Diet and Fitness Secret of Hollywood's A-List* (2004) and *The 5-Factor Diet* (2006), and *The 5-Factor World Diet* (2010) to help people who want to get celebrity results.

4. TRACY ANDERSON

The more publicity that has surrounded Madonna's chiseled arms and Gwyneth Paltrow's lean legs, the more people have wanted to know about Tracy Anderson's training methods, she is the exclusive trainer for both superstars. Anderson reportedly helped Paltrow lose her baby weight after Moses was born and Paltrow recommended the trainer to Madonna.

Anderson is an advocate of fusion training—mixing dance moves (she was a professional dancer) with more traditional exercises that allegedly melt inches fast. She invented new exercise systems that include bands, bars, and cubes. She has also designed the Hybrid Body Reformer (a pulley-system machine available only in her studios) that, as she claims on her website, works to "re-engineer the muscular structure." Her method's overall mission is "to strengthen the smaller muscle groups so that these muscles can pull in the larger muscles—which results in a lean figure." One way she suggests getting a lean figure is to never use weights heavier than three pounds, yet work to perform a hundred repetitions of each exercise.

For people interested in her method who do not live in the Los Angeles or New York City area (where her only studios are located) Anderson has a line of DVDs that include many of her signature exercises. Anderson's students are dedicated to exercising, most logging in six two-hour sessions weekly. So don't fret if you don't see Madonna's arms or Paltrow's legs when you look in the mirror. They've worked their butts off to look that way . . . literally.

5. DAVID KIRSCH

Most famously known for getting Heidi Klum runway-ready eight weeks after giving birth, David Kirsch has shown that his boot camp–style methods work. Klum followed his now famous New York Body Plan about which he has written three books and created numerous DVDs. Aside from training A-listers like Anne Hathaway, Ellen Barkin, Karolina Kurkova, and Liv Tyler, Kirsch is founder and owner of Madison Square Club, a fitness training and nutritional counseling center, and creator of a line of supplements. Once an attorney, Kirsch left his law career to pursue what he felt to be his true calling. It seems like he made the right choice.

6. BOB GREENE

If you're a disciple of Oprah then you've probably heard of her trainer, Bob Greene. Oprah has really propelled Greene's career into high gear, helping make his BestLife program wildly popular just by following it and promoting it. Everyone wants to be like Oprah! Greene has made numerous appearances on the *Oprah* show and is a contributing editor for *O The Oprah Magazine* and oprah.com. He has written numerous books, the first, *Make the Connection: Ten Steps to A Better Body—And A Better Life* (1996), was also coauthored by Oprah. The key to his program is making small but powerful lifestyle changes.

7. MANDY INGBER

How did Jennifer Aniston center herself after her split with Brad Pitt? She called yoga and fitness expert Mandy Ingber to whip her mind and body into shape. Ingber has also trained Helen Hunt, Brooke Shields, and numerous professional athletes, but Aniston is her most famous client. Aniston's figure is much-envied and at just over forty years old she looks ten years younger. What's her exercise regimen? A lot of yoga and running: every other day she has two-hour yoga sessions with Ingber that end with twenty minutes of cardio. On days she doesn't perform yoga she runs.

Ingber has practiced yoga since she was a child and has been featured in magazines such as *Vogue*, *Vanity Fair*, *Glamour*, and *Elle*. She believes, "having the body you want begins with loving the body you have." And she would like to help everyone access his or her inner athlete regardless of fitness level. She is a trainer who truly works on improving her clients' mental and physical well-being.

8. ROBERT PARR

Robert Parr has been in the health business for over twenty years, training Naomi Watts for her role in *King Kong*, Demi

Moore for her infamous nude *Vanity Fair* cover shoot (while pregnant), and Madonna seven days a week during the late 1980s, among many others. The longevity of his star-studded client list speaks volumes about the effectiveness of his training. His book, *Star Quality: The Red Carpet Workout for the Celebrity Body of Your Dreams* (2008), shares some of the secrets of his A-list clients. He admits that you have to be prepared to sweat because stars work hard for their bodies. You must constantly modify your routine or your body will adapt and will not change. Furthermore, he says that for a workout to be the most effective it must be at least an hour long. It may be hard but at least you know that if you're breaking a sweat you're not wasting your time.

9. TEDDY BASS

Previously a professional dancer and performer, celebrity trainer Teddy Bass combines his expertise in dance with Pilates and traditional training methods to create his own brand of exercise. Bass been featured in such magazines as *Allure, Cosmopolitan, Self,* and *Us Weekly* and has trained Cameron Diaz, Lucy Liu, and Christina Applegate. To sculpt their pefectly toned bodies he constantly changes up their workouts: one day the workout might be in the gym, the next it will move outside for hiking or kayaking.

His tips include working out on an empty stomach, traveling with water bottles to use as dumbbells for a quick workout, and exercising at least six days a week.

10. MICHAEL GEORGE

Michael George thinks of himself as a coach or educator more than merely a trainer, and his actions demonstrate that he doesn't just train his clients, but he tries to motivate and educate them as well. He has worked with such celebrities as Reese Witherspoon, Tobey Maguire, Sean Combs, and Dennis Quaid, but he also trains non-celebrity mortals as well.

Apart from personal training, George works as a consultant and coach, and as a motivational speaker at seminars and workshops as well. He is the author of *Body Express Makeover: Trim and Sculpt Your Body in Less Than Six Weeks* (2005) and the creator of the 2-in-1 Training System and B-Fit video series. George has often been featured on TV on CNN, Vh1, and numerous programs including *The View*, *FOX and Friends*, and *Entertainment Tonight*.

Fighting Fat

Though they won't admit it, most celebrities are on some diet or other most of the time. They're just as susceptible to fad diets as regular people, they just start out looking about twenty times more fit than most of the rest of us. The diets on this list are a mix of new diet crazes and the tried-and-true diets that keep celebrities coming back.

1. THE "BABY EATING" DIET

Don't worry, you don't eat babies on this diet, but you do eat their food. The November 2007 issue of *Marie Claire* magazine reported that the idea of substituting baby food for adult food originated with New York fashion designer Hedi Slimane. He allegedly eats baby food for days on end, though this is *not* recommended. Organic brand Earth Best has become popular with celebrity fans of this diet, such as Jennifer Aniston, Reese Witherspoon, and Marcia Cross. Witherspoon replaces one or two meals a day with baby food and Cross reportedly eats it in place of other snacks, which is how nutritionist Dr. Marty Edwards recommends it be used.

Baby foods are incredibly healthy. In order to make food easily digestible for babies they have no additives and they are full of vitamins. Add in the wide variety of flavors and the portion control and you'll never look at "baby" food the same way again.

2. **THE MACROBIOTIC DIET**

Despite sounding like a college level biology class, A-list celebrities, such as Gwyneth Paltrow and Madonna, have followed this nutritional plan. It's actually more of a lifestyle than a diet, and while it sounds scientific, the word macrobiotic is of Greek origin meaning "long life." Japanese educator, George Oshsawa, developed this diet from his belief that simple eating led to good health. Originally, his diet consisted of ten progressively restrictive stages, the last being that one consisted of only brown rice and water (at which point a long life might seem more like a curse!). These days that stage is no longer recommended. Today, the macrobiotic diet consists of the following: 50 to 60 percent whole grains, 25 to 35 percent seasonal vegetables, about 10 percent beans; fish and seafood, seeds and nuts, and local fruit should be eaten a few times per week. There is no caloric restriction, but part of the philosophy is to only eat when hungry and to chew slowly. All food should be organic of course, because, you know, a good celebrity diet should be expensive. No processed foods, dairy, meat, or caffeine are allowed and foods cannot not be microwaved . . . wait, how else is food prepared?

3. **THE ZONE DIET**

This diet is based on balancing the basic meal components: 40 percent carbs, 30 percent fat, and 30 percent protein. Proponents of this diet say that it allows for hormonal balance and control over the body's insulin production. Too much insulin, they claim, may prompt the body to convert carbs into fat and store it in your body.

In addition, the Zone Diet emphasizes closely monitoring caloric intake, not exceeding 500 calories per meal and 100 calories per snack. On a side note, however, a ZonePerfect Nutrition bar contains 210 calories, so is that supposed to be part of a meal rather than a snack? Jennifer Aniston, Cindy Crawford, and Courtney Love are fans of this diet plan. To make this way of eating easier, many celebrity clients have their meals delivered. This would be helpful if you can afford it because who wants to—or who even can—make all those calculations for each meal.

4. THE 3-HOUR DIET

Kind of like the Zone diet, but without the messy math, the 3-Hour Diet has exploded onto the media scene, being featured on *Oprah*, Vh1, and the *Today* show. Health expert Jorge Cruise constructed a diet that centers on eating the "right" foods every three hours, which stabilizes blood sugar and controls appetite. If you're starting to see a pattern about eating the importance of eating the right foods you aren't alone. Cruise's diet plan suggests eating a combination of carbs, protein, and fruits or vegetables at each mini-meal, with an emphasis on portion control. Celebrities like Jessica Biel and Jessica Alba have used this diet to slim down.

5. THE LOW-CARB DIET

Eating low carb is a way of life in Hollywood. While most people don't claim to be on Atkins anymore (that was *so* 2005) many watch the amount of carbs they consume. Celebrities who are trying to slim down or maintain a slender figure stick to a diet consisting primarily of lean protein and vegetables with a piece of fruit thrown in here or there. Some of the numerous stars that are proponents of low-carb eating are Angelina Jolie, Heidi Klum, Jennifer Lopez, and Rihanna, who said it all when she stated in an interview with *People* magazine in June 2007, "Carbs are the enemy."

6. THE RAW FOOD DIET

No, a raw food diet does not consist of totally raw foods. There are a wide variety of foods a "raw foodist" can eat; the only restriction is that foods be unprocessed, organic, and uncooked. Food can be heated up to 104 degrees, since the raw food theory suggests that heating food above this temperature removes some of the nutrients. Some raw enthusiasts eat raw and lightly cooked seafood, while others just say no to meat and dairy products.

Recently, raw food restaurants have popped up in L.A., touting gourmet raw meals such as lasagna, pizza, and quiche. Carol Alt, Susan Sarandon, Cher, and Alicia Silverstone champion the raw lifestyle and incorporate it into their diet to varying degrees. Alt is one of the strictest raw foodist among the celebrity set, having authored numerous books about the raw food lifestyle.

7. THE 5-FACTOR DIET

If you couldn't guess, the magic number on this diet plan is five: five weeks for results, five meals a day, five ingredients per meal, five minutes to prepare, five workouts per week (but no, not five minute workouts). It even allows for one cheat day per week. Wait, five meals a day, say about sixteen waking hours in a day, that's roughly a meal every 3 hours.

Although this diet is eerily similar to the 3-Hour Diet, it emphasizes the diet's composition and ease instead of meal frequency. However, *The 5-Factor Diet* book recommends eating every three hours to maintain blood sugar levels and increasing the metabolism. Trainer to the stars Harley Pasternak developed this diet plan that is responsible for many amazing celebrity bodies including Jessica Simpson (post–John Mayer), Eva Mendes, Kanye West, and John Mayer. If the diet ever goes out of vogue as Atkins did, Pasternak should get together with Jorge Cruise and see if they could rebrand this idea . . . again.

8. THE VEGETARIAN/VEGAN DIET

This diet is popular in Hollywood with musicians and actors alike. Vegetarians refrain from eating animals, yet may eat products that come from animals, such as dairy and cheese. Vegans do not eat any animal products. Famous herbivores include Pamela Anderson, Russell Simmons, Sir Paul McCartney, Alicia Silverstone, Carrie Underwood, Natalie Portman, Mary Tyler Moore, and Outkast's Andre 3000. Proponents of a meatless lifestyle claim improved health improved after eliminating animal products as well as clearer skin, a more fit body, and general improved feelings of well-being. Of course, there aren't any diets that claim you will feel and look worse while following them.

Many vegetarians also feel that eating animals promotes cruelty to animals. As Russell Simmons is quoted on goveg. com, "Cruelty is cruelty, whether it's cruelty to children, to the elderly, to dogs and cats, or to chickens."

9. THE JENNY CRAIG DIET

If there's one celebrity diet that you've heard of, it's probably Jenny Craig. They tout celebrity spokespeople in their ads more than any other diet on the market. Celebrities who have promoted Jenny Craig include Queen Latifah, Valerie Bertinelli, Kirstie Alley, and Monica Lewinsky.

Here's how it works: Jenny Craig sells prepackaged food to its clients so they have portions controlled for them. However, this diet doesn't leave you on your own. There are Jenny Craig weight loss centers around the country where clients meet each week to address three critical areas of weight loss: food, body, and mind. Jenny Craig aims to help clients develop a healthy relationship with food, an active lifestyle, and a balanced approach to life. If you're too busy to get to a center, you can have your meals delivered and it participate in meetings over the phone. They tailor the program to the individual and provides clients with the tools to maintain a healthy lifestyle, and at times an almost stalker-like involvement in their lives. Jenny Craig's cost varies, depending on the program and foods you choose. Because this diet uses celebrities spokespeople, if you want to know if the diet works, you can always keep up with their most recent photos thanks to the paparazzi!

10. THE COOKIE DIET

Whoo hoo! Pick up those Oreos and let's lose some weight! Not so fast. It doesn't work quite like that, but a girl can always dream right? This diet, which was created by Dr. Sanford Siegal, centers on a specific type of cookie, conveniently made by Dr. Seigal. Meals are replaced with his special diet cookies and diet shakes that curb the appetite. Here's how the diet works: Eat six diet cookies throughout the day and a sensible dinner. The cookies are available in a variety of flavors, each containing 90 calories. He recommends that dieters keep their caloric intake to 1,000 calories per day, thus ensuring more calories are exerted than consumed. While this diet may be effective—*American Idol* alums Jennifer Hudson and Kelly Clarkson have both had success on this diet—many experts caution that 1,000 calories per day is too few calories to remain healthy and that weight loss may be difficult to maintain if one strays from this cookie regimen. Of course if you can eat just one cookie at a time, or limit yourself to 1,000 calories per day, you probably don't need this diet.

Getting the Skinny

Well, when regular dieting just isn't enough, celebrities turn to diet tricks to help shed weight quickly or to keep from ruining their diets when nighttime cravings set in. To achieve starworthy perfection, try these tips.

1. THE MASTER CLEANSE
This extreme diet is also fondly known as "The Maple Syrup Diet" and "The Lemonade Diet." Numerous stars use this diet to shed pounds quickly for a role. Most famously, Beyoncé used this cleanse to drop twenty pounds for her role in the film *Dream Girls*. While this fast gives your digestive system a break, there are numerous downsides (feeling starved all the time for one). It is not something you can do long-term, but because water, cayenne pepper, maple syrup, and lemons are the only ingredients needed, you will save a lot on your grocery bill.

2. HOODIA GORDONII
Commonly referred to as the "size zero pill," Hoodia is an herbal appetite suppressant that tricks the brain into thinking you've just eaten. Reportedly, Eva Longoria, Teri Hatcher, and Nicole Richie are fans of this supplement. (Some [so far unverified] reports have even surfaced claiming that Richie

was addicted to Hoodia.) There are many Hoodia products on the market, in both pill and liquid forms, but many contain very little or only trace amounts of Hoodia. Reportedly, to be effective, the product should contain at least 750 mg of pure Hoodia.

In her book *Making the Cut* trainer Jillian Michaels explains that Bushmen in the Kalahari Desert have been using Hoodia for centuries to help ward off hunger during long trips, but she asserts that they do not eat it every day. The effects of ingesting Hoodia daily have not been thoroughly studied, but pharmaceutical companies see promise in this suppressant and are busily working to create a patented diet drug.

3. **VINEGAR**

While most people would consider vinegar a condiment that goes on food, Cindy Crawford reportedly drinks a little vinegar straight before she eats to reduce her appetite. This might seem extreme, but Dr. David Katz reported in *O, The Oprah Magazine* that the acidic nature of vinegar can slow digestion, prolonging the feeling of fullness. If drunk before or with foods with a high glycemic index, such as white bread and pasta, it makes them more filling, for it is thought the carbs enter the bloodstream more slowly. However, he is quick to add that too much vinegar could bother the stomach or esophagus, so you shouldn't drink more than three tablespoons of vinegar. If you don't think you can handle drinking vinegar straight, just putting vinegar over your food can help suppress appetite as well.

4. **ICE CUBES**

Ice cubes aren't merely used to cool drinks anymore, some celebrities are eating them as snacks. What more could you want? You consume water, keep your mouth busy, and actually burn approximately forty calories melting an ice cube. Renée Zellwegger reportedly snacked on ice cubes to help her lose weight after her role as Bridget Jones. Mariah Carey regularly chews ice cubes when she's tempted to snack between meals. While ice has no calories, chewing it tricks the brain and mouth into thinking it is being fed. Some argue that chewing ice cubes is damaging to teeth, so perhaps chewing on crushed ice would be safer, but make sure to consult with your dentist before chewing ice on a regular basis—and don't forget to some eat real food as well!

5. BRUSHING TEETH

How do celebs like Pamela Anderson and Matthew McConaughey maintain their perfect physiques? Well, ok, so there are probably many factors that go into it, but one way they keep their diets on track is by brushing their teeth after every meal. Reportedly, a different taste after eating signals your brain that the meal is over. However, it seems like McConaughey might take this idea too far, for he says, "I have a toothbrush in my car, in my bedroom, bathroom, and kitchen." Yes, he has in fact been spotted brushing while driving.

6. SLEEPING

Lack of sleep is often tied to obesity, and celebrities such as Penelope Cruz have taken this to heart. Cruz reports that she makes a point to get twelve hours of sleep each night. And while experts say that sleeping in itself will not help you lose weight, but not eating for half the day could lead to consuming fewer calories. However, Cruz also said she stopped smoking and eating junk food, so that could account for some of her weight loss as well.

7. GRAPEFRUIT OIL

The *Daily Mail* reports that Jennifer Lopez and Carmen Electra carry vials of grapefruit oil to help with weight loss. Apparently, studies have shown that animals exposed to grapefruit aroma, which affects liver enzymes, for fifteen minutes three times a day showed a reduction in appetite and body weight. Additionally, grapefruit oil has therapeutic properties and has been used as an antidepressant, antiseptic, diuretic, disinfectant, and lymphatic stimulant.

8. NATURAL DIURETICS
Celebrities are wild about natural diuretics that clean out the system and help stave off bloating. Asparagus is a natural diuretic and allegedly Owen Wilson eats at least two servings each day.

If you don't like asparagus, try dandelion tea, which is another natural diuretic that is used by Madonna and Gwyneth Paltrow. It contains many minerals, such as phosphorus, iron, magnesium, calcium, and potassium. Dandelion also contains ingredients that act as antioxidants and anti-inflammatories. Taraxacin, found in dandelion, allows for liver and digestive system benefits.

9. HYPNOTHERAPY
British singer Lily Allen attributed losing two dress sizes to "hypno-dieting" which she claims helped her quit drinking and eating fattening foods. Hypnotherapy has been popular in New York and Los Angeles for a while and is getting more popular in London. According to www.hypno-diet.com, hypnotherapy aids the "unconscious part of you that will help you make the changes you need to make."

This diet aid does not come cheap. The *Daily Mail* reported that each of Allen's sessions cost $600. That would buy a lot of time with a nutritionist and a trainer, both of whom would probably teach you the same lessons.

10. CAFFEINE
Whether it's an energy drink or coffee, celebrities are often photographed holding a caffeinated beverage. Why this obsession with caffeine? First, caffeine gives them energy that may be lacking without regular nourishment. Second, it can act as a meal replacement; these drinks are very filling while not adding many calories.

Body Art

Today it's not unusual to see a celebrity with a tattoo or two . . . or ten. While celebrity tattoos have become outrageously popular, some still manage to shock and awe. Either way, they still attract a lot of attention. The tattoos on this list are unusual and outrageous.

1. CHER

Cher was one of the first tattooed female celebrities. She got tattooed before it was hip for women to do so, but she wanted to make a statement. Cher admitted that she got her first tattoo after her divorce from Sonny Bono, to do something different that showed she was a free woman. Though Cher has gotten numerous tattoos—many of which she has since had removed—her first tattoo, a bouquet of flowers complete with a butterfly, is legendary because of its size and location across both of her buttocks. While this would be a place most celebrities keep covered in public, Cher's revealing outfits allowed the whole world a glimpse at her statement of independence.

2. LIL' WAYNE

Not only does rapper Lil' Wayne have unusual tattoos, tattoos cover most of his body. As of his May 2009 appearance on *The View* he claimed to have only two more spots for tattoos—his inner thighs. His oddest, and most visible tattoos are on his face. Above his eyelids are tattooed the words "Fear God." Between his eyes is the letter "C" and a cross, which could also have religious connotations. He has three teardrops below his eyes, which some think symbolize loved ones he's lost. The words "Misunderstood" and "I am Music" also adorn his face; it seems that Wayne speaks to the world through his tattoos. Maybe he's shy.

3. MEGAN FOX

Because she is a Hollywood newcomer, one may be tempted to classify Megan Fox's ink as her jumping on the tattoo bandwagon. But upon examination of Fox's tattoos, she goes outside the box of the typical "cute" tattoo that can be easily covered, and she would probably have these tattoos even if she weren't famous or it weren't cool.

She has Marilyn Monroe's face tattooed on her right forearm. She explained that Monroe was one of the first people she saw on TV, and instantly empathized with the tragic actress. A quote from Shakespeare's *King Lear* is tattooed on her back, a self-written poem is tattooed on the side of her ribcage, and "Brian" (her boyfriend's name) is tattooed on her lower stomach.

Fox doesn't seem worried about losing roles because of her tattoos, and displays them proudly on the red carpet.

4. STEVE-O

It's difficult for reformed *Jackass* star Steve-O to surprise people with his antics. Even sober he's a little crazy. However, some of Steve-O's tattoos are outrageous even for him. I mean, who would tattoo a giant picture of themselves on their back? Steve-O did! It comes complete with his signature. Almost as crazy is the flying phallus tattoo on his arm. He admits it was dumb and that he was told not to do it, but he loves that his arm will always have to be blurred on TV. Though he has numerous other tattoos, Steve-O's third absurd tattoo is the statement "I have a small weiner" made even funnier by the fact that "wiener" is misspelled, an error Steve-O admitted he did not notice for days.

5. MIKE TYSON

Boxer Mike Tyson's face tattoo created a lot of buzz and is one of the most famous celebrity athlete tattoos. The tattoo is reminiscent of Maori warrior tattoos, which represents who Tyson is at his core—a fighter. However, his face tattoo isn't Tyson's only unusual tattoo. He has three tattoos of famous people. One is of Arthur Ashe, the first black tennis champion. Another is of Mao Tse-tung, of whom Tyson is a big fan, going so far as to collect Tse-tung's writings. He got the tattoo after visiting Tse-tung's mausoleum. His final tattoo is of Che Guevara, a controversial revolutionary who helped Fidel Castro gain power in Cuba. Tyson explained that for him, these tattoos are powerful personal totems.

6. ANGELINA JOLIE

As Hollywood's most famous tattooed actress, Angelina Jolie's tattoos have been greatly discussed and have actually inspired tattoo fads. Her most well-known tattoo lists the geographical coordinates where each of her children was born on her left shoulder (this has replaced the name of her former husband Billy Bob). On her left shoulder she has a Buddhist Pali incantation in Khmer script to protect her from bad luck. Between her shoulder blades she has the phrase "Know your rights," which some might assume is a testament to her humanitarian efforts. In reality it is the title of a song by her favorite band The Clash. Jolie's 8 by 12 inch tattoo on her back of a Bengal tiger is one of her newest tattoos and has made this particular tattoo one of the most popular in America. Jolie got the tattoo to celebrate her Cambodian citizenship, what reason does everyone else give?

7. NICOLE RICHIE

Nicole Richie's rosary tattoo around her ankle is another very popular tattoo among young American women. The delicate, intricately detailed tattoo matches her reformed image of the perfect, slim, fashionable socialite and mother—with an edge. However, another of her nine tattoos raises some eyebrows. On her left wrist Richie has the word "Virgin" tattooed. Supposedly, it represents her astrological sign, Virgo, but then why not just tattoo the word "Virgo?" Perhaps Richie expects people to read beyond the tattoo's literal meaning.

8. BRITNEY SPEARS

Poor Britney, she can't even get a tattoo done right. You'd think that a celebrity with millions of dollars would be able to go to a top-notch tattoo parlor, but Britney is proof positive that money can't buy you everything. To add insult to injury, she received not one, but two incorrect tattoos. First, and most famously, is the tattoo Spears got on her neck to represent her devotion to Kabbalah. The tattoo was three Hebrew characters, which she reportedly thought meant "healing," but experts said the characters were out of order and thus had no meaning. She had it corrected, but has since had the tattoo removed. The other tattoo that is incorrect is the Kanji character on her pelvic bone, which was supposed to translate as "mysterious" but was mixed up with the Kanji character for "strange." Well, at least it means *something*.

9. TOM ARNOLD

Tom Arnold's tattoos are both unusual and unfortunate. Luckily he could shell out the money to have them removed, and hopefully they are a painful reminder not to tattoo your current love all over your body. Sure many people regrettably tattoo the name of their "true love," but Arnold went a little overboard getting *four* Roseanne Barr–related tattoos, including a portrait of Roseanne's face on his chest. What was at the time an extravagant display of affection, which he proudly displayed throughout their short marriage, turned out to be painful and expensive reminders of love gone sour.

10. THE FELLOWSHIP OF THE RING

Filming *The Lord of the Rings* trilogy was a massive undertaking; all three movies were filmed one right after the other, giving the actors plenty of time to bond over their eighteen months together in New Zealand. Elijah Wood said in an interview with ABC News that the experience was so wonderful and profound that the actors decided to brand themselves. Eight of the nine members of the Fellowship of the Ring got matching tattoos to commemorate the project. The only member not to get the tattoo was John Rhys-Davies who played Gimli. All the actors got the same tattoo—the Elvin word for the number nine—but they were not all tattooed on the same place. Originally the tattoo was supposed to be kept secret among the fellowship, but not surprisingly, the news leaked before the movie even premiered.

You Are What You Wear

Every so often a new celebrity style icon emerges, influencing not only other celebrities' style, but also the style of the public and fashion industry itself. Some of the most powerful style icons of the past three decades are listed below.

1. DIANA, PRINCESS OF WALES

From the day she married Prince Charles in 1981 to her untimely death in 1997, Princess Diana's fashion choices were constantly scrutinized. At first Diana's style did not seem to be her own, for the multitude of tweed suits and puffy dresses she wore looked like they were made for someone twice her age. However, even her puffy sleeved dresses and shoulder padded suits became fashionable. Her 1981 meringue Elizabeth and David Emanuel wedding dress set the style for wedding dresses in the 1980s. Her constantly changing hairstyles became instant sensations.

By the 1990s, however, Diana had found her own style, leading her to become even more influential in the fashion world. She became an international style icon, one of the most photographed women in the fashion world, she became the face of British fashion, and elevated the British fashion industry both domestically and internationally. She wore sim-

Princess Diana and John Travolta showing off their dancing chops at the White House in 1985. *Ronald Reagan Library*

ple, yet sophisticated suits and gowns made of light fabrics. Even when wearing jeans she exuded elegance and grace.

2. MADONNA

After two decades in the music industry the Material Girl continues to make fashion headlines, but the 1980s was the height of her fashion influence. Teenage girls everywhere wanted to copy Madonna's funky, eclectic style. Teased hair, big (and numerous) accessories, banana clips, and fishnet and lace stockings are just some of the fashion trends this controversial singer has been credited with starting.

3. VICTORIA BECKHAM

Victoria Beckham was originally known around the world as Posh Spice, a member of the girl group The Spice Girls.

Beckham's stage name came as a result of her luxurious fashion taste, but even she admits that many of the outfits she wore back then she wouldn't be caught dead in today. Surprisingly, it took becoming the wife of the most famous soccer player in the world, David Beckham, and mother of three sons before her status in the fashion world skyrocketed.

Beckham has admitted that it took a lot of hard work for the fashion industry to take her seriously, but that work has paid off, as she is one of the most influential international trendsetters today. Not only does Beckham have the perfect body for fashion—she's rail thin—but she knows how to use it and is not afraid to try new styles. She is always photographed in heels and clothing that flatters her body, whether it is a mini dress or skinny jeans. Her famous bob hairstyle has been named the "Posh Bob" and has been copied by numerous celebrities, most famously Katie Holmes. In addition to participating in an ad campaign for Armani and being a global ambassador for Roberto Cavalli, she has brought her style to the masses through a line of jeans, sunglasses, and dresses, all of which have been enormously successful. Who doesn't want to be posh?

4. KATE MOSS

In the early 1990s Kate Moss ushered in a new era of modeling. Out was the healthy, all-American looking model as exemplified by Cindy Crawford and Christie Brinkley; in was Heroine-chic, waif-looking models.

Moss became an instant style icon and has remained so, receiving the Fashion Icon Award from the Council of Fashion Designers of America in 2005. Moss has been credited with wearing numerous trends before they were trends including skinny jeans, vests, mini dresses, ankle boots, hot pants, ballet flats, Ugg Boots, and waist-cinching belts. She has inspired many imitators like Lindsay Lohan and the

Olsen twins. Even Moss's drug bust in 2006, for cocaine not heroine, has not diminished her popularity.

5. LL COOL J

Ok, so LL Cool J may not be the obvious choice for a trend-setter. He's is no Jay-Z, Russell Simmons, or Sean Combs, but he was instrumental in the launch of mainstream hip-hop clothing, which paved the way for these modern day hip-hop fashion moguls. The FUBU (For Us By Us) brand was founded in 1992, which was the first brand marketed to African Americans. LL Cool J reportedly owned part of the company, and was central to the company's advertising, which at its most popular grossed $350 million yearly world-wide. Though the company has declined in U.S. popularity in recent years, and LL Cool J unsuccessfully attempted to start his own fashion line, his importance in the inception of retail hip-hop fashion should be noted.

6. KURT COBAIN

Nirvana, and more specifically the band's front man Kurt Cobain, was the embodiment of the grunge trend that was popular in the early 1990s. Trademarks of this trend included greasy hair, a disheveled/androgynous appearance, and a flannel shirt. Fans of grunge were a generally jaded audience who were anti–mainstream fashion, but once something becomes a trend doesn't that make it mainstream?

7. SARAH JESSICA PARKER

Sarah Jessica Parker's place on this list can be attributed to her role as fashionista Carrie Bradshaw in the television show and film *Sex and the City*. The role led people to pay attention to Parker's everyday and Red Carpet style, and she did not disappoint. Perhaps not as wild as the character she portrayed, Parker credits the show's stylist, Patricia Field for bringing out her inner fashion icon. She always exudes a sophisticated, edgy style and is not afraid to try new designers. Hamptons.com credits her with starting trends such as aviator sunglasses, nameplate necklaces, gloves, newsboy hats, and, of course, the rise of Manolo Blanhik shoes. In 2007 Parker put her stamp on the fashion industry, releasing her own clothing line, Bitten, which is marketed as budget-priced clothes and sold exclusively at Steve & Barry retail stores. Though Parker will always be associated with the infamous character Carrie Bradshaw, it is Parker's style that fans emulate.

8. JENNIFER LOPEZ

Us Weekly named Jennifer Lopez their Style Icon of the Year in 2007, but her fashion influence started long before that. Lopez was the original booty, making it acceptable and even fashionable to have a real-sized bottom. Though her style has definitely changed over the years, she brings a mix of street and glamour to Hollywood. She has made headlines with her red carpet style (think the infamous extremely low-cut Versace dress), which has led the fashion world to take notice of her everyday style as well. In 2001 she brought her fashion to the masses by pioneering the concept of a high-end celebrity brand, and it has become incredibly profitable, grossing about $300 million annually. Ultimately, Lopez's relatable body type and ever-changing style will solidify her place as a fashion icon for years to come.

9. PAT BENATAR

Pat Benatar was a top selling artist during the 1980s famous for such classic tunes as "Heartbreaker" and "Hit Me With Your Best Shot." She made fashion headlines before the likes of Madonna, displaying an edgy style that mixed rocker chick, disco, and glam and she pioneered such trends as dancewear, spandex, leggings, fringe, cut up shirts, shoulder pads, bold makeup, and wild hair. Years later when Benatar was asked by *Entertainment Weekly* about the inspiration for her fashion she stated, "I was never a fashion person. I was just putting together things I thought were nuts. And that I could afford."

10. MICHELLE OBAMA

America's newest fashion "It" girl, Obama's status has come as a result of her new position as first lady, which has made her the most visible American woman in the world. Though every First Lady lives in the public eye, not since Jackie Kennedy has a first lady's fashion caused such media and public frenzy. Though it may be too early to tell, Obama is well on her way to becoming an American, and perhaps even an International, fashion icon. Not only does the media follow her every fashion choice, but the American people are taking fashion cues from her as well. After she appeared on the *The Tonight Show* wearing a J. Crew dress and on *The View* wearing a White House/Black Market dress, both pieces sold out the next day—J. Crew's stock even went up. Her decision to wear various new designers has catapulted the careers of these unknowns. Controversy arose when Obama chose to wear arm-baring dresses. Then she went even further and wore shorts during a family vacation to the Grand Canyon in August 2009. The media was abuzz with opinions over whether or not this was appropriate. Really, give the lady a break—it's not like she wore hot pants to a state dinner! Of course, Obama's style will be eyed closely—and most likely highly imitated—while she is First Lady, but only time will tell the extent of her impact on American fashion.

They Wore What?

With all the millions of dollars that celebrities earn, you'd think they would have an army of people around to assist them in every little task, especially dressing for award ceremonies. This list includes celebrities who, despite the privileges afforded by their status, have strayed from high fashion when walking the Red Carpet. They either need to hire a stylist or fire the one they have.

1. CHER

Cher is known for her attention-grabbing fashion choices, making it impossible to pick just one. Two Oscar outfits stand apart from the rest, and were over-the-top, even for Cher. Both outfits (incidentally both were designed by Bob Mackie) made her look like she'd blend in better on a Las Vegas stage than at a Red Carpet event—let alone the biggest Red Carpet event in the film industry. In 1986 she chose a three piece outfit consisting of a shiny black skirt, a midriff baring top that looked like the top half of a dominatrix ensemble, and a huge spiky black headdress. In 1988, Cher won the Best Actress Oscar for her performance in *Moonstruck*. She went for a similar look, though technically covering her entire body. The Bob Mackie dress was made of black sheer material and

255

accented with thousands of beads. Only her unmentionables were left to the imagination. Though the dress received many negative reviews, it has been termed "Cher Chic" which I guess means anything goes if Cher wears it.

2. DEMI MOORE

In 1989 Demi Moore decided to add "fashion designer" to her résumé. She designed her own Oscar dress and the result was disastrous. It's unclear exactly what led her to believe that spandex biking shorts would be an appropriate red carpet look, but there they were. The "dress" consisted of black biking shorts, a long-sleeved black and gold bustier, and an open front black skirt with gold embroidery. There's a good reason why Demi Moore does not have a fashion line.

3. KIM BASINGER

Jumping on the design-your-own-Oscar-dress bandwagon, Kim Basinger wore a gown of her own styling for the 1990 Oscars. While it would seem difficult to imagine a worse outfit than Demi Moore's creation of the previous year, Basinger pulled it off. Basinger looked like she'd been mauled by an animal, or suffered from a split personality disorder. Maybe she just couldn't decide which look she wanted. Somehow, though, she managed to look into a mirror and say, "I look good!"

The offensive gown was made of white satin and had a full princess skirt—nothing out of the ordinary there. However, the top of the dress was where it went wrong. One side had a strapless, sweetheart neckline bodice with a long white glove covering her arm. The other side consisted of a white, long sleeved jacket with gold embroidery on the sleeve and buttons up the front. Think half Michael Jackson and half Cinderella. What damaged her look further, was that her hair was half up and half down, like she couldn't make up her mind in that department either, or like part of it had been pulled down by the wild animal mauling her.

Kim Basinger in her own unique creation at the 62nd Academy Awards. *Alan Light*

4. GEENA DAVIS

1992 Oscar nominee Geena Davis decided that the fashion taste of others would not dictate what she wore. She explained her odd choice in a *New York Times* article saying, "That gown fit my concept of dressing up for evening." If that's what Davis wears during nights out, she must stand out everywhere she goes. Granted, the low-cut white satin bustier top was beautiful, but the bottom half of the dress was a disaster. Not unlike a can-can dancer's dress, it was short and bustled in the front, flowing into a long bustled train of messy black and white fabric in the back. What's worse, she wore black tights and long white satin gloves. Davis is known for her beautiful long legs, but this dress did nothing to positively accentuate them.

5. CELINE DION
Celine Dion's fashion choice for the 1999 Oscars may have been to show that she can be edgy even if her music is not. That said, she could have at least taken the risk with something sexy. Instead, Dion decided to go out on a limb wearing a reverse white tuxedo designed by John Galliano for the House of Dior. To top it off she wore a white fedora. Though the suit showed off her beautiful back, the rest of her was completely covered by the baggy tuxedo jacket. On the up side, Dion was probably the only attendee who didn't have to fast for weeks to fit into into her Oscar outfit.

6. BJORK
Bjork's swan dress has become a legendary fashion faux pas. In 2001 Bjork's Oscar look wasn't just inspired by a swan, it was a swan. Of course, it wasn't a real swan, but the dress had been made to look like she was *wearing* a swan—it even had a beak. To complete the ensemble, Bjork carried an egg purse and actually dropped eggs along the red carpet. Bjork insisted that the Marjan Pejoski design was meant as a joke. The one positive result of this dress was that it was auctioned for charity after the event.

7. UMA THURMAN
The tall statuesque blond is typically a vision of loveliness on the red carpet. At the 2004 Oscars she was more like a vision from the Swiss Alps. The Christian Lacroix creation

was white and flowy with poofy white sleeves and a blue and gold vest that narrowed around her waist like a belt, ultimately making her look like she was wearing a belt and suspenders. Though Thurman still managed to look beautiful, it was difficult to notice with the costume-like dress that even she could not pull off.

8. KATE HUDSON

Kate Hudson is known for her bubbly personality and knock-out body, so it shouldn't be difficult for her to find a stunning dress for a red carpet event, or at least one that accentuates her natural beauty. But of all the dresses from which Hudson could choose, she decided on the one dress that didn't complement her at all. Twenty-one-year-old Hudson's choice of a grey-fringed capelet dress actually made her look old and dowdy, more like a Victorian matron than a young Oscar nominee. The perm-like poodle hairstyle didn't help matters either. It's one thing to look mature, but no one wants to look like an antique.

9. GWYNETH PALTROW

Gwyneth Paltrow has become a Hollywood fashion icon. Fashion critics wait with bated breath to see what she will be wearing on the red carpet, and fans try to emulate her sophisticated style. So when Paltrow appeared on the 2002 Oscar Red Carpet in an Alexander McQueen dress that made her look frumpy, everyone wondered what had gone wrong. It looked like she'd attempted a goth look with the dress's long black skirt, see through tank top, and heavy black eyeliner. What made this look even worse was that Paltrow slouched for pictures, which made her top appear very droopy. Paltrow is, in fact, only human, and we all make mistakes. It seems that she corrected this one and hired a new stylist, since this disaster has not repeated itself.

10. HILARY SWANK

When describing Hilary Swank the word "feminine" does not necessarily come to mind. But Swank's angular face, serious nature, and sculpted figure all allow her to achieve an elegance and even sexy appearance on the Red Carpet. Who can forget the gorgeous navy backless Guy Laroche dress in 2005? In 2003 it seemed that Swank tried to soften her appearance by wearing pink. No, not a pink dress, which might have worked fine; instead, she wore pink tulle over a white mini dress. The result was ballerina-looking mess. Apparently she was unaware that this look had already been done by Sarah Jessica Parker and Lara Flynn Boyle. And it didn't work for them either.

Celebrity
Life

Celebrity Do-Gooders

Celebrities often get a reputation for being spoiled by their wealth, which may at times be true. The millions of dollars they receive for their acting roles and concert tours is exorbitant, but some celebrities use their fame and fortune to benefit others. True, almost every celebrity has their own charity foundation or a particular cause they support, but the celebrities on this list are beyond generous with their money and their time, and seem to genuinely want to use their wealth and status to make a difference in the world.

1. ANGELINA JOLIE

Angelina Jolie has become known for her extensive charity work. While it may be en vogue for celebrities to perform charity work of some sort, Jolie seems to truly care about the organizations and people that she helps. Jolie has frequently commented that she first became aware of the humanitarian crises in Cambodia while filming *Tomb Raider* there. From there she began visiting refugee camps in various countries and working alongside other volunteers in impoverished regions. Unlike many celebrities, Jolie did not take the press with her or use her A-list status to receive special treatment.

She lived alongside other volunteers and really did much of her work under the radar of the paparazzi.

Anderson Cooper reported that Jolie gives one-third of her income to refugees and other causes. In 2003 she received the Citizen of the World Award from the United Nations Correspondents Association and in 2005 she was awarded the Global Humanitarian Award from the United Nations Association of the United States of America (UNA-USA) and was extended Cambodian citizenship because of her extensive conservation work there. She is now a Goodwill Ambassador for the UN High Commissioner for Refugees, and as reporter Anderson Cooper claimed, Jolie truly knows what she's talking about. She and her partner Brad Pitt started the Jolie-Pitt Foundation in 2006 to assist in humanitarian crises around the world. The foundation initially donated one million dollars to both Doctors Without Borders and Global Action for Children, and since then has donated millions more to a variety of charities. Jolie seems increasingly involved in her charity work and it wouldn't come as a great surprise if she eventually she gives up acting to devote all her time to humanitarian causes.

2. BRAD PITT

Aside from the Jolie-Pitt Foundation started with Angelina Jolie, Brad Pitt has his own charity work in which he is deeply involved. Pitt's work accentuates his interest in architecture and puts it to work to help others. Thus, Pitt is actively involved in the Make It Right Foundation, which he founded after Hurricane Katrina. It would have been easy to just throw money at one of the many projects to help rebuild New Orleans post-Katrina, but Pitt wanted to do it his way.

The Make It Right Foundation focuses on rebuilding the lower Ninth Ward, which was one of the regions most devastated by Katrina. The foundation even hosted an architecture

Angelina Jolie, with Brad Pitt and Kofi Annan, doing her part as UNHCR Goodwill Ambassador in 2006. *World Economic Forum*

competition for ideas on sustainable rebuilding. Pitt has met with President Obama to discuss rebuilding New Orleans, and travels to the region often to oversee his projects. It's not unusual to see Pitt talking to local residents and listening to their grievances. It is refreshing to see a celebrity that does follows through to personally make sure that the donations are put to good use.

3. MARLO THOMAS

Most famous for her lead role in the television series *That Girl*, Marlo Thomas has become known today for her extensive work as both the hospital's spokesperson and National Outreach Director, for the charity her father began, St. Jude Children's Research Hospital in Memphis, Tennessee. According to the St. Jude Hospital website, St Jude's helps children who have been recently diagnosed with cancer, certain hematological disorders, AIDS, congenital immunodeficiency syndromes, and genetic disorders. This hospital is at the forefront of research and treatments in these areas. A doctor must recommend a child for treatment at St. Jude and once accepted the hospital covers all costs, including accommodations and meals for the patients' parents and family members. In her positions, Thomas works relentlessly traveling around the world promoting St. Jude's to garner donations to keep this unique hospital.

4. DON CHEADLE

Famous for his roles in the *Ocean's Eleven* films, *Hotel Rwanda*, and *Crash*, Don Cheadle has become a major player in Hollywood. Simultaneously, he has become deeply involved in humanitarian work, primarily crusading for the end of genocide in Sudan (namely in Darfur) and Rwanda. CNN.com reported in May 2007 that Cheadle says it was while traveling in Darfur in 2005 and seeing atrocities first-hand that "left him a changed man" and made him reevaluate his privileged life. He not only donates his time and money to these causes, he also coauthored (with John Prendergast) the *New York Times* bestseller, *Not On Our Watch: The Mission to End Genocide in Darfur and Beyond* (2007), which inspired the Not On Our Watch foundation he founded with his *Oceans* costars that, according to the foundations website, is "committed to robust international advocacy and humanitarian assistance" and develops advocacy campaigns that bring attention to international crises.

In 2007 Cheadle was honored with the BET Humanitarian Award for his work for people in Darfur and Rwanda. That same year he and George Clooney received the Summit Peace Award, presented by the Nobel Peace Prize Laureates, for their work in Darfur. Cheadle was extensively involved in the critically praised documentary *Darfur Now* (2007), which sought to bring the Darfur conflict closer to Americans.

5. **GEORGE CLOONEY**

Though it might seem like Clooney has jumped on the refugee bandwagon with his close friend Don Cheadle, Clooney is walking the walk and talking the talk, so to speak. He doesn't just write out big checks, he doesn't use his involvement with this cause to further his star power or to clean up his image. On the contrary, Clooney is using his star power to increase awareness of the issue.

On *Oprah* Clooney acknowledged that he was slow to learn of the crisis in Africa, but when he finally did he wanted to learn first-hand. Accompanied by his father Clooney visited the area in 2006. They documented their experience in the film *A Journey to Darfur,* and all proceeds were donated to the International Rescue Committee. Clooney said that seeing the crisis first hand and the sheer hopelessness of the people was so much worse than reading about it, or even watching it on television. The Sudanese government would not let the Clooneys into Darfur—they won't even let UN officials in—so they had to settle for walking the border between Darfur and Chad (which was experiencing a coup at the time).

Since that trip to Sudan, Clooney has been a vocal advocate for the people of Darfur, trying to make Americans care; he believes that the people must convince the U.S. government to act. In 2008 Clooney was named Messenger of Peace by the UN, a title bestowed on individuals from fields of art, music, literature, and sports, who have agreed to help focus attention on the UN's work. Past recipients include Jane Goodall, Muhammed Ali, Michael Douglas, and Elie Wiesel.

6. **OPRAH WINFREY**

As one of the world's richest and most powerful people, it is nice to see that Winfrey is doing her part to give back. This one-woman industry was worth over $2.7 billion in 2008. And though Winfrey definitely lives the high life, *Business*

Week estimated that as of 2005, her foundations had given over $303 million to charities worldwide. Winfrey's generous giving has landed her at number one on The Giving Back Fund's Most Generous Celebrities list.

Aside from the foundations she's started—The Oprah Winfrey Foundation and Oprah's Angel Network—that give 100 percent of donations to charity (Winfrey foots the company bill), Winfrey gives generously to all those she sees in need. Recently she gave $1.5 million to charities in a New Jersey community and $365,000 to an underfunded school in Atlanta, Georgia. She gave $10 million toward rebuilding after Katrina. The list goes on and on.

Winfrey's most famous work has been in South Africa where she opened the Oprah Winfrey Leadership Academy for Girls to help women become leaders in their communities and have the opportunity to learn in a safe environment. Winfrey initially gave $10 million for the school's development, but ended up contributing $40 million to design the school to her exact specifications. She wanted the best of everything for these girls. While the school did encounter some negative publicity when a worker was accused of abusing the students, it has ultimately been a positive creation, and will likely be far from the last of Oprah's generosity.

7. PAUL NEWMAN

All the profits after taxes from the Newman's Own company—that produces organic foods and beverages—goes to various charities. The company's website touts that so far it has distributed over $280 million to thousands of charities around the world since its inception in 1982.

In 2008 Newman turned over the value of his ownership in the company—about $120 million—to be donated to charity as well. As was his way, Newman made this contribution quietly. It only became public because reporters got wind of it, not because Newman wanted to publicize his generosity. So, when you're browsing the grocery store, remember that purchasing a Newman's Own product is like donating to charity.

8. BONO

Front man of the band U2, Bono is one of the most famous singers in the world and has recently become one of the most famous activists as well. He was nominated for a Nobel Peace Prize for his humanitarian efforts to end the AIDS epidemic, and was named *Time* magazine's Person of the Year alongside Bill and Melinda Gates in 2005. He is involved in numerous campaigns and organizations, and has been since the 1980s, primarily focused on ending world hunger and AIDS in Africa. He participates in numerous concert fundraisers including the popular Live Aid concerts that raise awareness about African poverty. He began the Jubilee 2000 campaign that strives to cancel Third World debt. He started Debt Aids Trade Africa (DATA) in 2002 to work with religious groups on global disease and hunger issues and also established Product Red and the ONE Campaign.

Bono seems to understand that one influential person, one country, is not enough to solve these massive problems; instead, people must work together for there to be any hope of ending hunger and eradicating AIDS. With the hope of bringing together different groups to take action toward a common goal, Bono has met with the late Pope John Paul II, former U.S. President Bill Clinton, members of Congress, and has addressed the United Nations.

9. MICHAEL J. FOX

The Michael J. Fox Foundation was created as a result of actor Michael J. Fox's diagnosis of Parkinson's disease. Fox was diagnosed with Parkinson's in 1991 at the young age of thirty, but did not go public with his diagnosis until 1998. It took him that long to get through the denial and depression he experienced upon learning of his diagnosis.

Fox established the foundation bearing his name in 2000 and is now the largest private source of funds for Parkinson's research in the United States, having raised over $149 million for Parkinson's research. The foundation not only funds research to find a cure but also toward improving therapies for those living with this debilitating disease. Fox has put a face and voice to a disease that affects more than half a million people in the United States alone.

10. CHRISTOPHER REEVE

After the near-fatal horseback riding accident that left Christopher Reeve a quadriplegic, he lent his name and his support to what was then a little-known group called the American Paralysis Association. Originally founded in 1982 to fund research to cure spinal cord injuries and paralysis and to improve the quality of life for patients. According to the Christopher and Dana Reeve Foundation website the foundation has raised over $80 million toward its goal. Even while confined to a wheelchair and breathing with the help of a respirator, Reeve made himself a spokesperson for spinal cord injuries, and a group of people who are typically overlooked. Though Reeve died in 2004 and his wife, Dana, followed less than two years later, the work of the foundation continues.

Aussie Invasion

Australian actors in Hollywood were once marked by Paul Hogan's infamous role as the title character in the *Crocodile Dundee* films. As a result, many Americans thought of Australians as real-life Indiana Joneses. However, Australians are no longer stereotyped in Hollywood, and over the past twenty years there has been an influx of Australians finding fame in America such as the stars on this list. Where are actors Naomi Watts and Mel Gibson who are often associated with their Australian roots you might ask? Well, Gibson did not live in Australia until he was twelve years old, and Naomi Watts didn't move to Australia until she was fourteen.

1. NICOLE KIDMAN

Nicole Kidman is one of Hollywood's most versatile A-list actors who are of Australian heritage. She was actually born in Honolulu, Hawaii, but she and her family returned to her parents' native Australia when Kidman was three years old. She began acting and modeling at a young age, gaining fame throughout her homeland for her role in the classic Aussie holiday film *Bush Christmas* (1983), which led to numerous film roles in Australia. Kidman grabbed Hollywood's attention with her performance in the 1989 film *Dead Calm*, and upon seeing her, A-lister Tom Cruise, insisted that a role be created for Kidman in his upcoming film *Days of Thunder* (1990). Cruise and Kidman got to know each other intimately during filming and made their relationship official when they wed on December 24, 1990. Kidman continued to land acting roles in the U.S., even winning a Golden Globe award for her role in *To Die For* (1995). But for over ten years and while raising two children with him, she was primarily known as Tom Cruise's wife.

It wasn't until the dissolution of their marriage in 2001 that her serious acting and individual celebrity potential was uncovered. In 2001 she was named one of *People* magazine's Most Beautiful People. She landed roles in *Moulin Rouge* (2001), *The Hours* (2002), and *Cold Mountain* (2003), which were all critically praised; Kidman earned an Oscar for her portrayal of Virginia Woolf in *The Hours* and a Golden Globe nomination for her role in *Cold Mountain*. By 2005 she was among the highest paid actresses in Hollywood. She now has the power to pick and choose her roles, which she does, reportedly turning down lead roles in such hit films as *Mr. and Mrs. Smith*, *The Producers*, and *Chicago*. Despite some personal and professional setbacks, this fiery red-haired Aussie has persevered and come out on top. In 2006 she married fellow Australian, and American country singer, Keith Urban, and in 2008 they welcomed a baby girl, Sunday Rose.

2. HUGH JACKMAN

Hugh Jackman has become one of Hollywood's most sought-after leading men. While many can't imagine Hollywood without this seemingly perfect specimen, Jackman has only been in the Hollywood spotlight for ten years.

Born in Sydney, Australia, to English parents, Jackman attended the Western Australian Academy of Performing Arts from 1992 to1994, and upon graduation landed the lead role in the Aussie TV miniseries *Corelli* (1995), where he met his future wife. Jackman found some film work, and also took roles in a string of musicals, such as *Beauty and the Beast* and *Oklahoma*. It was not until 2000 when Jackman was cast in his life- and career-changing role: Wolverine. Because of a scheduling conflict, actor Dougray Scott dropped out of the *X-Men* film; producers replaced him with Jackman. The movie was an overwhelming success, and paved Jackman's way to Hollywood stardom. Offers for roles poured in. Reportedly Jackman had his pick of numerous roles for comic book–based films, but turned them all down. He diversified his resume by appearing in the romantic comedies *Kate and Leopold* (2001), for which he was nominated for a Golden Globe; *Someone Like You* (2001), Woody Allen's *Scoop* (2006), and lending his voice to characters in the children's films *Flushed Away* (2006) and *Happy Feet* (2006). Nonetheless, Jackman remains best known for his action film appeal. He starred in *Van Helsing* (2004) and reprised his role as Wolverine in two *X-Men* sequels, as well as the spin-off film *Wolverine* (2009).

Jackman has also won a Tony Award for his role in the Broadway musical *The Boy From Oz*, has hosted the Tony Awards three times, the Academy Awards in 2008, and was named *People's* Sexiest Man Alive (2008). His friendly personality, great looks, as well as his diverse body of work, make him admired by men and women alike, and his popularity assures that he will remain a Hollywood staple.

3. CATE BLANCHETT

Primarily known for playing characters with British accents, such as Queen Elizabeth I and Galadriel in the *Lord of the Rings* trilogy, Cate Blanchett is often thought to be of British origin. Her residence in England during her rise to stardom in Hollywood, could certainly have contributed to the confusion; Blanchett did not return to live in her native Australia until 2006.

It seems that Blanchett was destined to be an actress, for she achieved success almost immediately in Australia as well as in the U.S. Blanchett graduated from the Australian National Institute of Dramatic Arts in 1992 and began working with the Sydney Theater Company, receiving critical success quickly. She won the 1993 Newcomer Award from the Sydney Theatre Critics Circle and Rosemont Best Actress Award the same year. Along with stage acting, Blanchett also landed television roles. She appeared in her first feature film, *Paradise Road* (1997), alongside Hollywood actresses Glenn Close and Frances McDormand, and instantly caught Hollywood's eye. This led to the critically acclaimed and internationally recognized role as Elizabeth I in the film *Elizabeth* (1998). Blanchett received an Oscar nomination, and her career took off. In the mere ten years Blanchett has been in Hollywood she has garnered five Oscar nominations, winning Best Supporting Actress for her portrayal of Katharine Hepburn in *The Aviator* (2004). An extraordinarily talented actress she will doubtless be pursued by directors and producers for years to come.

4. RUSSELL CROWE

Russell Crowe is known for two traits: his versatility as an actor and his Aussie—not Irish—temper. Though he may scare off some people, his acting talent keeps him working. Crowe was actually born in New Zealand, but his parents moved their family to Australia when Crowe was four. He was a child TV actor, and his big break came in his late twenties when he landed the lead role in the film *Romper Stomper* (1992), bringing him into the spotlight of the Australian film industry.

As for his breakout role in Hollywood, Crowe allegedly has Sharon Stone to thank; Stone saw him in *Romper Stomper* and wanted him in her film *The Quick and the Dead* (1995). She went so far as to delay filming until

Crowe wrapped the movie he was then filming, *The Sum of Us* (1994). *The Quick and the Dead* became Crowe's first Hollywood film and led to films such as *Virtuosity* (1994), *L.A. Confidential* (1997), *Gladiator* (2000), and *A Beautiful Mind* (2001). Reports say that Crowe turned down the role of Wolverine in *X-Men*, which ended up being a big break for fellow Aussie, Hugh Jackman. He has garnered three Oscar nominations and five Golden Globe nominations, winning one of each. Though stories of his hot temper sometimes over-shadow his work, there is no question of Crowe's talent and work will find him for as long as chooses to stay in the game.

5. KEITH URBAN

This country superstar dreamt of Nashville as a child, having been introduced to American country music by his father at an early age. In exchange for free guitar lessons for his son, Urban's father allowed a guitar teacher to place an ad for his services in his store window. Urban instantly took to the guitar, participating in numerous musical and performing extracurricular activities. Australia's EMI branch released Urban's self-titled first album in 1991, which produced nu-merous hits in Australia. As Nashville had always been his dream, Urban set out to try his luck in the world's Country Music Capital in 1992.

Once settled in the country music capital of the world, Urban formed a band, The Ranch, which was quickly signed by Capitol Records. The group's 1997 debut album was well-received, but the band disbanded shortly thereafter and Urban was left earning money playing gigs as a guitarist on albums for such country superstars as Garth Brooks and the Dixie Chicks. While this was a much-coveted opportunity, Urban yearned to see what he could do center stage. Finally, he asked a friend who knew the intricacies of the Nashville music scene to produce Urban's self-titled solo debut album (yes, he has two self-titled albums). The gamble paid off, and the 1999 album went platinum, producing four hit singles, and leading to touring opportunities with such headliners as Faith Hill and Tim McGraw and Dwight Yokum. Urban's second album, *Golden Road* (2002), was even more successful, achieving triple platinum status and producing even more hits.

Urban's blend of rock and country has earned him critical praise—receiving Grammy nominations and winning numerous country music industry awards—and his good looks and relaxed attitude have led to an ever-growing fan base. And of course, his wife is A-list actress Nicole Kidman, which has helped extend Urban's fame to even non–country music fans.

6. HEATH LEDGER

Ledger was committed to acting from an early age, dropping out of high school at age sixteen to pursue his chosen career full time. After appearing on numerous Australian TV shows, including the soap opera *Home and Away* he made his Australian feature film debut in *Blackrock* (1997).

After his initial success down under, Ledger came to the U.S. to try his luck in Hollywood. His first role was in the romantic comedy *10 Things I Hate About You* (1999) costarring Julia Stiles. The movie was a hit with teen girls everywhere and made Ledger an instant teen heartthrob. Offers for roles in romantic comedies poured in, but Ledger was less than thrilled about his prospects. In order to avoid being pigeonholed into one genre, he chose smaller roles in *The Patriot* (2000) and *Monster's Ball* (2001). These roles earned Ledger more attention as a serious and versatile actor and led to his role in the controversial film *Brokeback Mountain* (2005), for which he received a Best Actor Oscar nomination.

Unfortunately in January 2008 Ledger died from an accidental drug overdose, cutting short what was sure to be a long and successful career. Ledger's final complete film was *The Dark Knight* (2008) in which he portrayed the Joker. He won over thirty posthumous awards for his performance, including an Oscar, a Golden Globe, and a SAG award for Best Supporting Actor.

7. TONI COLLETTE

Less well known than many of her fellow Australian actors, Toni Collette is as professionally accomplished as any actor on this list. She could be more famous in the Hollywood circle, but she has maintained ties to the Australian film industry, splitting her screen time equally between Hollywood and Australia.

Collette left school at sixteen and enrolled in a three-year program at Australia's National Institute of Dramatic Arts. She only attended the institute until landing her first film role in *Spotswood* (1992), for which she received a Best Supporting Actress nomination from the Australian Film Institute. She continued to hone her craft in the theater until she won the title role in the film *Muriel's Wedding* (1994). For her performance she won Best Actress from the Australian Film Institute, and Hollywood recognized her with a Golden Globe nomination. Though she didn't head for Hollywood immediately, she eventually made the move. She played a small role in the Hollywood film *The Pallbearer* (1996) and then landed a larger supporting role in the film adaptation of Jane Austen's *Emma* (1996) alongside Gwyneth Paltrow. Her performance in *The Sixth Sense* (1999) earned her an Oscar nomination, and though she had to turn down the title role in the film adaptation of *Bridget Jones's Diary* (2001) due to a Broadway commitment, she has had a successful string of Hollywood films including *About A Boy* (2002), *The Hours* (2002), *In Her Shoes* (2005), and *Little Miss Sunshine* (2006) that will likely continue.

8. JULIAN MCMAHON

Though the surname McMahon is Irish, and his ancestry is Irish, Julian McMahon is Australian. He grew up in a promi- nent Australian household, the son of Australia's Prime Min- ister from 1971 to 1972. As fitting a Prime Minister's son, McMahon attended college and entered law school. Bored in law school he left to pursue modeling and found instant success, landing a nationwide Levi Strauss commercial in Australia. His fame from modeling helped him clinch a role on the Aussie soap opera *Home and Away*. In 1991 he earned a role on the American soap *Another World* where he worked for two years before moving on to TV stardom on *Profiler* (1996–2000), *Charmed* (2000–2003), and *Nip/Tuck* (2003–2010) for which he earned a Golden Globe nomina- tion. McMahon's star rose even higher after costarring in the *Fantastic Four* films in 2005 and 2007.

While he may not be as famous on the big screen as some of the celebrities on this list, he has consistently worked in Hollywood since his arrival and his star power continues to rise.

9. ISLA FISHER

Isla Fisher is an up-and-coming actress of Australian import. Her first mainstream Hollywood role was in the hit comedy film *Wedding Crashers* (2005), for which she won the MTV award for best Breakthrough Performance. Primarily a co- medic actress, she struggled to break out in Hollywood and her persistence is paying off.

Fisher was raised in Australia and began appearing in commercials at age nine. Like her fellow Australian Julian McMahon, she also worked on the Australian soap opera *Home and Away* (1994–1997). She began working in the theater and landed the role of Mary Jane in the *Scooby Doo* (2002) feature film. She won the role without an American agent, but quickly acquired representation and subsequently, further work in Hollywood. Though not all of her films been big box office hits, she's seen success in a number of films, such as *Definitely, Maybe* (2008), *Horton Hears a Who* (2008), and *Confessions of a Shopaholic* (2009), which was her first lead role.

10. MIRANDA KERR

As one of the most famous models in the world, Miranda Kerr has been dubbed "the next MacPherson." She has the look of the hot girl next door, and that has served her well in the modeling industry. At age thirteen Kerr won a modeling competition for the Australian teen magazine *Dolly*, which gave her a taste of the industry. However, she did not continue to pursue modeling until completing high school. Upon graduation she signed with Chic Management in Sydney and was extremely successful in Australia. Her experience gave her the confidence to make the jump to the modeling major league—New York—where she signed with Next model agency. There she worked for numerous labels and magazines, but her career really took off when she landed a campaign for Maybelline cosmetics in 2006. Contracts with Clinique, Arden B, and, most famously, Victoria's Secret soon followed. She is now a Victoria's Secret Angel, one of the company's most visible models (and her relationship with actor Orlando Bloom only increases that visibility). In just a few short years Kerr has managed to become one of the highest-earning models in the world, ranking tenth in 2008. Kerr has started branching out from modeling, launching her own 100 percent organic cosmetic line, Kora, available at David Jones stores and online as of February 2010. The *Sydney Morning Herald* reported on February 16, 2010 that a clothing line and other products are already in the works as well.

Not Lost in Translation

People of Spanish-speaking heritage have been coming to America for decades and giving English-speaking celebrities a run for their money. Not only are the celebrities on this list amazing talents, but their foreign culture and exotic accents enhance their mystique.

1. SHAKIRA

Shakira Isabel Mebarak Ripoll, known throughout the world as simply "Shakira," is the highest-selling Colombian singer and the second most successful female Latin singer, having sold over fifty million albums worldwide.

Growing up with seven half-siblings, Shakira was a natural entertainer. She needed to find a way to receive attention in such a large family. She began writing songs at age eight and signed her first record contract at age thirteen. However, success did not come overnight for Shakira, which may be part of what keeps her grounded in the midst of her current fame. Her first two albums sold approximately one thousand copies each. Her third album, *Pies Descaleos* (Barefeet) was released in 1995 and was a departure from the pop genre and had a more rock sound, which she said was heavily influenced by Nirvana, Aerosmith, and Tom Petty. The change paid off and *Pies Descaleos* has sold over five million copies worldwide according to Shakira's official website. This success catapulted her into the spotlight in the Spanish-speaking world. *Dónde están los ladrones?* (Where Are the Thieves?) (1998), her fourth album, even sold over a million copies in the United States.

However, to achieve success in America, Shakira picked up and moved to Miami where she taught herself to write songs in English. Relocation turned out to have been a wise choice, and in 2001 Shakira released her first English-language album, *Laundry Service*, which rose to number three on the U.S. charts and sold more than twenty million copies worldwide. She released two more albums—one in Spanish and one in English—in 2005, and another in 2009, furthering her success. Only in her early thirties, Shakira has won two Grammys and seven Latin Grammys and this talented singer, songwriter, and dancer will likely remain a worldwide presence for many years to come.

2. RICKY MARTIN

Ricky Martin became famous in America with his smash hit "Livin' La Vida Loca" (1999) that took radio stations by storm. But Martin was no newbie to fame and success, already having established his singing career in the Spanish-speaking world. Originally from Puerto Rico, Martin rose to fame when as a member of the boy band Menudo. He toured with this group until he was eighteen—the group's age limit. From there he went to New York to attempt a solo singing career, while simultaneously pursuing acting. He landed roles on stage, as well as on the Spanish soap opera *Alcanzar una Estrella*, and the American soap opera *General Hospital*. He released two solo albums during this time, which made him a well-known solo singer in the Spanish world. He skyrocketed to fame when his song "The Cup of Life" was chosen as the theme song for the 1998 World Cup. The song hit number one in sixty countries. However, he did not break into the U.S. market until the single "Livin' La Vida Loca" off his first English album in 1999 debuted at number one. Martin has continued to release Spanish and English albums, with a new English album slated for release in 2010, and though other songs have been moderate hits in the United States, none have become the craze that was "Livin' La Vida Loca."

3. ANTONIO BANDERAS

Antonio Banderas doesn't just have the looks and the moves on-screen that make women swoon, but he is also a political activist and a former soccer player. Initially, Banderas dreamed of becoming a professional soccer player, but when he broke his foot at age fourteen that dream was shattered. As an alternative he became involved in theater, eventually performing with a traveling theater troupe that was arrested numerous times for their performance of banned plays; they refused to give in to government censorship.

Banderas's initial break came when director Pedro Almodovar noticed Banderas on stage and cast him in *Laberinto des Pasiones* (1982). This film led to further collaboration between the two, eventually landing Banderas in Almodovar's Academy-Award nominated film *Mujeres al borde de un ataque de nervios* (Women on the Verge of a Nervous Breakdown) in 1988. Banderas's Hollywood debut came with a role in *The Mambo Kings* (1992) and because Banderas did not speak English he learned his lines phonetically. However, his big Hollywood break came the following year when he played Tom Hanks's lover in *Philadelphia*. Since then Banderas's most recognized performance has been as Zorro, though he has appeared in many other films, including the *Shrek* movies as the inimitable voice of Puss in Boots. Slowly but surely Banderas has become a Hollywood fixture.

4. JAVIER BARDEM

Coming from a long line of Spanish actors, Javier Bardem jumped into the family business at an early age, acting in his first role at age six, and he never looked back. In 2000 Bardem received international recognition for his performance in *Before Night Falls*, which earned him a place in Oscar history as the the first Spanish actor to be nominated for an Academy Award (Best Actor). In 2008 he achieved another Oscar milestone when he won the Academy Award for Best Supporting Actor for *No Country for Old Men* (2007). Bardem takes his craft quite seriously and has no desire to be typecast as a heartthrob. To that end, he has turned down roles in blockbuster films such as the James Bond film *The World Is Not Enough* in favor of more challenging, independent roles.

5. PENÉLOPE CRUZ

Penélope Cruz also hails from Spain. Though Bardem was the first Spanish actor to win an Academy Award, in 2009 Cruz joined Bardem in making Academy history as the first Spanish female to win an Oscar—coincidentally in a film in which she costarred alongside Bardem—Woody Allen's *Vicky Cristina Barcelona* (2008).

Cruz got her start in the entertainment industry as a dancer in Spanish music videos and then as a Spanish TV host. She even acted in the erotic TV series *Secie Rose.* (How many of you are now putting this book down and trying to find episodes on the Internet?) In 1992 Cruz made her film debut in *Jamón jamón* for which she received international recognition and offers for more roles that further elevated her status her within the Spanish film industry.

At twenty-five Cruz made the leap across the pond to try her luck in Hollywood. She immediately won a role in *All the Pretty Horses* (2000) and then director Cameron Crowe who noticed her performance in the hit Spanish film, *Abre los Ojos* (1997), immediately cast her in his English remake of the film, *Vanilla Sky* (2001). In this film she acted alongside A-lister Tom Cruise, who also became her first public Hollywood romance, garnering a lot press and headlines for this previously little-known actress. Cruz took roles in more mainstream Hollywood films, such as *Captain Corelli's Mandolin* (2001) and *Sahara* (2005) where she hooked up with her second A-list hunk, Matthew McConaughey—all of which added to her Hollywood celebrity profile. With her feet firmly planted in Hollywood, Cruz has recently returned to acting in films outside the mainstream such as *Bandidas* (2006), *Volver* (2006), and *Vicky Cristina Barcelona* (2008).

6. ANDY GARCIA

Andy Garcia was only five when his family fled their native land of Cuba for Miami, hightailing it out of there as Castro came to power. Disinterested in college after only a year, Garcia moved to Los Angeles to try his hand at acting. As is typical of many aspiring actors, Garcia worked as a waiter while waiting for his big break. What was atypical in Garcia's case is that his big break actually came. Garcia landed a role in the film *The Mean Season* (1985) opposite Kurt Russell and his career took off. He was chosen over such seasoned actors as Val Kilmer, Alec Baldwin, and Charlie Sheen for the role of Vincent Mancini in *The Godfather: Part III* (1990), which also earned him an Oscar nomination. He is known to be fiercely guarded about his privacy and personal life, and has never had any desire to be part of the Hollywood scene. Garcia has continued to be very much in demand, and has been known to turn down roles because he refuses to participate in a project he does not believe in. His ability to stick to his principles has made him one of the most respected actors in the entertainment industry.

7. **CARLOS SANTANA**

Carlos Santana hails from Mexico, but in 1961, at the age of fourteen, his family relocated to San Francisco. Though Santana had grown up around music, this move had a major impact on how his music was influenced, as well as his future career in the music industry. His music was obviously heavily influenced by Latin music, but also rock, jazz, and blues, making his sound unique.

In 1966 Santana formed the Santana Blues Band with two street performers. The band achieved instant popularity when it performed at Woodstock in 1969. This performance also landed them a record deal with Columbia Records. Ironically, Santana says he does not remember the performance because he was under the influence of LSD. The band's second album went to number one and sold over four million copies worldwide.

The band's heyday seemed to be in the 1960s and 1970s, but they made a resurgence in the 1990s when they began collaborating with young, popular artists of that era. Their 1999 album *Supernatural* that featured collaborations with Dave Matthews, Wyclef Jean, and many others sold over twenty-five million copies worldwide and won nine Grammy Awards. It was a clear demonstration that Santana's inimitable sound and style still appeal to modern audiences, with only a little updating.

8. **GLORIA ESTEFAN**

Gloria Estefan is another Cuban who immigrated to Miami upon the rise of Fidel Castro. Estefan said she originally got into music as an escape from the hardship of her family life after her father returned from Vietnam and was diagnosed with multiple sclerosis. However, music did not become a career until she met her future husband who was looking for a lead singer for his band. Upon hearing Estefan sing he asked her if she was interested. With Estefan singing, the group soon landed a record deal, which led to four Spanish language albums and much success throughout the Spanish-speaking world. Their first album with songs in English was *Eyes of Innocence* (1984) and from it came the singles "Dr. Beat" and "I Need Your Love" hit the Billboard charts. The follow-up album, *Primitive Love* (1985), was even more successful charting even more singles.

Estefan had been the primary draw for many years, and in 1989 she began being billed as a solo artist, though the band still backs her up. In 1990 Estefan's tour bus crashed and she suffered a broken vertebrae. After extensive rehabilitation she returned to the stage ten months later for a year-long world tour, which was followed by the release of four albums in four years. Estefan continues to perform and produce hits in both Spanish and English.

9. SALMA HAYEK

Actress, producer, and director Salma Hayek grew up in a prosperous Mexican family. At the age of five she decided she wanted to become an actress after seeing the film *Willy Wonka and the Chocolate Factory*. However, acting did not become a serious passion until she dropped out of college to pursue it. She quickly landed the lead role in the Spanish soap opera *Teresa* (1989), which made her a celebrity in Mexico. However, in 1991 she quit the soap and left Mexico to try her luck in L.A. Unfortunately success was not instantaneous the second time around.

Her break was sheer luck, for director Robert Rodriguez saw her on a late night Spanish talk show, liked her spirited nature, and decided to cast her in his upcoming film *Desperado* (1995) opposite Antonio Banderas. The film was a hit and got her attention in Hollywood. Hayek continued to play roles in both funny and serious films and has built an impressive resume and achieved critical acclaim as an actress and producer. Her relationship with Robert Rodriguez and his family has grown as well, for not only has she appeared in more of his films but she is also godmother to his children.

10. ENRIQUE IGLESIAS

Now known primarily for his secretive romance with tennis hottie Anna Kournikova, Latin heartthrob Enrique Iglesias is actually a very successful artist worldwide. Son of Spanish singing sensation Julio Iglesias, who sold over three hundred million copies of his seventy-seven albums, Enrique had a lot to live up to. Born in Madrid, Spain, the Iglesias family moved to Miami when Enrique was eight. He was very secretive about his desire to pursue music and insisted on auditioning for a record contract under the name Enrique Martinez, not wanting to tread on his father's success. Enrique landed a contract with a small label, thus proving to himself that he was talented. However, his albums were released under his real name.

Enrique's first two albums were in Spanish and made him known throughout the Spanish-speaking world. It wasn't until the single "Rhythm Divine" off his third album that he broke into the English market. His fourth album contained the smash hit "Hero" that made him a star in America. So far, Iglesias has sold forty-five million copies worldwide, has achieved two number one hits on the Billboard Hot 100 chart, and a record nineteen number one singles on the Billboard Hot Latin Tracks chart. Though Iglesias is not very visible on the American music scene today, he continues to release music in both English and Spanish and tour around the world.

A Mind Is A Terrible Thing to Waste

Think you know which celebrities are the most educated? Then the list below might just surprise you. Some celebrities you'd think were college educated didn't even finish high school while others have significant academic achievements.

1. QUENTIN TARANTINO

Tarantino is famous for his innovative directing style. He has received wide critical praise for his films including *Reservoir Dogs* (1992), *Pulp Fiction* (1994), and *Kill Bill Vols. 1 and 2* (2003 and 2004). However, unlike most directors these days he did not cultivate his directorial skills in school. At fifteen Tarantino dropped out of high school and earned his film education by watching movies while working at a video store in Manhattan Beach, California. It was at this time that he began writing screenplays.

2. TOMMY LEE JONES

Though this native Texan often plays "tough guy" characters, he is an Ivy League graduate. Jones graduated cum laude from Harvard University with a B.A. in English. While there he was good friends and roommates with future vice president Al Gore. An interesting aside here: Erich Segal, author of the book-turned-movie *Love Story* (starring Ryan O'Neal and Ali MacGraw) claims that O'Neal's character Oliver Barrett IV, was based on *both* Jones and Gore.

3. GENE SIMMONS
Simmons earned an education degree from Richmond College on New York City's Staten Island. He even taught in the city before his music career took off. While teaching and working various other jobs, he performed with numerous bands around the city. How cool would it be to be able to claim one of your teachers was the guy with the long tongue from KISS?

4. WEIRD AL YANKOVIC
Musician Alfred Matthew Yankovic, aka Weird Al, is known for his song parodies and accordion accompaniment. Yankovic graduated from high school as valedictorian at only sixteen. He continued on to college and earned a degree in architecture from California Polytechnic State University in San Luis Obispo. Realizing that architecture was not the best career fit for him, he transformed musical interests into a career. Throughout high school and college Yankovic had written song parodies—some of which were even played on the radio—and in fact developed a small cult following. Not long after graduation he signed a record deal and never looked back.

5. HUGH HEFNER
Known as the founder of the *Playboy* empire (as well as for his revolving door of girlfriends living in his mansion) Hefner took the time to educate himself before pursuing his dream of being the most famous playboy in America. He earned a degree in psychology from the University of Illinois, Urbana-

Champaign in less than three years. It seems he wasted no time partying his way through school knowing that more exciting adventures awaited him.

6. HILARY SWANK

Hilary Swank is a two-time Oscar-winning actress. She plays no-nonsense roles, and appears to be incredibly level-headed and serious. She must have a wild side too, since she dropped out of high school. When asked why she dropped out, Swank explained that she didn't like the rules and was often chastised for excessive talking. She does not advocate dropping out of school, however while promoting the movie *Freedom Writers* in which she plays a teacher she said that she believes education is important and would encourage her own children to complete school.

7. NICOLE KIDMAN

Nicole Kidman also comes across as someone who plays by the book, but like Swank, Kidman dropped out of high school at sixteen to pursue acting full-time. It seems that under her polite and mild-mannered façade lies a bit of a gambler. No question her bet has certainly paid off!

8. SACHA BARON COHEN

Funnyman Sacha Baron Cohen, known for creating such extreme characters as Ali G and Borat, has a serious side as well. This British comedian attended England's prestigious Cambridge University earning a degree in history.

9. HALLE BERRY

Halle Berry is one of the most respected actresses in Holly-wood, but for all her eloquence, there's no high-dollar educa-tion to thank. Berry attended Cuyahoga Community College in Michigan, and received a two-year degree in Broadcast Journalism. These days, young Hollywood upstarts shoot for

Sacha Baron Cohen not skipping a beat as Borat. *Michael Bulcik/SKS Soft GmbH Düsseldorf*

Ivy League colleges, but Berry shows that you do not need a fancy college degree to be intelligent.

10. MATTHEW MCCONAUGHEY

Though he exudes a more outdoorsman than collegian image, McConaughey earned a film degree from the University of Texas at Austin. Being an actor, he was certainly interested in film, so the degree may not have been a big stretch for him.

TMI (Too Much Information)

A sex tape can be as rejuvenating for a celebrity's lacklus-
ter career as a reality television show can. The typical
celebrity sex tape (though not for all on this list) features
a wannabe or has-been celebrity, generates a good deal of
media attention, and can often lead to money—either in the
form of revenue from tape sales or from legal reparations.
Few celebrities admit to leaking the videos, but it makes
one wonder, especially when their celebrity status soars
afterwards.

1. PAMELA ANDERSON
Pamela Anderson is a celebrity sex tape pioneer, being
among the first celebrities to have such a video that went
public. Furthermore, she has not one but *two* public sex
tapes. The first tape that went public was made on her honeymoon with Tommy Lee, and was allegedly stolen from
their home. The couple sued the distribution company, Internet Entertainment Group, and received $1.5 million plus
attorney fees as compensation. The company continued to
sell the video, and it continues to be one of the most popular
celebrity sex tapes.

Anderson's second sex tape was uncovered after the first,

but takes place before her 1995 marriage to Lee. This video costars Poison front man Bret Michaels. Though a video clip was available over the Internet for a short time, and *Penthouse* magazine featured frames of the video in its March 1998 issue, Michaels and Anderson have continued to work to block the film from distribution. They won an injunction, but continue to fight distribution companies that crop up. Michaels's adamant stance against this tape's distribution leads to speculation about what exactly is on this tape. Michaels, now the star of the reality show *Bret Michaels Rock of Love*—where Michaels frequently hooks up with contestants—isn't exactly the model of sexual discretion.

2. **PARIS HILTON**

Though Pam Anderson was the original sex tape queen, Paris Hilton forged a new path through her sex tape scandal: *becoming* a celebrity *because of* a sex tape. Prior to the release of her sex tape, *1 Night in Paris* in 2003, Hilton was merely an heiress, indistinguishable from other wealthy American girls. However, the release of her sex tape right before the debut of her reality show *The Simple Life* gave Hilton media attention she had never previously attracted.

Rick Salomon, the "costar" of the video, was the party that released the tape, while Hilton was reportedly upset over its distribution. Each sued the other: he for defamation of character and she over the tape's release. The parties settled out of court. Hilton received $400,000, her percent of the profits, and the video can still be legally purchased. However, Hilton said she has never actually seen the money owed her for the tape. The tragedy of it all, Hilton says, is that upon the release of the video she knew she would never be able to follow in Princess Diana's footsteps. Were they ever even on the same path?

3. ROB LOWE
Rob Lowe's 1988 sex tape was one of the earliest public celebrity sex tapes. On that singular sex tape were two separate incidents. One included Lowe as part of a threesome in a Parisian hotel with a female model and another man. The other incident on the tape was the headline grabber. It featured Lowe with two girls, one of whom was underage. The story goes that when Lowe was in Atlanta for the 1988 Democratic National Convention he made a slight judgment error when he picked up two girls at a club and took them back to his hotel. They proceeded to have an entertaining evening, even filming the events. Lowe was unaware that one of the girls was underage, since she had used a fake ID to get into the club. A lawsuit ensued, and was subsequently settled out of court. Shortly thereafter Lowe checked himself into rehab for addictions to alcohol and sex. It may also have been an effort to breathe life back into his career, which took a nosedive after his sex tape controversy.

4. KIM KARDASHIAN
Kim Kardashian is another socialite whose sex tape, *Kim K Superstar*, popped up on the Internet. Kardashian's film partner was then-boyfriend Ray J, better known as the brother of R&B singer Brandy. He has since gone on to star in his own Vh1 reality show *For the Love of Ray J*. In 2007 *Page Six* reported that a Kardashian/Ray J sex tape was sold to Vivid Entertainment for one million dollars.

Two weeks later, Kardashian filed a lawsuit against the distribution company on the basis that the film was sold without her permission or consent. She demanded damages, court costs, and all profits from the sale. Initially, the film's distribution was temporarily halted. Ultimately, the case was settled out of court and Kardashian was richly compensated, receiving a reported five million dollars in return for consenting to the tape's distribution.

5. DUSTIN DIAMOND

Best known for his role as Screech on *Saved by the Bell*, Dustin Diamond cashed in on his 1990s fame by filming, narrating, and selling a sex tape entitled *Screeched*. The "film" tells a lovely story of two girls from a bachelorette party who accompany Diamond back to his hotel room for a night of fun. Celebrity news source TMZ called the tape "unique and entertaining," though other reviews were not as glowing, referring to the point-of-view style of filming as "poor" but with "realistic" dialogue. Realistic? Really?

6. VERNE TROYER

Actor Verne Troyer is best known for his role as Mini-Me in the Austin Powers films. In 2008 a video of Troyer having sex with his then-girlfriend was leaked onto the Internet. E! Online reported that TMZ posted part of the video and was subsequently sued by Troyer, along with two porn distributors, for twenty million dollars. His reasoning for the hefty suit, as well as his request to halt all sales of the video, was that "he [would] suffer irreparable harm to his reputation."

Troyer's request was granted and he received a temporary injunction against distribution without his consent. So who leaked the video? Initially news sources speculated that Troyer had leaked the video for monetary gain, but his ex-girlfriend eventually admitted that she leaked the tape. Troyer continued his lawsuit spree by filing a twenty million dollar lawsuit against her citing abuse.

7. COLIN FARRELL

In 2005 the story broke that a fifteen minute sex tape existed featuring Hollywood's resident bad boy Colin Farrell and *Playboy* Playmate Nicole Narain. The tape was allegedly two years old, and Farrell filed a suit against Narain who had made the film public. MTV.com reported that Farrell alleged that she had promised the video would remain private and he was suing for damages, for an injunction prohibiting the sale and distribution of the video, and for a temporary restraining order. His request was approved and the video only briefly appeared online before the website was shut down. Farrell settled with Narain out of court.

8. FRED DURST

Front man for the band Limp Bizkit, Fred Durst's heyday was in the late 1990s and early 2000s when he was linked to such starlets as Britney Spears, Christina Aguilera, and Paris Hilton. By 2005 Durst was out of the media spotlight when a sex tape featuring him was leaked. He blamed it on fall-out from a massive T-Mobile hack, implying that the video had been shot on his cell phone, which sounded suspect. Apparently it wasn't illegal for the video to be available on the Internet, but when Gawker.com "hosted" the video Durst sued for eighty million dollars. Nothing came of the suit. Durst actually ended up apologizing to the website, sending them flowers, and fading back into obscurity.

9. KATE MOSS

The Kate Moss/Pete Doherty sex tape is probably best left to the imagination. Though Kate Moss might be pleasant to look at, the same can't necessarily be said for her pasty, drugged-out, former boyfriend Pete Doherty. The *New York Post* reported that Doherty contacted British ITVZ network to shop an idea for a television show where he would tell all about his relationship with Moss, and allow them to use the home videos as well. Allegedly the network considered paying one million dollars for the show. These videos were never released, but London's *The Sun* reported that an upset Moss had gone so far as to contact lawyers to keep the couples home videos at home. Some reports state that Moss even destroyed the tapes to keep them from being made public.

10. BRITNEY SPEARS

There are two alleged sex tapes starring Britney Spears. The first made the news in 2006 when reports surfaced that Spears's then-husband Keving Federline had a sex tape of himself and Britney and was using it as leverage in their divorce. Federline's attorney maintain that these reports were false.

One-time paparazzo turned Spears's boyfriend Adnan Ghalib is the alleged owner of the second Spears sex tape. The video allegedly runs two hours long, takes place in Mexico, and features a pink-wigged Spears. In 2008 Ghalib told *Heat* magazine, "There is such a tape. But I won't discuss prices for hypothetical inquiries." This guy is holding out for big bucks.

Mental Meltdowns

The celebrities on this list are proof positive that sometimes it isn't easy being in the spotlight 24/7. The pressure to look perfect, act charming, and stay at the top of their craft becomes overwhelming for some, causing them to crack. These unfortunate celebrities cracked in public, altering their career and greatly influencing the public's opinion of them. Some have managed to overcome this setback, while others seem as if they will be branded by it for life.

1. DAVE CHAPPELLE

Dave Chappelle became famous for his comedy show *The Chappelle Show* that premiered on Comedy Central in 2003. His career took a giant leap when he signed a fifty million dollar contract with Comedy Central prior to the show's third season. One day, during taping, Chappelle walked off the stage and never returned. He left the country immediately and flew to South Africa. Rumors abounded that Chappelle had checked himself into a rehab clinic in South Africa, but in an interview with *Time* magazine two weeks after his disappearance, Chappelle insisted that he went to South Africa to "find a quiet place." He also specified that was staying with a friend, not in a rehab clinic. Chappelle explained his actions by stating that he had become overwhelmed by feelings of responsibility for his work and "[he] felt like [he] was really pressured to settle for something [he] didn't necessarily feel like [he] wanted."

When Chappelle returned to the U.S., he moved away from the Hollywood limelight and currently lives on a sixty-five acre farm in Ohio. He continues to perform stand-up comedy, but has realized that money does not equal happiness.

2. ALEC BALDWIN

It's no secret that Alec Baldwin and Kim Basinger's divorce included a nasty custody battle over their daughter, Ireland. But their family issues came under intense media scrutiny when TMZ released a recording of a voicemail message Baldwin left on his daughter's phone in April 2007, which painted him as anything but Father of the Year. The contents of the voicemail included Baldwin calling Ireland a rude, thoughtless pig; threatening to fly from New York to Los Angeles to straighten her ass out; as well as calling her mother a thoughtless pain in the ass. The public was outraged, and Baldwin's blaming the leak on Basinger and insisting that obviously he was really mad at someone else (probably Basinger) did not help his image. To return to the public's good graces, Baldwin issued a public apology explaining that he was "driven to the edge by parental alienation for many years." Nonetheless, Baldwin's visitation rights were temporarily suspended.

However, there does not seem to be any permanent damage, for father and daughter have been spotted together around Los Angeles in the years following the event. In an interview for the July/August 2009 issue of *Playboy* Baldwin admitted that he considered suicide after the rant was leaked, but said it was his ex-wife who convinced him to live. No, it wasn't a thawing of their feud, but the thought that if he killed himself Basinger would have "won."

In February 2010, Alec and Ireland were back in the news again. This time, according to the February 12, 2010 edition of the *Daily Mail*, Alec and Ireland had argued and he threatened to take some pills. Ireland called 911 and he was taken to the hospital where he was quickly released. What actually happened is unclear however and Baldwin's representatives claim that it was all a misunderstanding on "one person's" part—presumably meaning Ireland or Basinger.

3. WINONA RYDER
Winona Ryder looks doe-eyed and innocent, so it surprised everyone when she was arrested in December 2001 for shoplifting five thousand dollars of clothes from Saks Fifth Avenue in Beverly Hills. What made this A-list actress steal? In a 2007 interview with *Vogue* magazine Ryder blamed her indiscretion on an addiction to painkillers she obtained from a "quack" doctor she'd visited for a broken arm. She explained that the pills left her in a state of confusion, and further stated that she never touched the pills after the incident. However, in court her defense lawyer claimed that Ryder "did it to prep for a film role." The judge sentenced her to 480 hours of community service and three years probation.

After her arrest, Ryder took a break from acting, moving to San Francisco to be near her parents and live under the radar for a while. She returned to the big screen in *A Scanner Darkly* (2006), and has continued to work regularly. Ryder now buys her clothes.

4. MEL GIBSON
Mel Gibson's meltdown took place on the side of the road and with the help of copious amounts of alcohol. In July 2006 Gibson was pulled over under suspicion of drunk driving. He

made anti-Semitic and sexist remarks, claiming that Jews are responsible for all the wars in the world, and calling a female officer "sugar tits." Gibson was arrested, and TMZ reported that his antics continued even at the police station.

Gibson quickly issued an apology stating that he "said things [he does not] wish to be true and are despicable." He also checked into rehab, opting for an outpatient recovery program, to deal with this alcoholism relapse. Though Gibson seems to have remained sober over the past few years, he has not jumped back into Hollywood's good graces. Once an in-demand actor, Gibson has worked little since this incident. He is, however, slated to star in the 2010 film *Edge of Darkness*, which will indicate whether Hollywood, and audiences, can forgive and forget.

5. MICHAEL RICHARDS

Everybody loved crazy Kramer on *Seinfeld*, but Michael Richards, the man who played Kramer, saw how quickly one's popularity could plummet. Richards was performing stand-up at The Laugh Factory in West Hollywood, a seemingly routine occurrence. However, that night there were some audience members heckling him, and Richards lost his temper, going on what was interpreted as a racist rant. And it didn't go on for a few seconds. He continued his offensive tirade for minutes while most of the audience stood up and left.

There was immediate backlash over the remarks and Richards quickly began damage control. He apologized via satellite on Letterman's *Late Show*, explaining that his remarks were fueled by anger not racism. However, that explanation only led to more debate. Richards continued to try to repair his image by calling Al Sharpton and Jesse Jackson, even appearing on Jackson's radio show. However, in July 2007 Richards announced that he was retiring from stand-up comedy, and he has continued to stay out of the limelight. Most people agree that it will take a long time for this impromptu outburst to blow over.

6. ANNE HECHE

Anne Heche has always been a little eccentric, but she went from eccentric to downright crazy on August 19, 2001, (allegedly the day after she and Ellen Degeneres split) when she appeared on the doorstep of a home in Fresno, California, saying that her car had broken down. She then asked to take a shower, and made herself right at home in the strangers' living room. The residents were rightfully concerned and called the police. When the police arrived Heche declared that she was God, and said she would take everyone to heaven in her spaceship.

In her aptly titled autobiography, *Call Me Crazy*, published later the same year, Heche explains that the incident was a result of mental illness fueled by ecstasy and stemming from child abuse she endured at the hands of her father. Heche told *People* magazine that the incident snapped her out of her fantasy world and led her back to the path of sanity.

Though this is definitely Heche's wackiest incident, she remains eccentric . . . to say the least.

7. WHITNEY HOUSTON

Vocal powerhouse Whitney Houston seemed to have the world at her fingertips. Throughout the 1980s and 1990s she sold over 140 million albums, making her the fourth best-selling female artist in the United States. However, as the 1990s drew to a close, people began to notice a change in Houston. She was late for interviews and rehearsals and canceled concerts and talk-show appearances. However, in spite of her behavior, Houston signed a one hundred million dollar record contract with Arista records—the biggest record deal in history.

During a now-infamous interview with Diane Sawyer, Houston's odd behavior surfaced when Sawyer squarely asked about Houston's recent conduct. "Is it alcohol? Is it Marijuana? Is it cocaine? Is it pills?" Houston replied that it had been all these substances at various times, but was adamant that she never used crack, yelling, "Crack is whack!" This outburst, as well as her admitted drug use, confirmed many people's suspicions about Houston's personal battles.

Though Houston released an album in 2002 and a Christmas album in 2003, they were not as successful as her earlier albums. Afterwards, she receded from the spotlight, making appearances only rarely, which did not go far to promote her sanity. Now Houston is poised to make a comeback. She's reportedly clean, sober, and single, with a new album that released in late 2009. Hopefully she will return to the level of greatness of which her fans know she is capable.

8. BRITNEY SPEARS

Probably the most famous meltdown of recent years is that of Pop Princess, Britney Spears. She seemed a bit crazy to rush into marriage to backup dancer Kevin Federline and then have two children within two years of marriage, but her mental status seemed to be improving when she filed for divorce from Federline.

However, after her split with Federline she spiraled out of control. In November 2006 she was seen partying (sans panties) with socialite Paris Hilton. Not a great sign, but not necessarily an insane action for a newly single celebrity gal. On February 16, 2007, she was officially labeled as "crazy" when she went to a salon and had her head shaved. According to a February 2007 issue of *Us Weekly*, Spears went to a tattoo parlor immediately after her . . . haircut and when an employee at the tattoo parlor asked her why she shaved her head Spears responded, "I don't want anyone touching me. I'm tired of everyone touching me." It's not exactly clear how the two are connected but, what is clear is that Spears was having a difficult time dealing with her life in the spotlight.

Spears spent the rest of February and March in and out of rehab, but treatment did not improve her mental health. Her erratic behavior continued during photo shoots, performances, and even while driving, which ultimately led her to lose custody of her children. The pinnacle of her mental meltdown came on January 3, 2008, when police were called to her home in Beverly Hills because Spears refused to hand over her children as required by the custody arrangement. She reportedly barricaded herself in a bathroom with her youngest son Jayden. Once she emerged, she was taken to Cedars-Sinai hospital and underwent two days of psychological evaluation. *People* magazine was told by sources very close to the Spears family that they speculate that Spears suffers from bipolar disorder. *Newsweek* also discussed the possibility that Spears is bipolar on its website in January 2008, but this diagnosis has not been confirmed. After her release, a judge appointed her father conservator of her estate, a position he continues to hold. This move has gotten Spears back on track, being a responsible mother, even making home-cooked meals for her boys!

9. CHRISTIAN SLATER

Christian Slater was a teen heartthrob in the late 1980s and early 1990s, playing bad boy roles that made girls swoon. He is also no stranger to run-ins with the law, having been arrested in 1989, charged with evading police, driving under the influence, assault, and driving on a suspended license; and again in 1994, charged with criminal possession of a weapon while trying to board a commercial airplane with a 9mm pistol. However, his previous arrests do not compare to the incident that took place at a party in August 1997 when Slater punched a woman (whether she was his then-girlfriend or an ex-girlfriend is unclear), bit a friend in the stomach, and attempted to take a gun from a police officer. Slater was eventually subdued by police and charged with battery, resisting arrest, and drug offenses. According to the January 23, 1999, issue of the *Guardian* his initial police statement was, "The Germans are all coming. And they will kill us." Slater claims he has no memory of the incident, which is quite possible, for tests showed the presence of cocaine, tequila, and vodka in his system, and a blood alcohol level of .24, which is three times the legal limit.

Slater spent over one hundred days in rehab before serving fifty-nine days in jail, followed by another ninety days in rehab. He stayed out of trouble for some time following his meltdown, and focused on rebuilding his once-envious career. But in 2005 he was arrested again, this time for allegedly harassing a woman on the street while intoxicated. Despite this setback, Slater continues to work in Hollywood, though he has never reclaimed the A-list status he enjoyed early in his career. Slater was once quoted as saying, "Work is my hobby, staying sober is my job." Hopefully if his hobby is a little neglected, that means he's succeeding at his job.

10. MARIAH CAREY

Mariah Carey's red-hot career hit a snag in 2001 while promoting her film debut *Glitter* and its accompanying soundtrack. Carey had been going at full-steam for over ten years, so it is no shock that such a fast-paced life finally took its toll on her. What was unfortunate was that it was that it all caught up with her in public. Rumors ran rampant concerning Carey's questionable mental health after an appearance on MTV's *Total Request Live* on July 21, 2001. First, while handing out popsicles to the audience she began a strip tease. Then she gave an odd interview to host Carson Daly when she said, "I just want one day off where I can go swimming and eat ice cream and look at rainbows." The final straw was when she followed up the TV appearance by writing on her website, "I just can't trust anybody anymore right now because I don't understand what's going on. . . . I'm desperately trying to get out of this room. . . . I'm gonna take like a minute off. . . . Nothing's wrong." These turned out to be famous last words, before Carey was hospitalized on July 25, and then again on September 4. There was speculation that she attempted suicide, but in an interview with *Marie Claire* magazine for their March 2006 issue, Carey insisted it was a physical breakdown due to extreme exhaustion. She just needed a break to take care of herself, something she had neglected to do for a long time.

It seems like Carey's breakdown really has been a break-*through*, as she calls it. After a few years out of the public eye, Carey returned with her album *The Emancipation of Mimi*, and Carey returned to her former glory, where she remains.

"It" Destinations

We all see the pictures of celebrities frolicking on beaches and sailing the ocean blue. But details such as where exactly celebrities vacation and if "regular people" can afford to vacation there too are usually left out. This chapter explores some of the most frequented and most exclusive celebrity vacation spots—and yes, they will make the vacations we take look paltry in comparison.

1. MEXICO

Mexico is one of the most frequented celebrity vacation spots, namely because of it's proximity to Los Angeles. There are numerous vacation spots in Mexico, and they range from ultra exclusive to more accessible.

One of the most exclusive vacation spots in Mexico is the Cuixmala resort, which is situated on a 32,000-acre nature reserve. There is a wildlife sanctuary on the grounds and 12,000 kinds of plants, birds, and animals (including pumas and jaguars). Celebrities such as Madonna and Mick Jagger have vacationed here, most likely in one of the luxury private villas, which can be rented for upwards of $16,000 per night. However, the more budget-friendly choice would be to stay in one of the resort's *casitas*, which can be rented for as little as $400 per night during the off-season.

Another popular celebrity spot in Mexico is the Four Seasons Resort Punta Mita, located near Puerto Vallarta. All the typical resort amenities can be found here, such as a spa and golf course, but unlike many resorts you can also rent a yacht by the day. Rooms start at $625 and all are *casitas* ranging from one to five bedrooms. Starting at approximately $5000, you can have a private residence.

Cabo San Lucas is the most-visited Mexican vacation spot among celebrities, for its close proximity to L.A. and its young and hip atmosphere. Numerous celebrities have been spotted here, such as Eva Longoria-Parker and Jessica Simpson. In another generation, Ernest Hemingway and John Wayne frequented this Mexican destination. Oliver Hudson, Kate Hudson's brother, married at the One & Only Palmilla Resort, which is one of the highest-rated resorts in Cabo. Room rates run from $500 to $9,000 dollars a night, and each of the 172 rooms offers privacy and an unobstructed view of the ocean. A 24-hour personal butler service is on hand to fulfill your every request and each room has a telescope for star or ocean gazing. With fabulous resorts like these it's no wonder celebrities take advantage of our Mexican neighbor for quick sun-soaked getaways.

2. MAUI, HAWAII

Hawaii in general is a top vacation destination for celebrities, many of whom own property in some part of Hawaii. Maui in particular seems to be where many A-listers, such as Kate Hudson and Owen Wilson, choose to relax. The Four Seasons Resort Maui sits on 15 acres along the planned resort community of Wailea and is often booked solid, which is not surprising seeing as how it has hosted numerous celebrities such as Oprah, Britney, Governor Arnold Schwarzenegger, and Pamela Anderson. In 2007 the resort underwent a $50 million dollar face-lift, and hosts a giant courtyard with three pools, and luxurious marble bathrooms. Numerous amenities are available to visitors, including daily kids programs, a game room, fitness classes, twice-daily housekeeping, L'Occitane bath products, and complimentary poolside cabanas, where staff members come by and spritz you with Evian water to keep you refreshed. All those extras almost justify the $475 to $12,000 per night rates.

3. ST. TROPEZ, FRANCE

Located on the French Riviera in the south of France, St. Tropez boasts the largest number of celebrities per square foot (yes, even more than Hollywood!). Of course its small size (less than six square miles) aids this statistic. Why does this little spot attract so much star power? Ingela Ratledge, features editor for *Life and Style* magazine, says, "It's the ultimate in decadent living and Old World Hollywood glamour" stemming from the likes of 1950s model/actress Brigitte Bardot.

Near Nice and Cannes, this ultra exclusive hot spot was where Pam Anderson and Kid Rock rekindled their romance that led to a short-lived marriage in 2006. Jay-Z and Beyoncé, Rod Stewart, Bruce Willis, and the Beckhams have all visited here. P. Diddy visited by yacht, which is a popular form of lodging in St. Tropez. Johnny Depp's permanent residence is located near St. Tropez, where he and his family can live media-free. Though St. Tropez can be visited on a budget, if you want to live it up like a celebrity where celebrities abound, you need a hefty bank account and style.

4. THE HAMPTONS, NEW YORK

Everyone has heard of the Hamptons, and that's because it's the hottest vacation spot in the northeast. Everyone who's anyone goes to the Hamptons from Memorial Day to Labor Day. While many wealthy people rent extravagant beachfront homes for their stay, those who cannot afford private homes, yet want to rub elbows with celebrities, rent rooms in a house. Numerous celebrities (mostly New York–based) own elaborate properties in the area, such as Jerry Seinfeld, who owns a massive $32 million dollar estate, Sarah Jessica Parker and Matthew Broderick, Stephen Spielberg, Kelly Ripa, and Howard Stern.

While the Hamptons may not be an exotic location, its proximity to New York City makes it a quick weekend getaway for city folk and a relatively easy commute in and out of the city for people who must travel into the city for work while staying in the Hamptons. Some of the rich and/or famous cut their commute short by making use of New York City's Heliport and getting to the city in about forty minutes. For the rest of us it's about a two-hour drive, which can be doubled during peak travel times. The Long Island Rail Road runs directly between the Hamptons and the city, which makes for a much more relaxing commute. The other mass-transit option is the New York tradition of the Hampton Jitney: upscale bus service from Manhattan directly to various points in the Hamptons.

Aside from proximity, the Hamptons allows for vacationers to experience quiet suburban life away from the city, such as lying on the beaches and buying fresh produce at the farmers market. It also offers a luxurious lifestyle including elite social events and exclusive restaurants and clubs. In this way, many vacationers can network while on vacation. It's a two-for-one: Manhattan with sand.

5. ST. BARTS—ANGUILLA

Often called the "island of beautiful people" because of the numerous celebrities and wealthy people who vacation there, St. Barts wins hands-down for a traditional and luxurious Caribbean vacation. Celebrities such as Tom Cruise, Harrison Ford, Daniel Craig, and Miranda Kerr are among the numerous glitterati that flock to the island—especially during the winter holidays. Victoria's Secret once used the island location for a catalog photo shoot. A typical St. Barts day consists of sunning oneself on one of the island's twenty-two beaches, followed by shopping at the many designer boutiques, and then dining at one of the island's fabulous restaurants. As St. Barts is a French colony, it is known for its excellent French cuisine and wine. Among the numerous luxury hotels, is the Hotel Guanahani and Spa, which has hosted Arnold Schwarzenegger, Bon Jovi, and Penelope Cruz.

Anguilla, a British territory, is a small (16 miles long by 3 miles wide) Caribbean island that has been hailed as the "new" St. Barts. The much smaller tourist population on Anguilla allows celebrity guests much more privacy than its more popular neighbor, St. Barts. Seclusion, however, is another matter as all thirty-three beaches on the island are public, making stars easily accessible and part of the "general population." But personal space is respected: it says a lot when Beyoncé can lounge on a public beach and not be harassed by fans or paparazzi.

Numerous other A-list celebrities enjoy the tranquility of this island including Donatella Versace, Richard Gere, Susan Sarandon, and Robin Williams. Most prefer to rent private villas, but numerous high-end hotels also cater to the rich and famous, such as Malliouhana Hotel ($400 to $2,000 per night), Cap Juluca ($600 to $10,000 per night), and the St. Regis Anguilla, which boasts a 10,000-square-foot spa. If you're on a budget you can rent a condo or villa for anywhere between $240 and $8,600 per night.

6. ASPEN, COLORADO

If stargazing (not of the celestial variety) is what you crave, spend your Christmas vacation in Aspen, Colorado. It combines small town charm with A-list tourists and amenities.

It's the classic celebrity ski town. Kate Hudson and her family have spent numerous Christmases in Aspen and Jack Nicholson has been a regular since the 1970s. Will Smith, Kevin Costner, Michael Jordan, Mariah Carey and Nick Cannon, and Bill and Hillary Clinton regularly hit the slopes here. It's typical to walk through the little town and see stars window shopping or lunching at a café right there among the simple folk.

Many celebrities own homes here or rent them for their stay, but hotels such as Hotel Jerome cater to the celebrity and jet set as well. Oprah, Cameron Diaz, Donald Trump, and Johnny Depp have all been spotted at Hotel Jerome where rooms range from $500 to $2,000 per night. The Little Nell and the Sky Hotel also offer A-list accommodations.

7. SOUTH BEACH, MIAMI

Celebrities who vacation in South Beach are going to see and to be seen. This is not the place for privacy and exclusivity. Furthermore, it is also not a town for people looking for a quiet and peaceful getaway. This hotspot tends to cater to the younger celebrity set who can keep up with the hectic nightlife. The most popular time for celebrities to descend upon Miami tends to be around the New Year's holiday, many even hosting New Year's Eve events at the hottest nightclubs. With all these stars and wannabe stars, dressing to impress (the bouncer) is a must to secure entry into the ultra exclusive clubs.

South Beach has also grown in celebrity status because a growing number of movies and television series are being filmed on location there, and because celebrities such as Jennifer Lopez and Marc Anthony, Matt Damon, Alex Rodriguez, and Anna Kournikova all own homes in Miami. Where stars stay in South Beach depends on their mood. Most celebrities make at least one stop at the Shore Club, which houses a Nobu restaurant and the famous Skybar. The Setai Hotel is relatively new and is the preference of celebrities who want to escape the party scene and who seek a bit of privacy. The Ritz-Carlton is a celebrity staple, they claim because they "go to great lengths to meet and exceed the expectations of even [their] most particular guests." The Mandarin Oriental Hotel is where Janet Jackson goes for spa treatments and Tom Cruise and Katie Holmes stay during trips to South Beach. Finally, Casa Casuarina, Gianni Versace's former home (made infamous when Versace was shot and killed on the doorstep), has been turned into an exclusive restaurant and hotel. Apparently, any celebrity that has ever been to Miami has been there at some point or other.

8. BORA BORA, FRENCH POLYNESIA

Bora Bora is a tropical paradise in the Pacific that is surrounded by a beautiful lagoon and a barrier reef. It is close to Tahiti, but celebrities prefer Bora Bora, for its remoteness and intimacy, the island being only 11.3 square miles. Eva Longoria-Parker and Tony Parker, and Nicole Kidman and Keith Urban, all stayed there the same week and shared the same hotel. While the Parkers were merely vacationing, Kidman and Urban were honeymooning. The A-listers hotel of choice? The St. Regis Bora Bora. Allegedly the newlyweds booked the Royal Estate Suite, which is a three bedroom, 13,000-square-foot villa with a private pool, Jacuzzi, steam room and sauna, and private beach. All rooms come with 24-hour butler service and every villa is positioned over the lagoon—so even though Eva and Tony didn't have as posh a villa as Mr. and Mrs. Urban did, they didn't have it *too* bad.

9. FIJI ISLANDS

Fiji is a cluster of small islands located in the South Pacific. Celebrities travel to this remote location when looking for privacy and romance. The only way to get to the island is by boat, which makes for a virtually paparazzi-free vacation. One of the most popular places in Fiji is Turtle Island. Numerous famous couples have honeymooned at the Turtle Island Resort including Britney Spears and Kevin Federline, Jessica Simpson and Nick Lachey, and Reality TV couple Trista and Ryan Sutter. Though the resort sits on 500 acres, there are only 14 bungalows. You can probably stay there and never see another guest if you don't want to. This extreme privacy comes at a high price, though most visitors are more than happy to pay up for true peace and quiet, which averages about $2,000 per night. Don't worry, this price also includes meals, massages, and drinks as well.

Another popular celebrity retreat in Fiji is the Wakaya Club and Spa located on the 2,200-acre Wakaya Island. Celebrities such as Keith Richards and Demi Moore and Ashton Kutcher have stayed here. It is even more exclusive than Turtle Bay Resort, offering only ten cottages. Each is 1,625 square feet and is situated just steps from the ocean. The resort is all-inclusive, thus their nightly rates include all meals and beverages, laundry service, fully stocked mini bar, two scuba tank dives per day, use of golf course, and much more. While there is no television or phone access in any of the cottages, wireless Internet access is available all over the island, so it's not totally cut off from the world. So how much does this piece of paradise cost (where the minimum stay is five nights)? The cheapest cottage is approximately $2,000 per night, while the Vale O villa will run you about $8,000 per night. Keep in mind, these rates do not include the 12.5% value-added tax the Fijian government adds.

10. NECKER ISLAND, BRITISH VIRGIN ISLANDS

Necker Island is for the celebrity who is serious about vacationing alone, or at least about having complete control over whom he or she will see while on vacation. Virgin Group founder Richard Branson owns this 74-acre island and rents it out in its entirety for $51,000 per night. The Great House is the main living space, though there are two Bali Studios beneath it for guests as well. In total there are fourteen bedrooms and bathrooms and a staff of thirty-one to fulfill guests' every desire. Everything available on the island is included. Chef service, use of all equipment, and even a yacht for a day when you stay for five nights. For the price tag, it better be pretty darn amazing. Super celebrities Mel Gibson, Oprah Winfrey, and Stephen Spielberg are among the privileged that have shelled out for this ultimate private retreat.

Spilling the Beans

What's even better than celebrity news? Celebrity news straight from the horse's mouth, that's what. Though the version of events is of course from the celebrity's point of view, and so it's not exactly a neutral perspective, it's still exciting to hear stories from the primary source. Below are some of the most gossip-worthy memoirs that dish the dirt.

1. TORI SPELLING

Tori Spelling not only grew up as the daughter of one of television's most successful producers, she was also a cast member on one of the hottest teen television dramas of the 1990s, *Beverly Hills 90210*. Her 2008 autobiography *sTORI Telling* received attention for its honesty about events on the set of *90210* and about her personal life, in particular her rocky relationship with her parents. In the book Tori claims that everyone—except for her—basically slept with everyone else on the *90210* set. She also accuses her mother of having an affair during the months leading up to Tori's father's death. However, Tori doesn't paint herself the picture of innocence, admitting that she slept with her current husband Dean McDermott while she was still married to her first husband, Charlie Shanian. Whether or not Tori's recounting of events are entirely true, the book elicited reactions from both her *90210* costars and mother, putting Tori in the media spotlight. The success of Tori's first book led to *Mommywood*, which was published in 2009.

2. MAUREEN MCCORMICK

Marcia Brady was the epitome of the wholesome girl next-door image. Maureen McCormick, the actress who played Marcia Brady on the iconic television series *The Brady Bunch* from 1969 to 1974, was associated with the same squeaky-clean image. That is she was until McCormick published her 2008 memoir *Here's the Story: Surviving Marcia Brady and Finding My True Voice*, which details her drug use and sexual escapades during her years on *The Brady Bunch*. She also opens up about her un-Marcia-like life once the series ended: battling cocaine addiction, depression, an eating disorder, as well as dysfunctional relationships. After reading this book, watching *The Brady Bunch* will never be the same.

3. DREW BARRYMORE

Most teen personalities should never publish a memoir. Really, how many noteworthy experiences could they have? Generally speaking, not nearly enough to fill up an entire book. Drew Barrymore is the exception to this rule. Her 1990 autobiography, *Little Girl Lost*, told of a girl with more harrowing experiences than most of us will have in a lifetime—and she was only fifteen. Barrymore tells of a childhood where she rose to fame at age six; became a regular at hot spot Studio 54 before she was ten; snorted cocaine, smoked cigarettes and marijuana, and drank as a pre-teen; entered rehab twice; and attempted suicide. All this, before the age of fifteen. With so many trials and tribulations in a mere fifteen years, how many volumes will her complete life story will fill?

4. JENNA JAMESON

What could be more titillating than a porn star's memoir? One of the most famous porn stars Jenna Jameson set out to give the lowdown on her life and chosen profession in her provocatively titled autobiography *How to Make Love Like a Porn Star: A Cautionary Tale* (2004). It was an instant best-seller, claiming a spot on *The New York Times* Best Seller list for six weeks. This six hundred-page tell-all, detailing Jameson's first thirty years, gives a behind-the-scenes glance into the porn industry and insight into her relationships with various famous men. However, according to the *New York Times* Sunday Book Review, there is a lot of unnecessary information in this book. Jameson includes numerous "diary entries" as well as an entire adult film contract and a list of her favorite songs. It seems Jameson didn't realize that anyone interested in reading this book is in it for the dirt.

5. JANE FONDA

Jane Fonda was a popular model and actress in the 1960s and 1970s who also became known for her controversial stance on the Vietnam War. At first she was one of many celebrities who supported anti–Vietnam War efforts and organizations, but when she visited North Vietnam, her activism escalated. Fonda was photographed sitting on an anti-aircraft battery, she took part in North Vietnamese radio broadcasts, and proceeded to call certain American POWs liars and hypocrites. The backlash was significant. Fonda's autobiography, *My Life So Far* (2005), details these events, as well as her career in the entertainment industry and her family life. She apologizes for her previous statements about Vietnam Veterans and the anti-aircraft battery photo, though she stands by her trip and views in general.

6. BROOKE SHIELDS

Brook Shields's memoir *Down Came the Rain: My Jour-*

ney Through Postpartum Depression (2005), detailed her struggle with postpartum depression after the birth of her first child in 2003. The book received a lot of press after it sparked a heated war of words between Brooke Shields and Tom Cruise. Both celebrities worked the print and television media circuit, promoting their side of the issue. Cruise spoke out against postpartum depression and criticized Shields for using prescription medication to help her recover. Though Cruise and Shields were at odds for a year, the debate worked to promote Shields's book and turn public attention toward a newsworthy subject.

7. BARBARA WALTERS

Barbara Walters has worked as a journalist for over five decades, and has covered many important events during that time. At the age of eighty she is still a working journalist, though now she picks and chooses her assignments, seeming to prefer focusing on celebrity, rather than political, drama. Walters's 2008 memoir, *Audition*, tells of her rise in the competitive, male-dominated world of journalism, as well as her personal life and relationships. Walters does not hold back, breaking the news of an affair with married U.S. Senator Edward Brooks in the 1970s, and giving her side of the story about the controversial departures of her cohosts on *The View*, Star Jones and Rosie O'Donnell. Walters's best-selling memoir gives today's readers a glimpse into the exciting and controversial life of one of the first female television journalists.

8. MARILYN MANSON

Alternative rock singer Marilyn Manson is better known for his creepy goth appearance than for his musical talents. When this oddball celebrity published his autobiography *The Long Hard Road Out of Hell* in 1998, it became an instant success because many people were interested in gaining insight into the real Manson. What were his thoughts on life? How did he come to be this well-known, and somewhat scary, persona? The picture of Manson in all his creepy glory was enticing as well. Surprisingly, the book was favorably reviewed. *Rolling Stone* magazine called it "funny, appalling, and disturbing;" *Newsweek* found it "unimaginably perverse and demented;" and *Us Weekly* referred to it as a "fascinating, sleazy account of his coming of age and assent into damnation." Who wouldn't be immediately, and yes, a bit morbidly, curious?

9. ERIC CLAPTON
Rock legend Eric Clapton stunned the world with his soul-baring book *Clapton: The Autobiography* (2007). By nature Clapton is reserved and private, but his autobiography let fans know of the struggles he has experienced throughout his career. Aside from detailing his career, he comes clean about his drug and alcohol addictions, suicide attempts, love life, and the untimely death of his young son. *Clapton* received rave reviews.

10. MADONNA
Madonna has not yet published her autobiography, but her brother, Christopher Ciccone's 2008 tell-all, *Life with My Sister Madonna*, has only heightened curiosity about Madonna's "real life." For many years Ciccone was Madonna's right hand man, so, he definitely had insider access to Madonna during much of her career. It seems that their falling-out occurred when Madonna began dating Guy Ritchie in 1998. Considering the current animosity between brother and sister, the truth of Ciccone's tell-all certainly comes into question. Maybe its best to simply take it as one insight into Madonna's character. Regardless, it's an entertaining read about the world's favorite material girl.

Blog All About It

Thanks to the Internet, there is no shortage of information of any kind, least of all of celebrity gossip. Currently, in fact, there are so many celebrity news sites and blogs that searching for the latest scoop can be overwhelming. Many sites are repetitive and run together into an unmemorable blur, but the following blogs stand out from the crowd.

1. WWW.TMZ.COM

TMZ is both a television show and a celebrity news blog. All the stories they cover on the show are available on the web site, just without the witty banter. TMZ employs its own paparazzi, and features clips of their out-takes. According to the web site, the name "TMZ" is an acronym for the 1960s term "Thirty Mile Zone," which referred to the studio-designated zone for monitoring filming in Hollywood. Just as the offices of the Association of Motion Pictures and Television Producers was at the center of that zone, TMZ markets itself as the center for entertainment news. Known for its exclusive stories and video footage, TMZ is indeed at the cutting edge of daily Hollywood news. It was recognized by *Newsweek* as the Breakout Blog of 2007 and has established itself as one of the best sources for the most up-to-date celebrity information.

2. WWW.PEREZHILTON.COM

Perez Hilton began his blog in 2005 as an unknown and over the past four years has become a celebrity himself, making his own headlines. His blog tracks the latest celebrity news with Hilton adding his own snarky takes on the topics. His outspoken nature has landed him in feuds with members of the Black Eyed Peas—Fergie was upset about comments Hilton made about her on his web site, which led to a physical altercation between Hilton and the band's Will.i.am—and former Miss California 2009 Carrie Prejean. The fact that Hilton is now a Hollywood insider himself makes his blog even more subjective, for he is no longer a neutral observer. When all is said and done, a blog is just one person's opinion, so Hilton is just giving readers his point of view—and it's always entertaining.

3. WWW.EONLINE.COM

E! is the only television channel solely devoted to Hollywood, so it should have a information-filled web site—and it does not disappoint. Not only is the E! web site continually updated with the most timely celebrity news stories, there are a lot of fun features such as a Twitter box—so you can read what popular celebrities are twittering about; blogs about the inside scoop on TV shows; and the latest celebrity parties. The web site and the E! News nightly celebrity news program aren't exactly the same, with some stories appearing on the news program before being posted to the web. However, the web site gives more details about TV scoop and celebrity fashion.

4. WWW.POPSUGAR.COM

PopSugar is the celebrity gossip page for a slew of "Sugar"-

related web sites, comprehensively called OnSugar. While PopSugar features celebrity happenings, and links to stories on other celebrity gossip sites, it stands apart with its numerous celebrity features. It features individual pages for today's hottest celebrities complete with recent photos and news stories. There are also links to news about the current celebrity expectant moms, celebrity sightings, and fun polls. Thus, this site is incredibly comprehensive and is perfect for people interested in celebrity life, and not merely the news of the day. Another great feature of this website is that it has links to the other "Sugar" websites, such as FabSugar (fashion), BuzzSugar (entertainment), LilSugar (mom and kids), and SavvySugar (money). It's essentially an online magazine, free and at your fingertips 24/7/365. Though not every sugar site has a celebrity angle it can be addictive—just like sugar!

5. WWW.PINKISTHENEWBLOG.COM

This blog is run by Trent Vanegas out of Detroit, Michigan. But just because it isn't close to the celebrity action of L.A. or New York doesn't mean he's not up to date on celebrity happenings. This blog does not monotonously report news stories, it also infuses comedy into its reports. Furthermore, this blog reports some out of the way stories, so it's a useful supplemental news source to the big celebrity news blogs that report the major stories of the day—or bury smaller stories. This blog has been positively reviewed by numerous legitimate news sources such as the *New York Times*, *The Village Voice*, and *Entertainment Weekly*.

6. WWW.HOLLYSCOOP.COM

HollyScoop.com is set up like an online newspaper. This allows the top stories in each category to be plainly visible, a departure from most celebrity gossip sites that merely feature the overarching celebrity news on their home page with links to other categories. HollyScoop's homepage features such categories as Hot Topics, Photo Gallery, Style, TV, Movies, Music, and Featured Videos, with pictures or story tags below each. This site makes it easy to be "in the know" about all aspects of the entertainment industry.

7. WWW.THESKINNYWEBSITE.COM

This web site has a strict celebrity focus: "celebrity weight, diet, exercise, and body gossip." These topics are front and center in Hollywood, so it is only fitting that there be a web site completely dedicated to celebrity bodies. TheSkinny home page sports numerous tabs, which include: Diets, Thin, Skinny, Gain, Scary Skinny, and Curvy. Each tab takes you to stories about celebrities that are in these categories. This site is incredibly addicting and could very well be a bad influence on the weight-obsessed.

8. WWW.HOLLYWOODHEARTBREAKER.COM

HollywoodHeartbreaker.com's tagline, "Breaking News on Broken Hearts," says it all. When you just want in-depth coverage of Hollywood's most talked about hookups and splits (ok . . . mostly splits) HollywoodHeartbreaker.com is the place to go. Its focus on celebrity relationships means you don't have to sift through all the other "news" that can clog other celebrity gossip sites. The site's coverage of celebrity relationships is extensive and will satisfy your relationship news craving.

9. WWW.HOTMOMMAGOSSIP.COM

HotMommaGossip.com is radically different from most in this category. It touts itself as edgy, yet clean, so it's acceptable to read if you have children in the room. This web site is the tasteful celebrity gossip site, taking the high road of the celebrity gossip spectrum (if there is one) with their slogan "We try to play clean, not mean." This site comments on most of the day's most intriguing news stories, and they do so humorously, not maliciously. This does however make it less comprehensive than the gossip websites without a conscience.

10. WWW.THEHOLLYWOODGOSSIP.COM

While many celebrity gossip sites try to be more journalistic in their delivery, bloggers on TheHollywoodGossip.com give opinions on their featured stories. And though this blog typically features the same stories as other celebrity blogs, it is comprehensive in its coverage and funny in its delivery. Furthermore, the site has pages dedicated to fashion, hairstyles, and celebrity babies.

Selected Sources

WEBSITES
www.AssociatedContent.com
www.CNN.com
www.Eonline.com
www.FitSugar.com
www.Forbes.com
www.howcelebritiesloseweight.com
www.IMDB.com
www.PageSix.com
www.People.com
http://pregnancyandbaby.sheknows.com
http://www.randomhistory.com
www.TheInsider.com
www.TMZ.com
www.UsMagazine.com
www.Vh1.com

MAGAZINES
Harper's Bazaar
In Touch
Life and Style

Marie Claire
New York Magazine
Rolling Stone
Vanity Fair
W

NEWSPAPERS

Los Angeles Times
New York Post
The Telegraph

BOOKS

Braudy, Leo. *The Frenzy of Renown: Fame and Its History.* New York: Oxford University Press, 1986.

Ciccone, Christopher and Wendy Leigh. *Life with My Sister Madonna.* New York: Simon Spotlight, 2008.

Jameson, Jenna and Neil Strauss. *How to Make Love Like a Porn Star: A Cautionary Tale.* New York: HarperCollins, 2004.

Manson, Marilyn. *The Long Road Out of Hell.* New York: Harper Entertainment, 1999.

Spelling, Tori. *sTORI Telling.* New York: Simon Spotlight, 2008.

Walters, Barbara. *Audition: A Memoir.* New York: Alfred A. Knopf, 2008.

Index

About the Author

Marjorie Hallenbeck-Huber graduated from George Washington University with Bachelor degrees in English and International Affairs. She earned a Master's degree in English from the University of Tennessee, Knoxville. She is a self-proclaimed celebrity enthusiast and an avid reader of celebrity blogs and magazines, including TMZ.com and *US Weekly*. She currently lives in Herndon, Virginia, with her husband, daughter, and two cats.